IMAGES
of America

PLEASANTS COUNTY

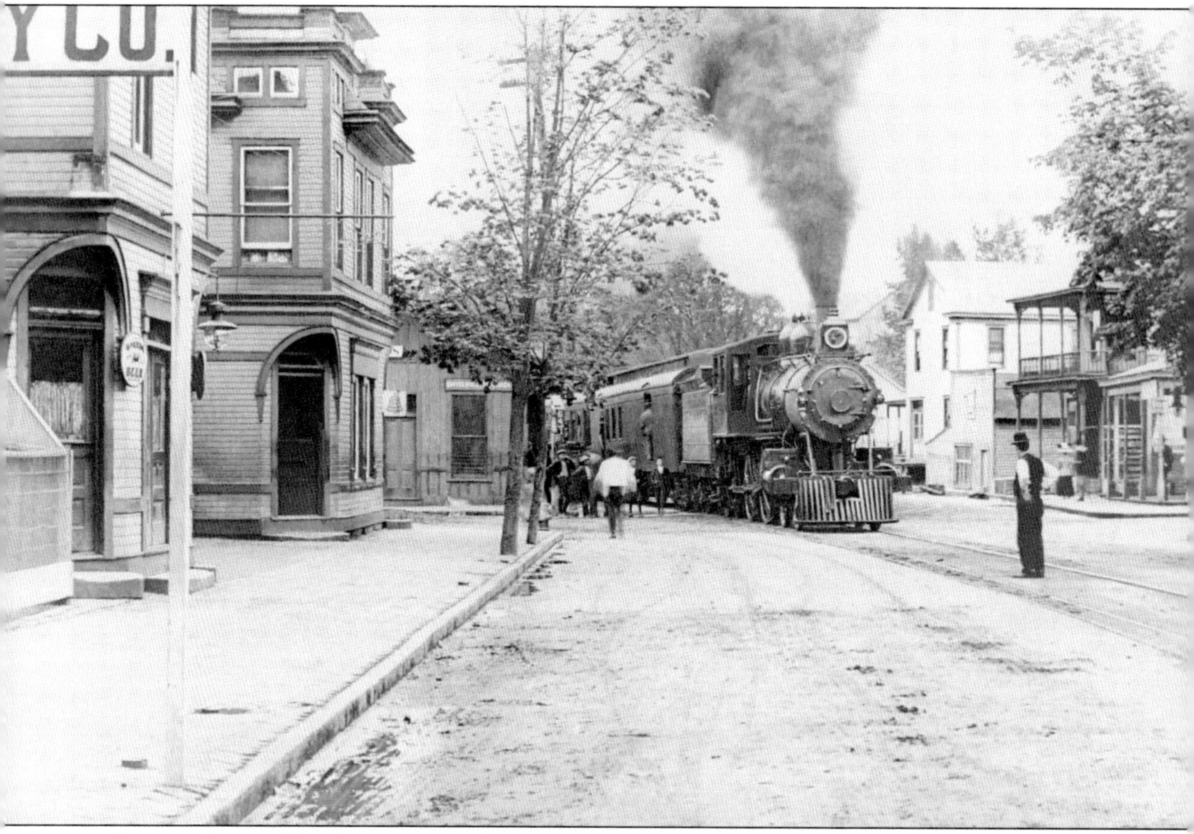

On the Cover: The St. Marys B&O Depot was located on the corner of Second and Clay Streets across from the Howard Hotel. After the hotel burned, the Main Theater was built. The theater building was converted into the Food Giant, a local grocery store, which still remains. This picture was taken about 1901. (Pleasants County Historical Society, courtesy of West Virginia Division of Culture and History State Archives.)

IMAGES
of America

PLEASANTS COUNTY

Ellen Dittman Pope
and Ruth Ann Dayhoff

ARCADIA
PUBLISHING

ISBN 978-0-7385-6816-4

Published by Arcadia Publishing
Charleston SC, Chicago IL, Portsmouth NH, San Francisco CA

Printed in the United States of America

Library of Congress Control Number: 2008941476

For all general information contact Arcadia Publishing at:
Telephone 843-853-2070
Fax 843-853-0044
E-mail sales@arcadiapublishing.com
For customer service and orders:
Toll-Free 1-888-313-2665

Visit us on the Internet at www.arcadiapublishing.com

This book is dedicated to the people of Pleasants County for the preservation of their history and especially to all of the parents and teachers who have instilled the love of learning into those who read this book.

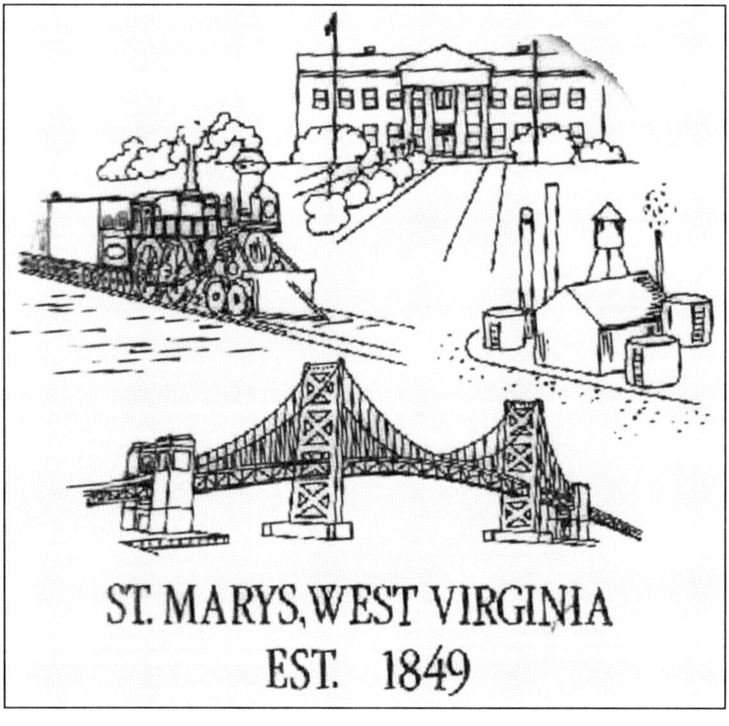

Several motifs have been designed throughout the years to represent Pleasants County. Each one has included at least three of these drawings. This design, by Carla Wince, was taken from a button submitted by Sandra Cronin. It has also been painted as a mural on the wall of our city building. Another version was used on the front cover of *The History of Pleasants County to 1980*. (Courtesy of Sandra Cronin.)

Contents

Acknowledgments

We want to express our thanks and gratitude to all who have assisted us in the gathering and assembling of the materials for this book. We would like to give a special thanks to Rev. Daniel Simmons, the photographer of many of our photographs. Other individuals we would like to thank are as follows: Sonya Adams, Debra Basham, Dale Brown, Janet Butler, Esther Carroll, Andrew Clovis, Evelyn Clovis, Theadore Clovis, Carla Conoway, Sandra Cronin, Thelma Davis, Lyle Dayhoff, Barbara Dean, Mary Ellen Dittman, Elaine Elliott, Bob Enoch, John Evans, Dorothy Evans, Priscilla Fleming, Linda Fluehardy, Steve Green, Mildred Hardin, Pat Hays, Ed Hicks, Becky Ingram, Paul Ingram, Barbara Johnson, Delores Kemp, Anthony Lauer, Jeff Little, Joe Mahaney, David McCain, Ruth Ann McPeake, Richard Moore, Mike Naylor, Shirley Newbrough, Lee Ogdin, Wanda Payne, Daniel Pitts, Eleanor Poling, Brenda Poynter, Jim Procopio, Wilber Rae, Kitty Renner, Judy Roden, Mary Sue Ross, Frank Sellers, Ruby Sellers, Fonda Sigler, Anna Mary Thacker, Larry Webb, Charles Weekley, Tom Weekley, Holly West, Louise Wherry, Delno Winland, Bob Withers, Betty Wolfe, and William Wolfe.

We give a special thanks to the staff of Arcadia Publishing (Lindsay Harris, Maggie Bullwinkel, and Luke Cunningham), whose help and patience was vital. Besides the individuals who provided assistance, several organizations made collections of photographs and information available to us. These are listed below in alphabetical order. To save space, these collections will be abbreviated in the courtesy lines. When in question about an abbreviation under a picture, please refer to the abbreviation key below.

Abbreviation Key:

James Edwin Green Collection (JEGC), Dale Brown
Hazael Coleman Williams Collection (HCWC), Mark Williams
Pitts/McCollum Collection (PMC), Daniel Pitts
Pleasants County Historical Society Collection (PCHSC), West Virginia Division of Culture and History State Archives
Pleasants County Public Library Collection (PCPLC), Eleanor Poling
West Virginia Department of Natural Resources (WVDNR), Janet Butler
West Virginia Division of Culture and History State Archives (WVDCHSA)
West Virginia University Archives Library Collection (WVUALC)

INTRODUCTION

The first native settlers along the Ohio River in the area of present-day Pleasants County were the Mound Builders, also known as the Adena people. Once Adena mounds numbered in the hundreds, but only a small number of Adena earthen monuments still survive today. There are several documented mounds in Pleasants County. These mounds served as burial structures, ceremonial sites, historical markers, and possibly gathering places. The mounds were built using hundreds of thousands of baskets full of specially selected and graded earth. These early settlers knew this area was a wonderful place to live. They cultivated pumpkin, squash, sunflowers, and goosefoot and gathered several edible seed grasses and nuts. The wild game was plentiful, and they hunted deer, elk, black bear, woodchuck, beaver, porcupine, turkey, trumpeter swans, and ruffled grouse. These people represented a high civilization for their time. They were noted for their agricultural practices and pottery. All of this shows what creative and intelligent people our first settlers were.

During the early 1600s, Pleasants County was used as a hunting ground by the Ohio-based Shawnee and Mingo tribes. The Mingo people were not actually a Native American tribe, but a multicultural group of Native Americans who established several communities within present-day West Virginia. A high concentration of artifacts has been found on Middle Island. Throughout Pleasants County, artifacts were discovered when fields were plowed. The flint found at several prehistoric sites came from local sources, such as the Hughes River flint in Ritchie County. The total assemblage of early artifacts from prehistoric Native American culture indicates to archeologists that the ancestors of the Native Americans were in Pleasants County for more than 10,000 years, occupying hilltop and river sites along the major waterways. These were the same sites first selected by our county's first white settlers.

Robert Cavelier de La Salle was probably the first European to set foot in what is now Pleasants County. He sailed down the Ohio River in 1669. There is mention of an English fur trader who is said to have lived on Middle Island in 1765. George Washington explored the area in 1770. There is a marker commemorating his coming located on the banks of the river in St. Marys by the Creel House.

The first permanent white settlers were a pair of French brothers, Jacob and Isaac LaRue. They built a cabin at the mouth of Middle Island Creek in 1790. (They are buried on Middle Island in a small cemetery.) At that time, the entire area was a wilderness. It was still subject to depredations by small bands of marauding Native Americans, but in 1794, the establishment of small bodies of militia at several frontier points, such as Marietta, brought some degree of safety. The first white child born to the area was Hannah, the daughter of Isaac and Hannah Hughes LaRue. In 1797, Basil Riggs settled above Raven Rock narrows and, starting in 1810, built a gristmill, which was run by water on Riggs Run. It could grind 25 to 50 bushels a day and for a long time enjoyed the custom trade of settlers throughout the area. The principal crops of the county were wheat, corn, oats, and most varieties of grain, vegetables, and tobacco. There were immense quantities of valuable timber throughout the interior of the county and along the Ohio River and Middle Island Creek. A lot of the timber had been cut along the waterways into lumber, staves, and cross-ties. There was a ready market for all of those products. Jacob LaRue erected a sawmill on Broad Run about two miles from the river. Throughout the county, large tracts of coal, sandstone, limestone, and oil lands had only been partially developed. There were strong indications that there was iron in the area also.

Pleasants County was formed in the winter of 1851 from portions of Wood, Tyler, and Ritchie Counties. It was named in honor of Hon. James Pleasants, a member of the House of Representatives in Congress from Virginia (1811–1819) and the governor of the state in 1822. The county's population began to increase as several more families moved into the area. The first school was taught by Nancy Daily, and she had 10 to 12 pupils. This school was held in 1808 in a little log building 12 by 16 feet located near the mouth of Middle Island Creek. The first court was held in the home of Alexander H. Creel. He was appointed commissioner on behalf of the court to find a suitable site for a permanent courthouse. He donated $700 toward the building of the public square, courthouse, and jail. George Sharp and John Stewart bid $5,300 to erect and complete the courthouse, clerk's office, and jail by 1852. Alexander delegated that the seat of justice would be on his farm near the foot of Middle Island Creek on the Ohio River. The town was then named St. Marys after Creel's vision of the Virgin Mary on his trip down the Ohio. Thomas Browse produced the governor's commission as county surveyor for a term of seven years, took the oaths, and paid the security required by law. Alexander had Thomas survey and lay out the streets of the new county seat.

The oil industry is probably the oldest continuous industry in the community. The early beginnings were in small quantities, gathered from surface pits and sold to wholesale druggists for medical uses under the name Seneca Oil. But throughout the country, Pleasants County was known to have some of the richest and biggest producing wells in the United States.

Many businesses were opened, such as the Exchange Hotel, Cain House, Wells Hotel, Reynolds Inn, and many more. There were churches, schools, a newspaper, and entertainment of all kinds. St. Mary's was on its way to be a bustling city. Many little towns were settled in the county, like Hebron, Belmont (also known as Parkerville), Shultz, Grape Island, Arvilla, Raven Rock, and Willow Island. If Alexander Creel could come back and visit St. Marys and Pleasants County now, he could see that his vision of a prosperous community had been realized. He would be a very proud man because the people of the area today honor him for his foresight, honesty, and courage to prepare a place for all of us. He would be surprised at changes that have taken place and how people have worked together to build this community into what it is today. We love Pleasants County, our home, a wonderful place in which to live!

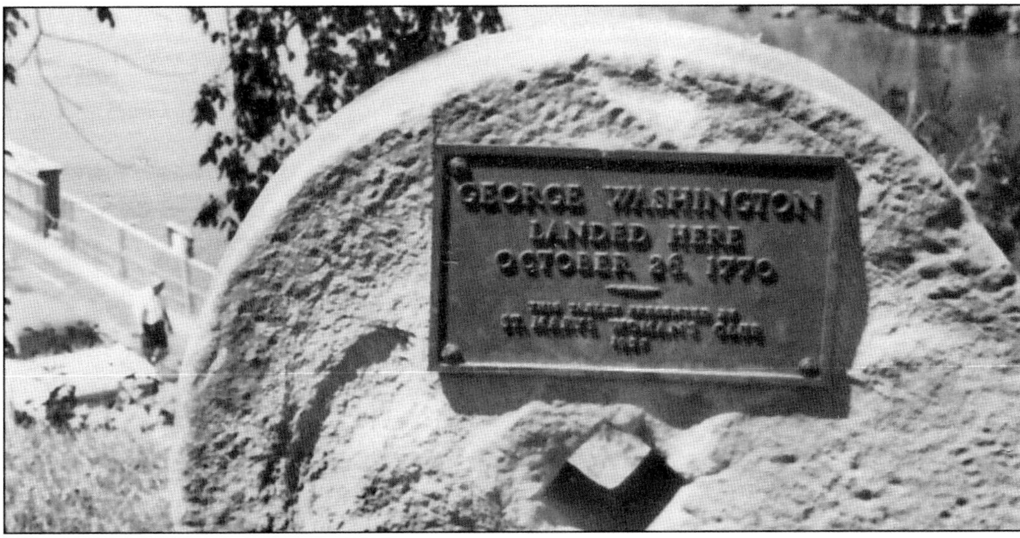

This millstone near the Creel House marks the spot commemorating George Washington. When Washington traveled down the Ohio River in 1770, he noted that there were several islands, some of which contained 100 or more acres. He also liked the fact that the fishing was great and the land looked productive. In his journal, everything he wrote described Middle Island and Middle Island Creek. (Courtesy of Rev. Daniel Simmons.)

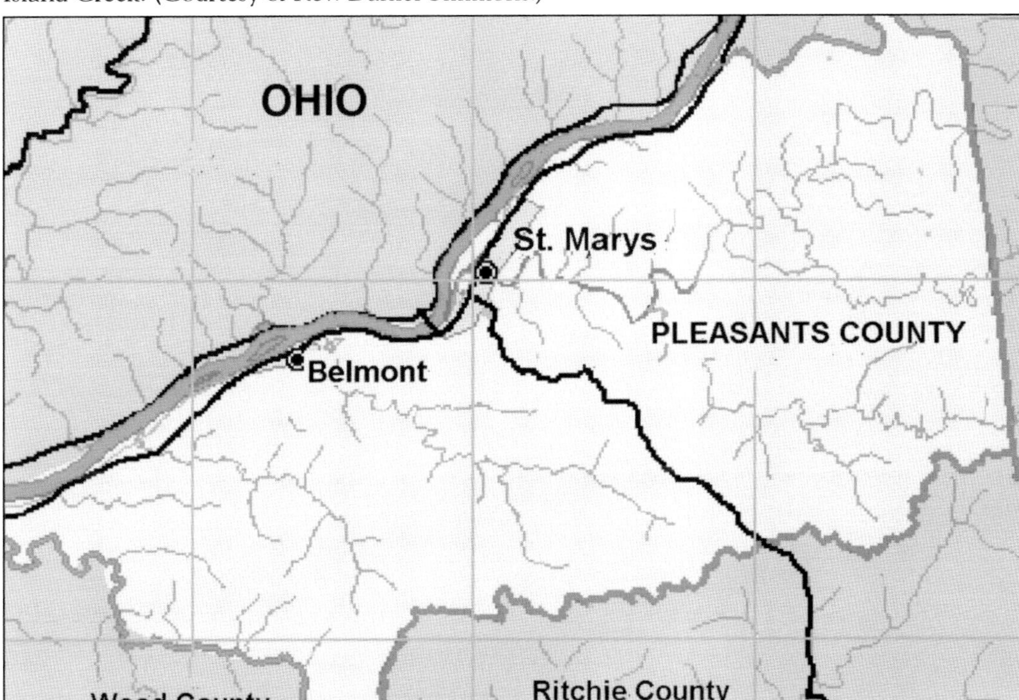

In January 1842, Thomas Browse went to the Union School House to discuss forming a new county. In September 1846, this surveyor of Tyler County began making a map for the new county. Pleasants County was formed from portions of Wood, Tyler, and Ritchie Counties and named in honor of James Pleasants, governor of Virginia. It is one of the smallest counties in West Virginia. (Courtesy of Ruth Ann Dayhoff.)

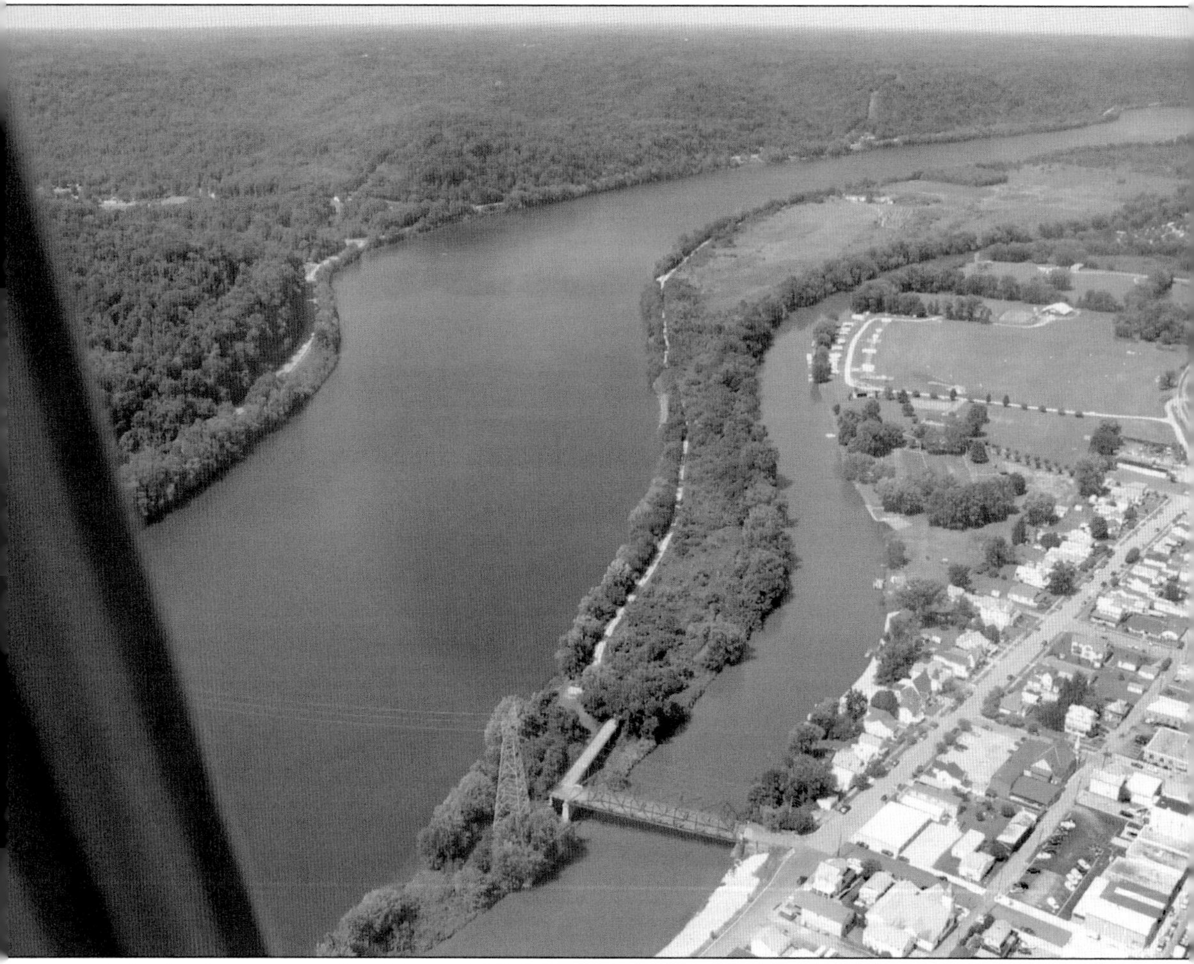

This bird's-eye view of St. Marys, Middle Island, and the Ohio River will perhaps help the reader to understand why Alexander Creel was so impressed by this place as he traveled down the Ohio, which means "Beautiful River." This photograph was taken from a helicopter by Janet Butler as she studied the island as one of the wildlife sanctuaries in West Virginia. Although Creel observed it from a floating vessel in an undeveloped state, he made a mental note to come back and establish the community and county that now exist. His vision of the Virgin Mary and her message inspired him to complete this task. It was several years before this dream started to come true, but in due time, his perseverance paid off. View the bridge from the island to the city. Follow the road to the end and find the marina. The railroad track to the right and the buildings below show the layout of the lovely town of St. Marys, West Virginia. (WVDNR, courtesy of Janet Butler.)

One

Moundbuilders, Native Americans, and Founders

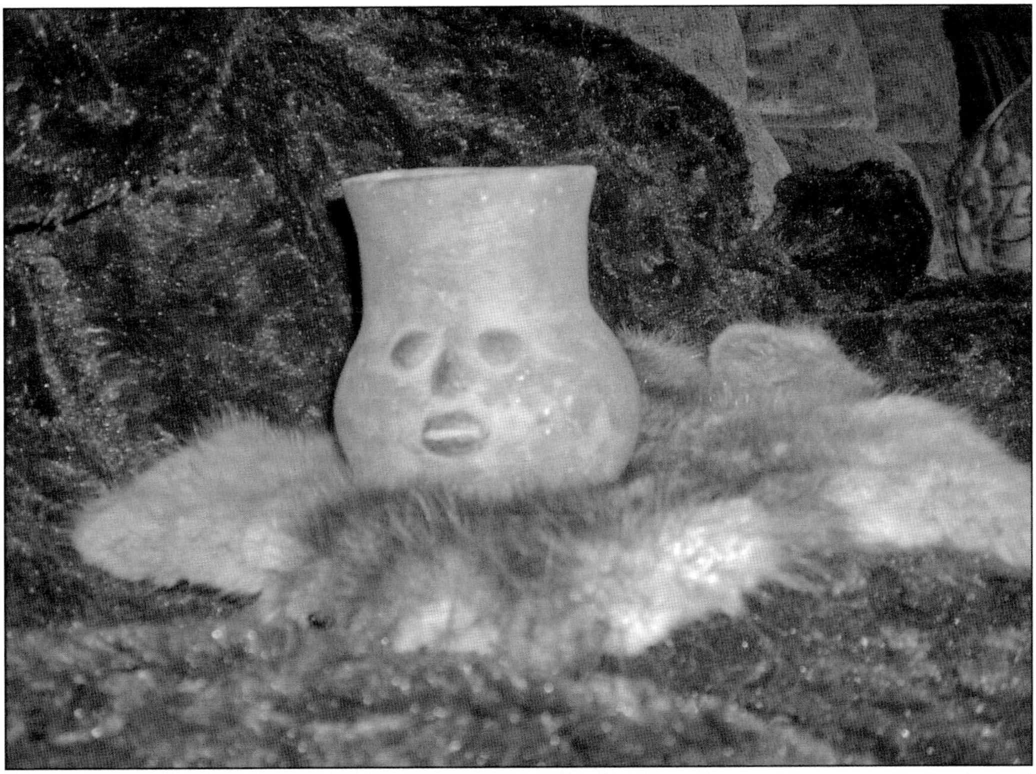

This pottery, from an Adena mound, was carbon-dated by the West Virginia University Archeological Department. Tests indicated it is over 10,000 years old. It was once owned by George Riggs, formally the local sheriff and police chief of St. Marys and a noted collector of Native American artifacts. He gave it to author Ellen Dittman Pope, who was working with the Cub Scouts to propitiate their love of Native American history. (Courtesy of Ruth Ann Dayhoff.)

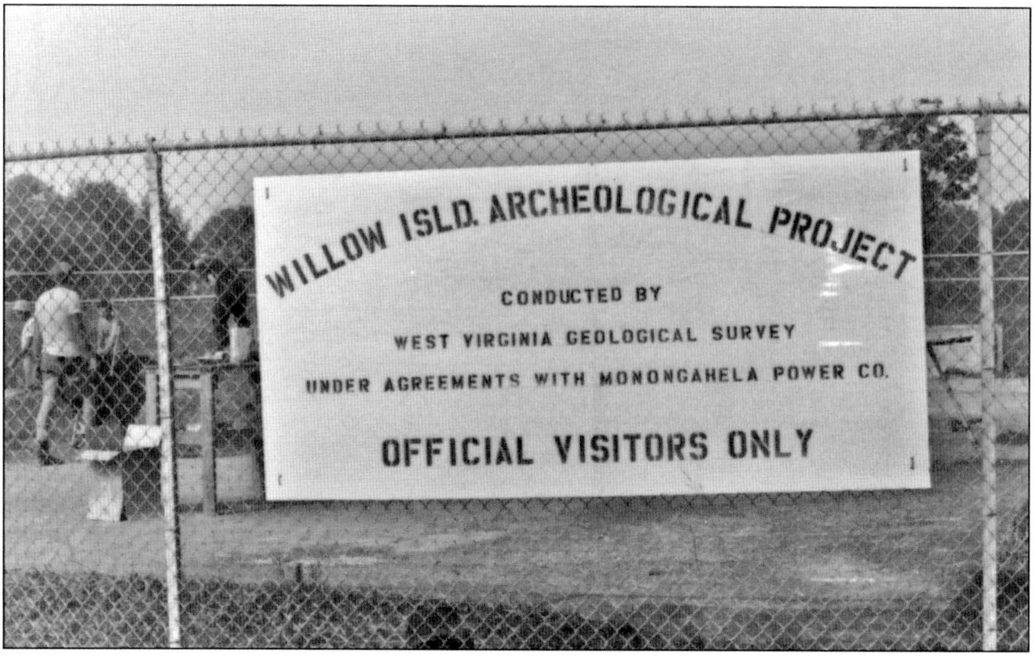

This mound being excavated was located on the property of the Monongahelia Power Plant. Great care was taken to protect and preserve the artifacts found in this Adena mound, called the Willow Island Archeological Project. Below, archeological students learn how to properly excavate a historical site. Patience and perseverance was necessary because of the delicate nature of the task. Tools used in the project ranged from the size of an ordinary shovel to tools as small as a toothbrush. This fact, along with hot weather, made the job at hand quite arduous. The artifacts found were distributed to historical collections and museums within the state. (Both courtesy of Rev. Daniel Simmons.)

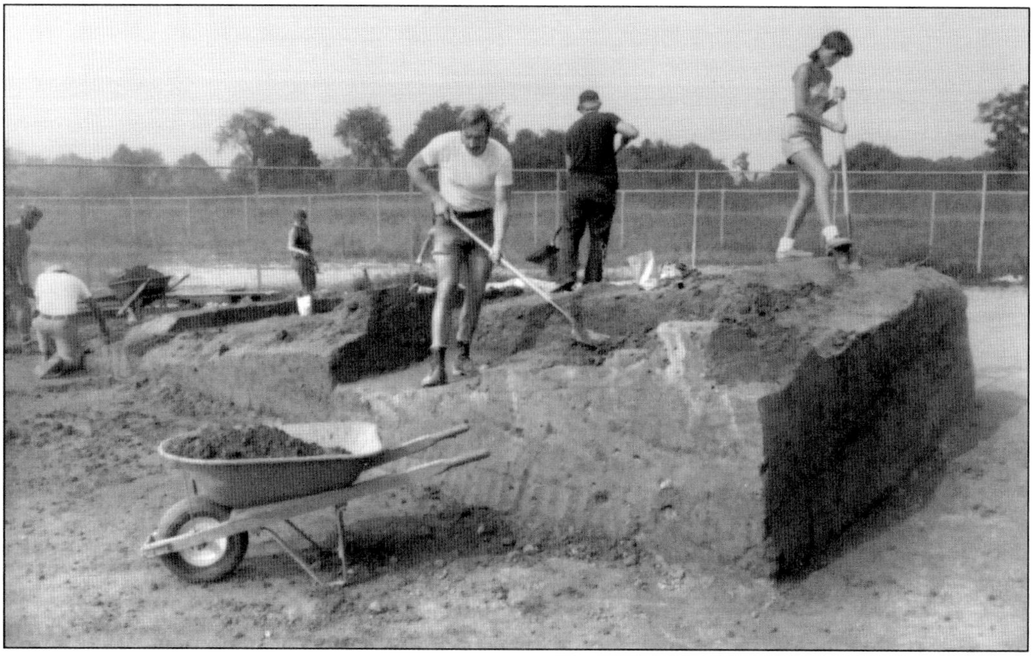

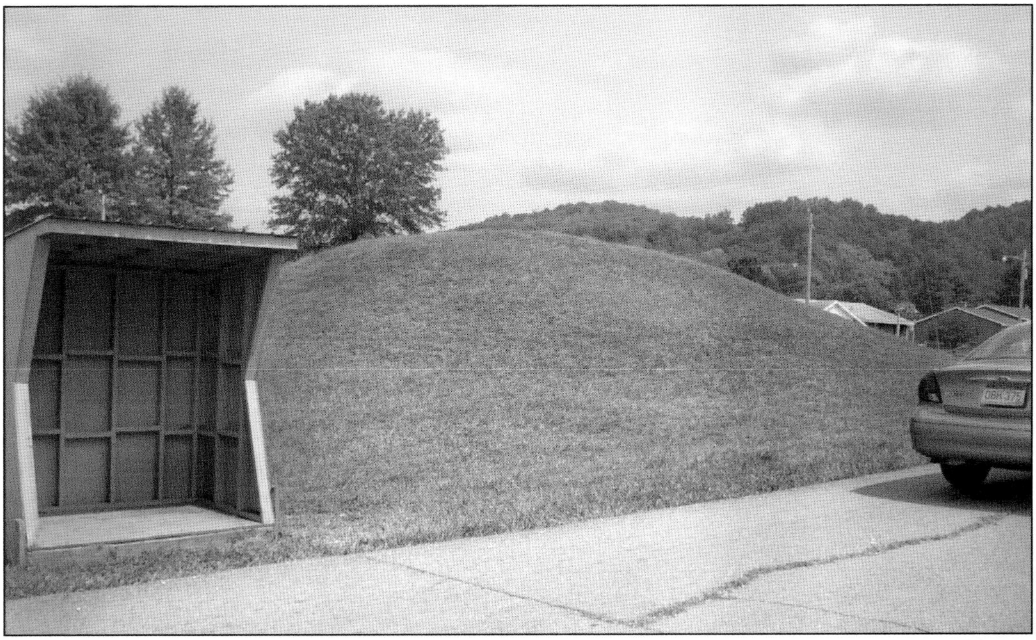

Reynolds Mound, located two miles north of St. Marys, is named after the Linden Reynolds farm on which it is located. The mound is of Adena origin. The Adena civilization, 1000 BC to 200 AD, lived in the Ohio Valley, and they were the first of three mound-building peoples. When someone died, they covered the body with red paint and then placed useful objects around it. They then cremated the body and covered the ashes with earth. The mound would grow higher as new bodies were added. The sign at the mound on the Cytec property below reads, "*Prehistoric Aboriginal Ceremonial Mound.* Many Indian relics were removed from this mound which was built by a civilization preceding the Indians discovered by the first white settlers." Standing by the mound is author Ellen Dittman Pope. (Both courtesy of Ruth Ann Dayhoff.)

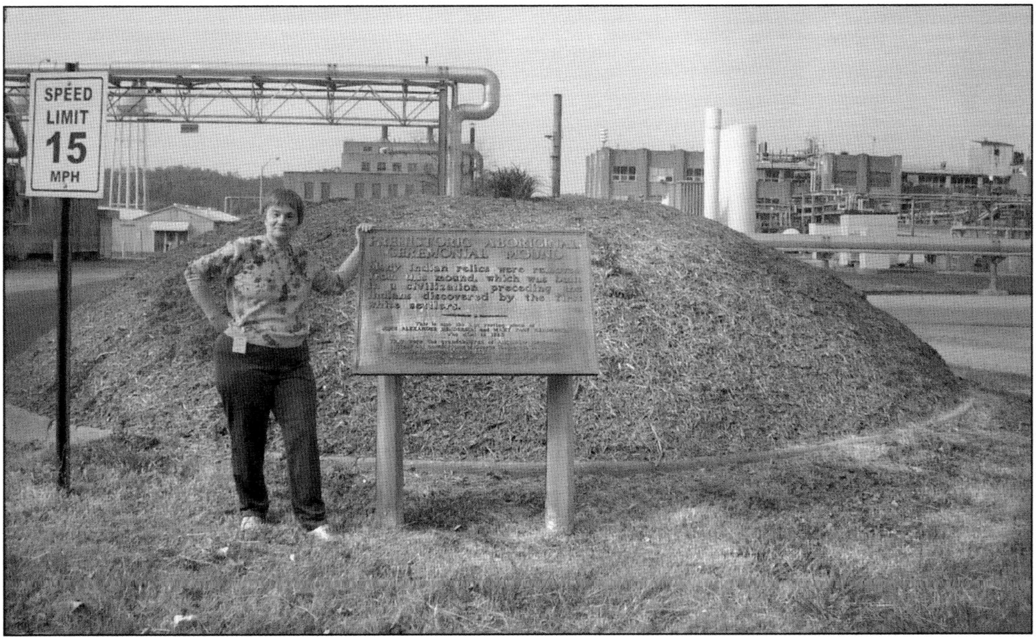

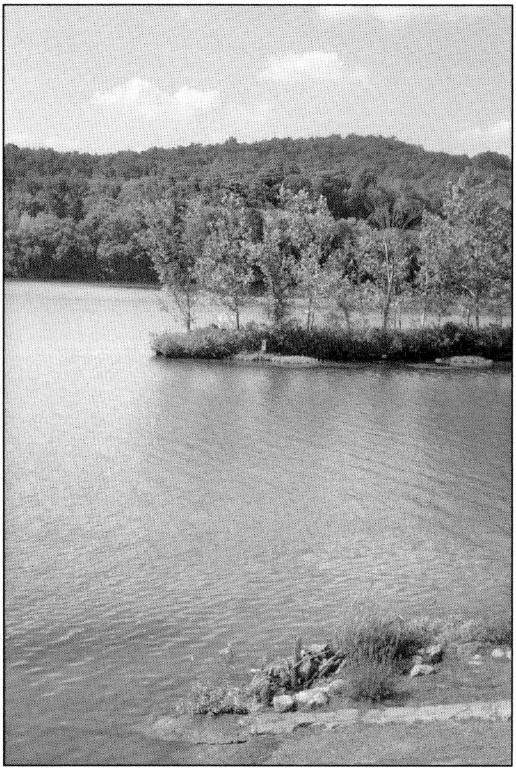

Middle Island and Middle Island Creek mark the location along the Ohio River where the county seat of Pleasants County, St. Marys, is located. Jacob and Isaac LaRue settled the island in 1890. The island is now a protected wildlife sanctuary where visitors may encounter rabbits, foxes, deer, and birds of all kinds, especially ducks and Canadian geese, which now dominate the area. (Courtesy of Ruth Ann Dayhoff.)

Scout leaders Joan Spencer Stewart (left) and Ellen Dittman Pope (right) dressed up to pose in front of this arrowhead arrangement. The arrowheads in the frame were found on Middle Island with the help of George Riggs, former police chief and sheriff. The exception is the large arrowhead in the right-hand corner, which was found by Tony Parsons, Ellen's son, when he was seven years old along Sled Fork on Cow Creek. (Courtesy of Delno Winland.)

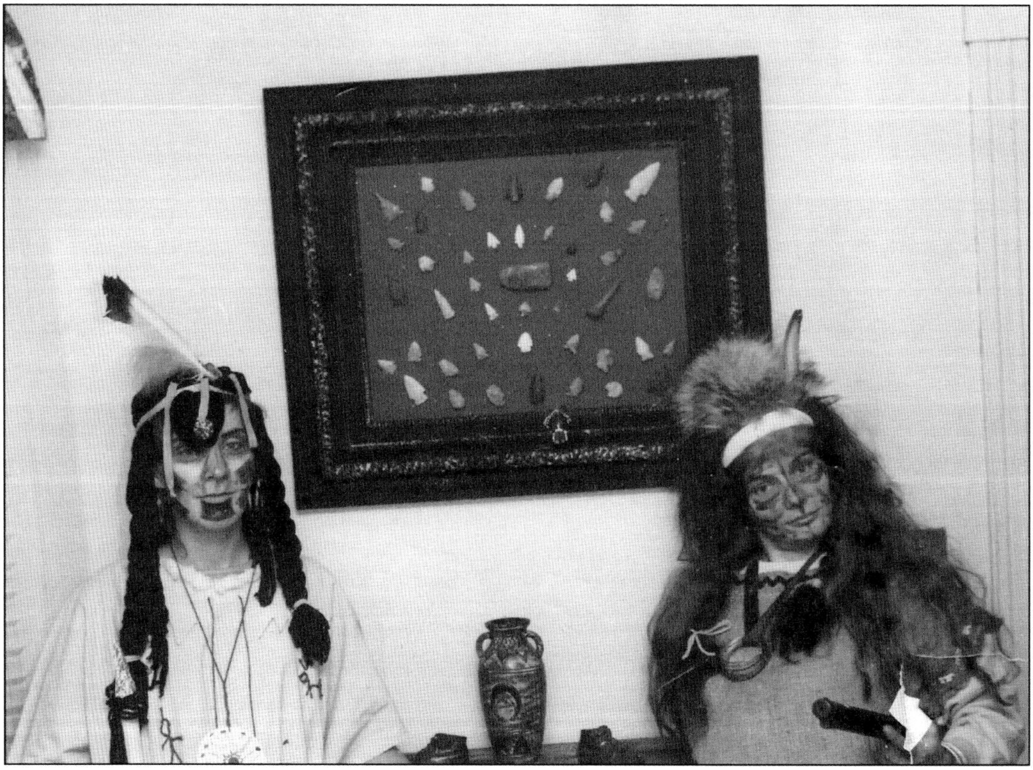

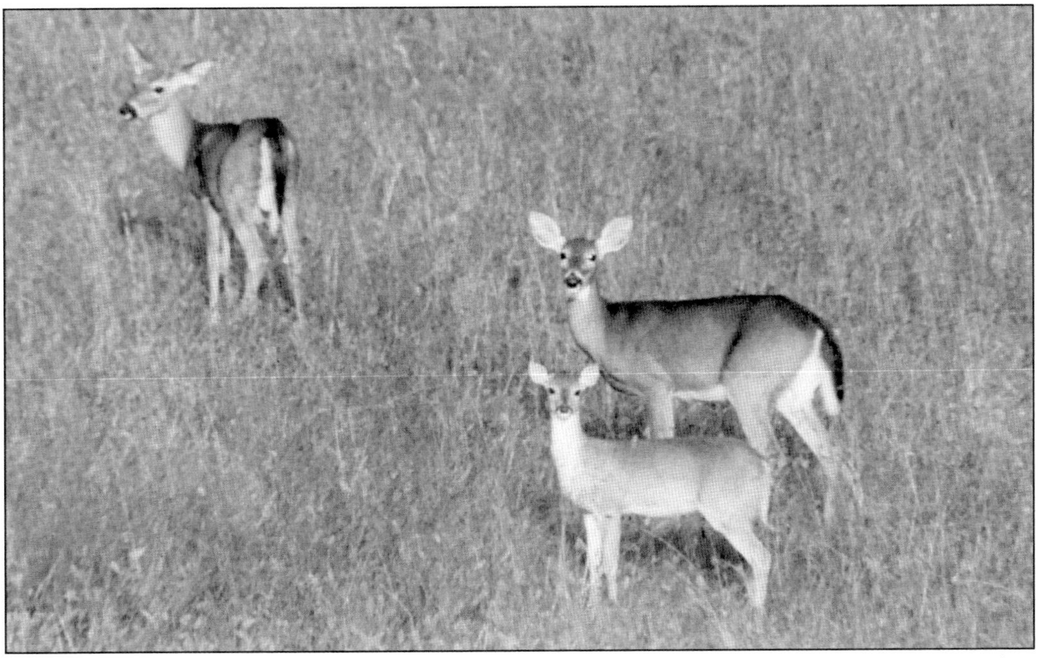

The Mound Builders, Native Americans, and early settlers depended upon the natural game that was abundant in this area. Deer hunting has continued to provide food for many inhabitants of the region. Other game has included bear, rabbit, squirrel, turkey, and even buffalo. Bones of such a variety have been found in the excavation of the mounds. (Courtesy of Rev. Daniel Simmons.)

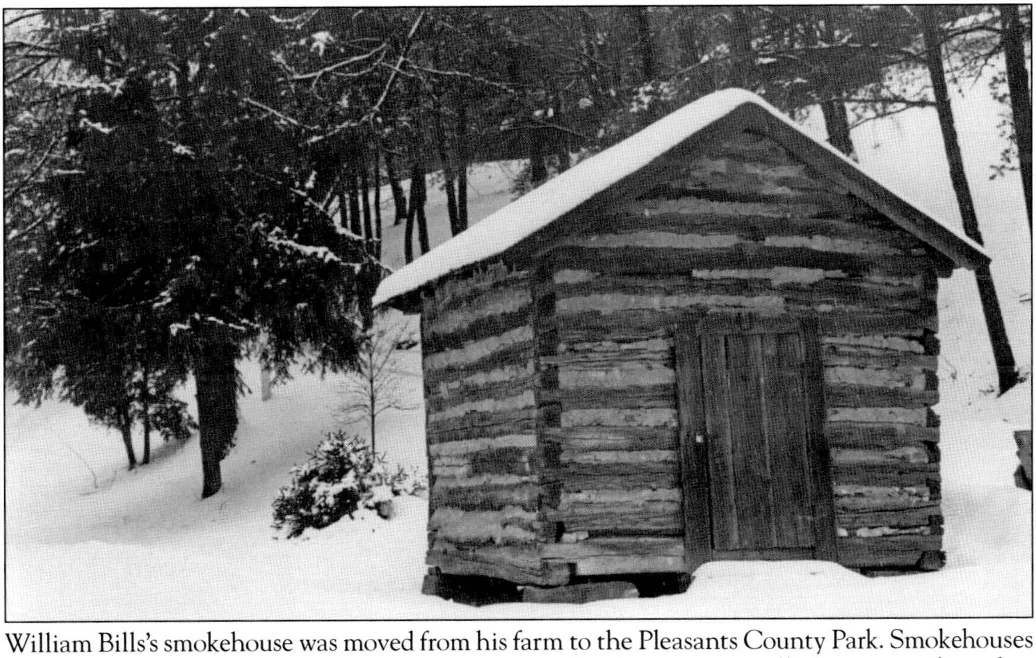

William Bills's smokehouse was moved from his farm to the Pleasants County Park. Smokehouses were used to cure and preserve meat products. A settler's home was usually a one-room log cabin with a rough stone fireplace and mud chimney reinforced with sticks to provide heat. Floors were bare earth or sometimes hewn puncheons or split wood. Furniture was made using an axe, hatchet, or auger. (Courtesy of Rev. Daniel Simmons.)

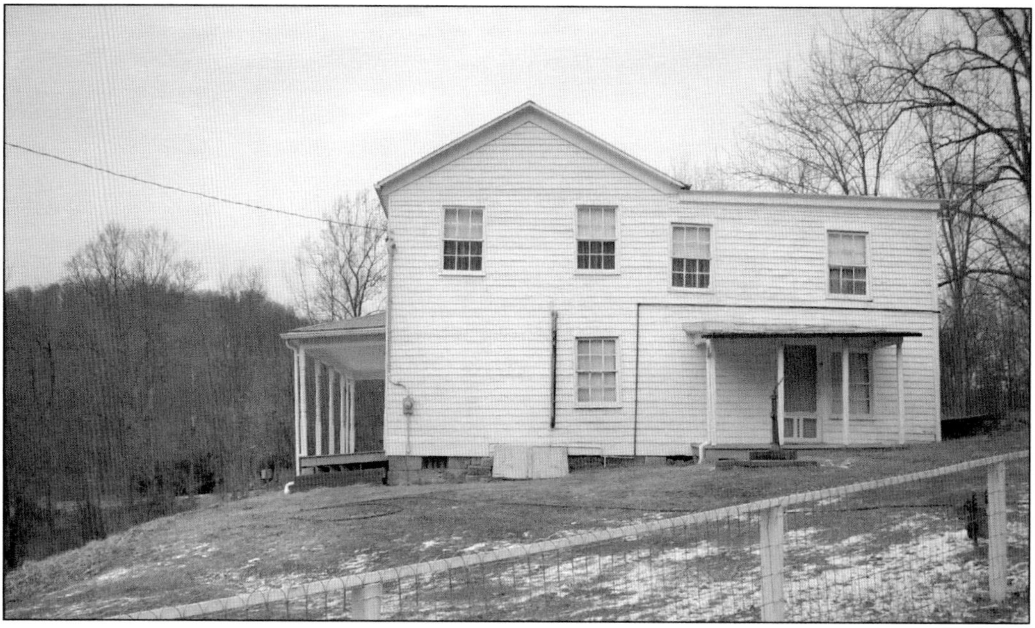

The LaRue house is located at the mouth of Broad Run. It was built in 1848, the third house built by the LaRue family. Jacob and Isaac LaRue moved to the area in 1790 and settled in a cabin at the mouth of Middle Island Creek. Jacob built a sawmill at the mouth of Broad Run, where the home above still stands. Isaac and Hannah Hughes LaRue had the first white child born in this vicinity, a daughter named Hannah. (Courtesy of Ruth Ann Dayhoff.)

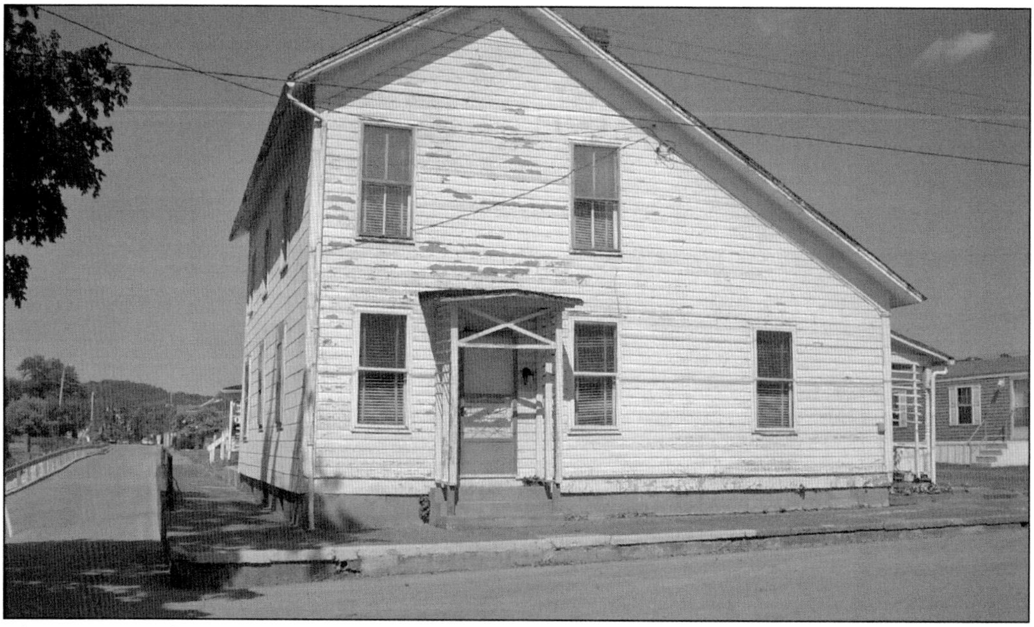

The Carpenter house was the first home built in St. Marys. Located on the corner of First and Creel Streets, it was owned by H. A. Carpenter. The Logan brothers erected it between 1849 and 1850 and used it as a mercantile store and a home. At the same time, the large brick building on the opposite side of Creel Street was erected and occupied by A. H. Creel. (Courtesy of Ruth Ann Dayhoff.)

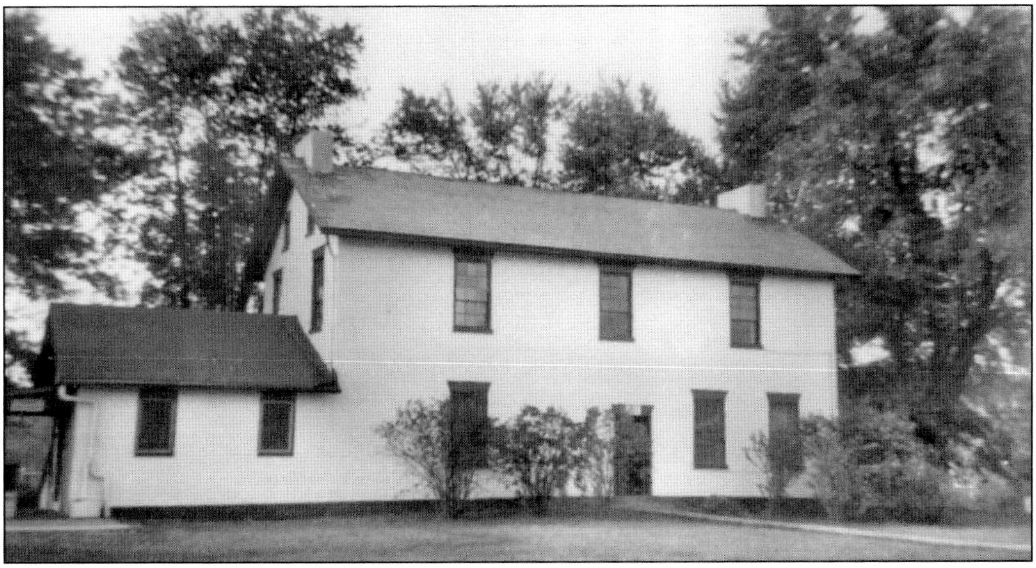

The Henderson house is located on the Cytec Willow Island Plant property. In 1814, Alexander Henderson built this gracious brick home in what was then known as Salama, Virginia. It was built with hand-made bricks and has walls 16 inches thick. The windowpanes are made of hand-blown glass. The Hendersons bought some slaves and began clearing the area. (Courtesy of Adolph "Charlie" Dittman.)

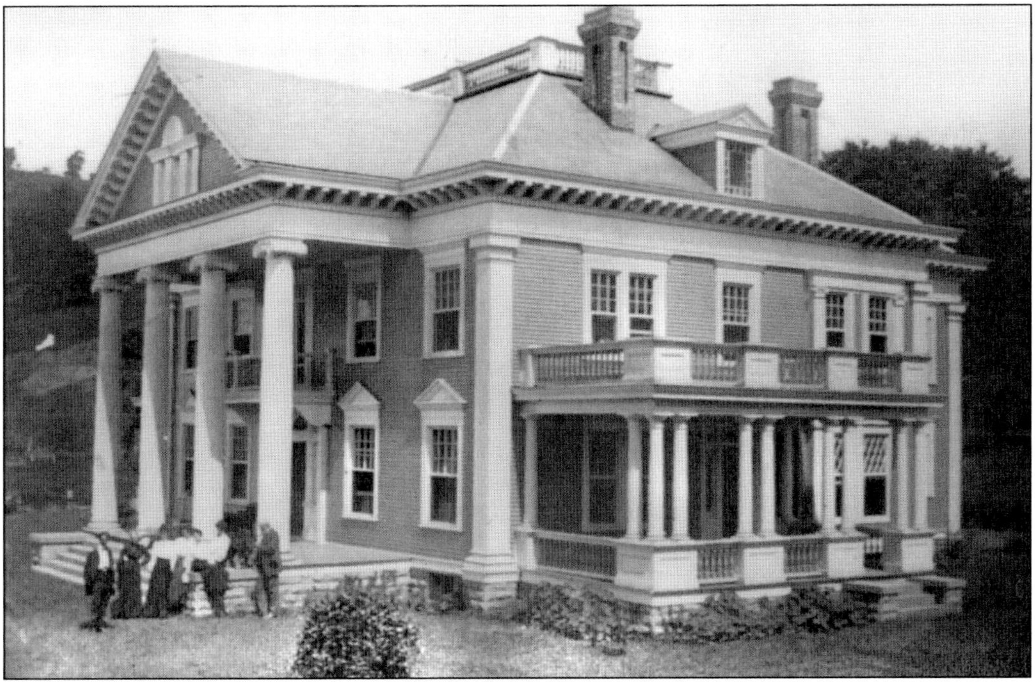

Thomas Browse and his wife, Eliza, built a small cabin in 1831. They had moved to America from England. Thomas built this beautiful mansion for his wife about four miles north of St. Marys at Spring Run. They had tenant farmers as well as several slaves. He surveyed the town of St. Marys. This exceptional landmark of Pleasants County burned to the ground on March 1, 1949. (St. Marys Correctional Center, courtesy of Sherry Burton.)

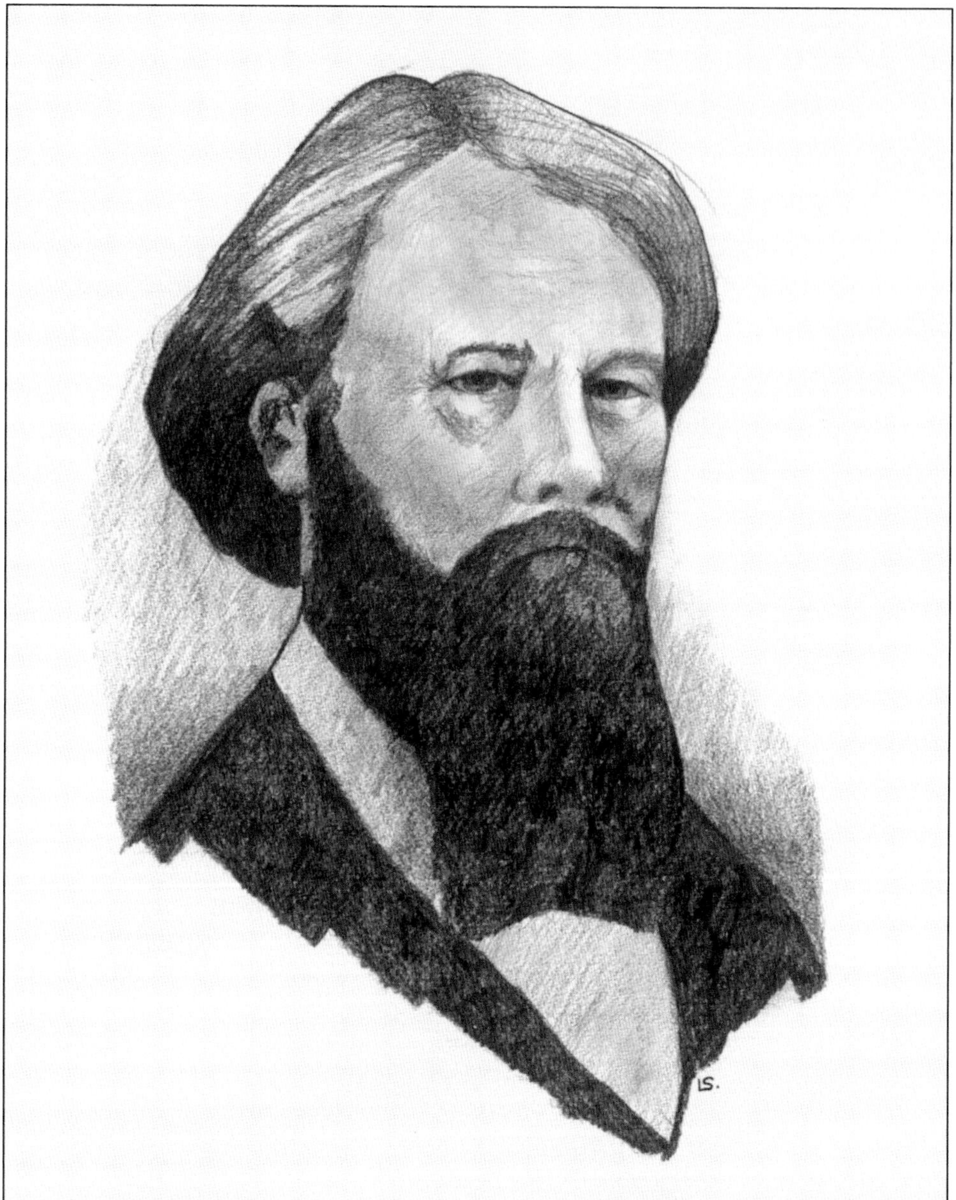

Alexander Herbert Creel, founder of St. Marys, was the son of George and Mary Creel. Born in 1738 in Virginia as the eighth child of a family of 10, he moved into Wood County, Virginia, now West Virginia. While traveling to Wheeling, he had a vision of the Virgin Mary, who told him to look at the Virginia side of the river. She said, "You will behold the site of what some day will be a happy and prosperous city." The moonlight allowed him to see the lower end of Middle Island. The memory of his vision never left him. His father, George, purchased the land on which St. Marys now stands. After his father's death in 1825, Alexander sold this land to Mr. Pickens, and it was known as Picken's Bottom. In 1849, he repurchased the land that is now St. Marys. This portrait was drawn by Leonard Savage, a world-renowned artist, from a photograph of the Creel portrait by an unknown artist. Kitty Gorrell, former owner of the Creel House, took the photograph of the original portrait. (Courtesy of Leonard Savage.)

Two

Early Businesses and Vital Industries

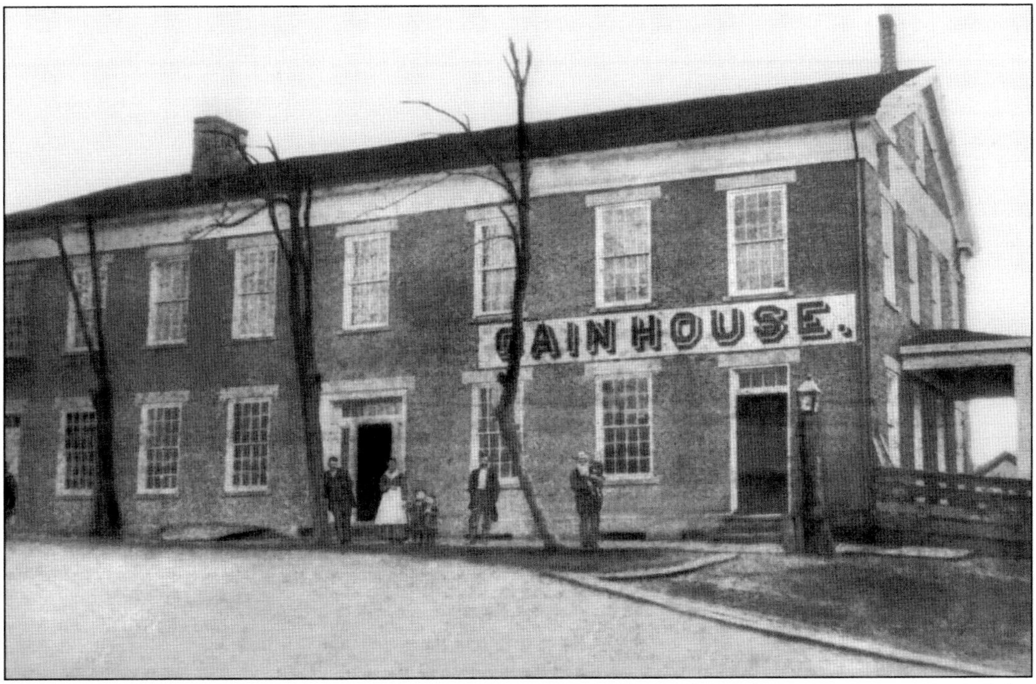

The Cain House, used as a store, hotel, and tavern in the early 20th century, was named for Zachariah Cain, who operated the tavern. It was built in 1839 by Alexander Creel and is usually now referred to as the Creel House. In the photograph, Zachariah Cain is holding his son, Zachariah Jr., the great-great-uncle of Steve Green, a local resident of Belmont. (Courtesy of Steve Green.)

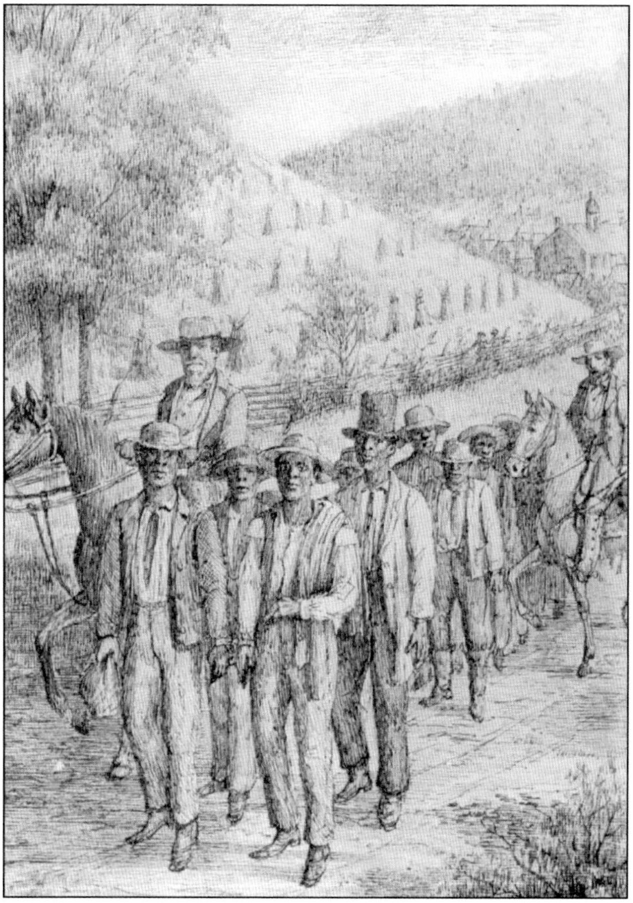

In 1847, Joseph H. Diss Debar sketched this picture depicting slave drivers and slaves walking between Clarksburg and Parkersburg. These slaves would have walked through the Vaucluse area and possibly have been auctioned off at the slave market at Vaucluse. Alexander and John Henderson, sons of the wealthy Dumfries merchant Alexander Henderson Sr., owned the largest number of slaves in the area. Alexander Creel purchased slaves from the Hendersons at the courthouse in Parkersburg. A slave cemetery is located on Route 2 south of St. Marys on the Abicht property. Underground Railroad historian Henry Burke has substantiated this in his book, *Washington County Underground Railroad* (Arcadia Publishing). Below is a photograph of the Abicht home, built between 1850 and 1860. The cemetery is behind the house. (Left Joseph H. Diss Debar Collection, courtesy of WVDCHSA; below courtesy of Ruth Ann Dayhoff.)

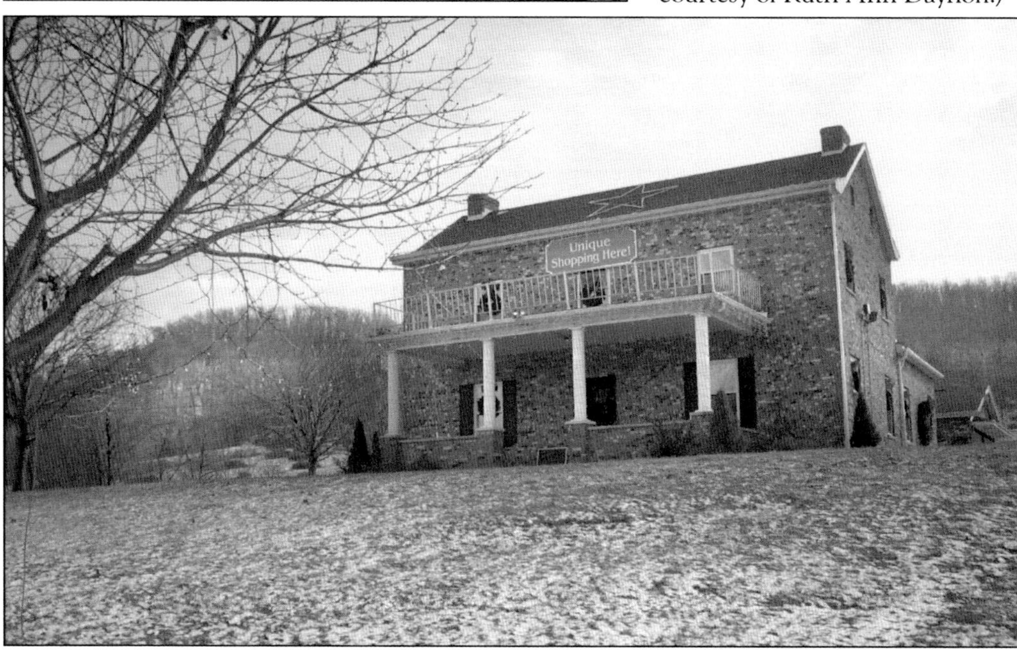

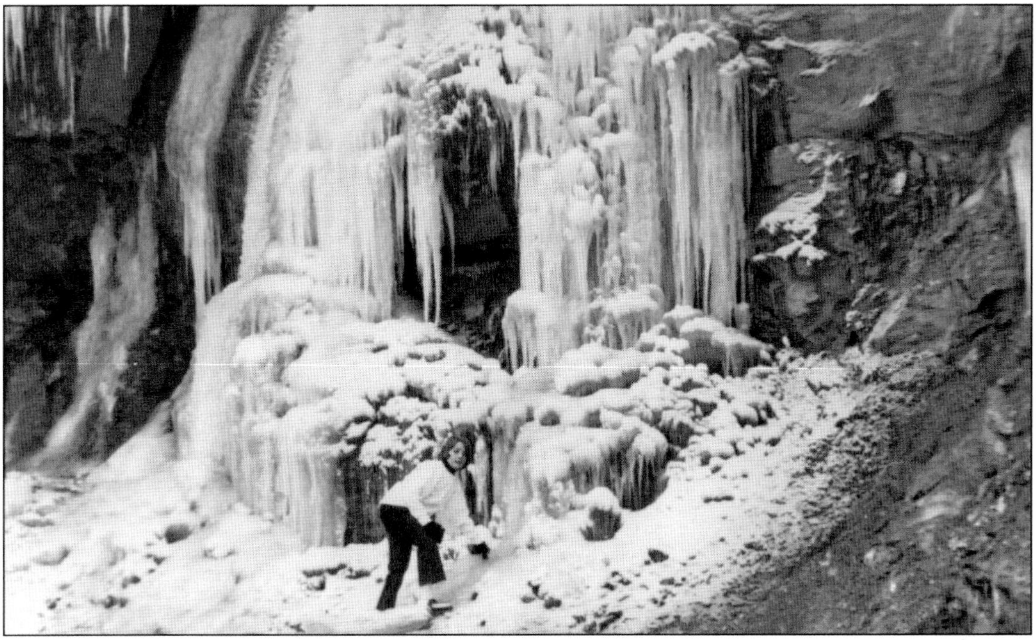

Founded in 1817 by Alexander Creel, Vaucluse was the first town and river port in Pleasants County and even rivaled Parkersburg in its commerce. A disgruntled slave burned it down. Later the flood of 1852 wiped it out. Creel's father, George, purchased the land on which St. Marys is founded. Alexander sold the land at his father's death and purchased the property where Vaucluse was settled. Population increased rapidly, especially the wagon trade to flatboats and steamboats. Rebecca Simmons climbs up frozen rocks beside Route 2 in the Vaucluse area, located a mile south of St. Marys at the mouth of Green's Run. Below, about the first thing a settler did was to clear land and cut wood for a home. Timbering was a vital business, not only for the construction of buildings but for other related businesses. (Above courtesy of Rev. Daniel Simmons; below courtesy of Ruth Ann Dayhoff.)

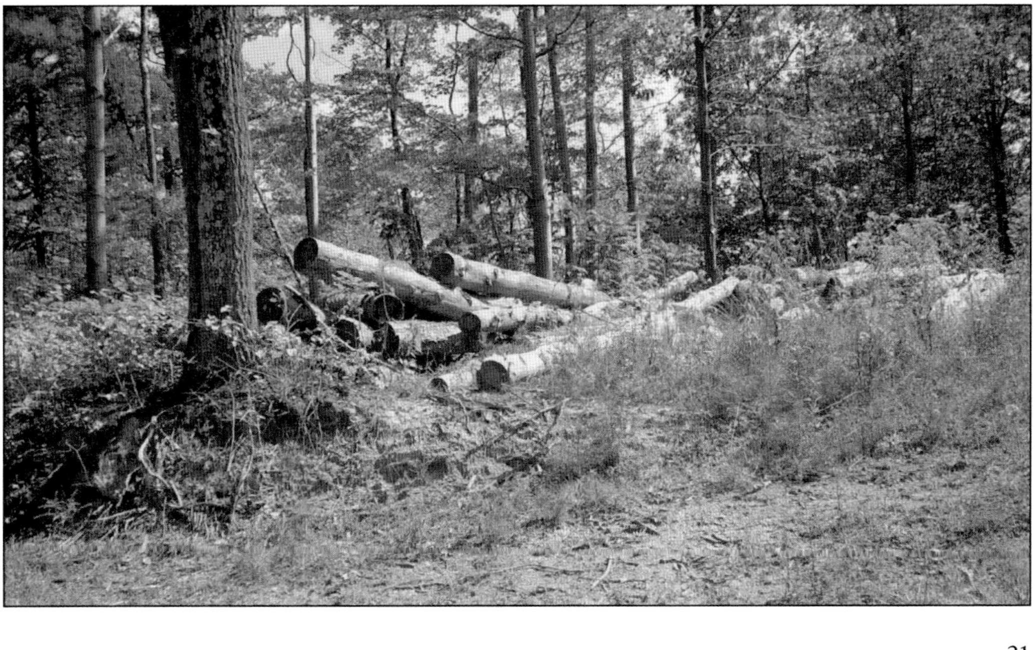

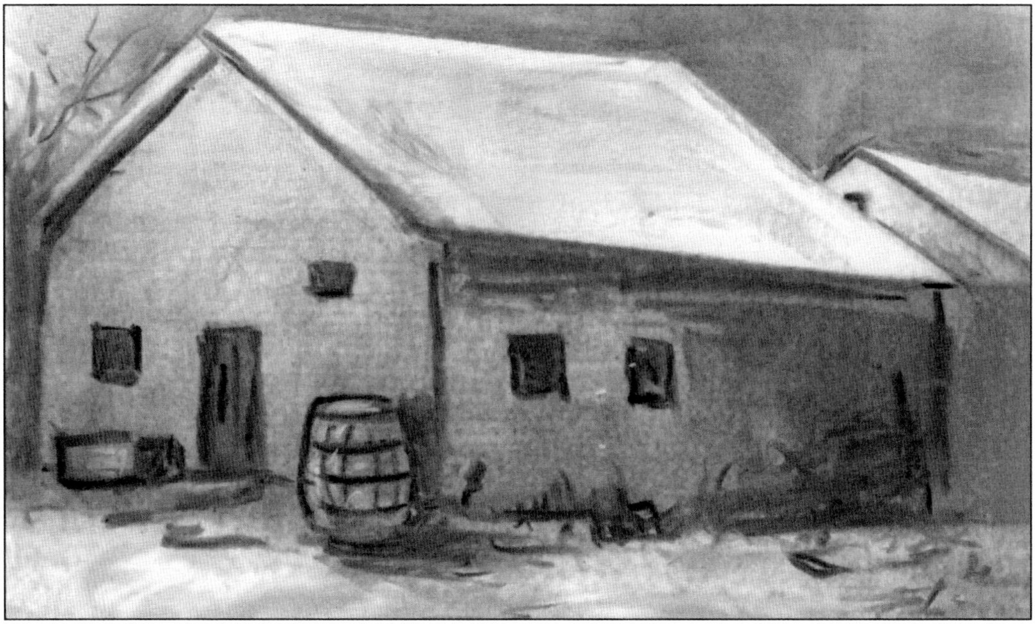

One industry depending on timbering was the cooper shop. Shops produced wooden barrels for storing oil, hides, water, and so on. For almost 20 years, coopering was the main industry of the county. This charcoal sketch by Ruth Ann Dayhoff shows a shop formerly located behind the Cain House. In the 1870s, about 10 cooper shops in St. Marys employed most of the men who worked outside of their farms. (Courtesy of Ruth Ann Dayhoff.)

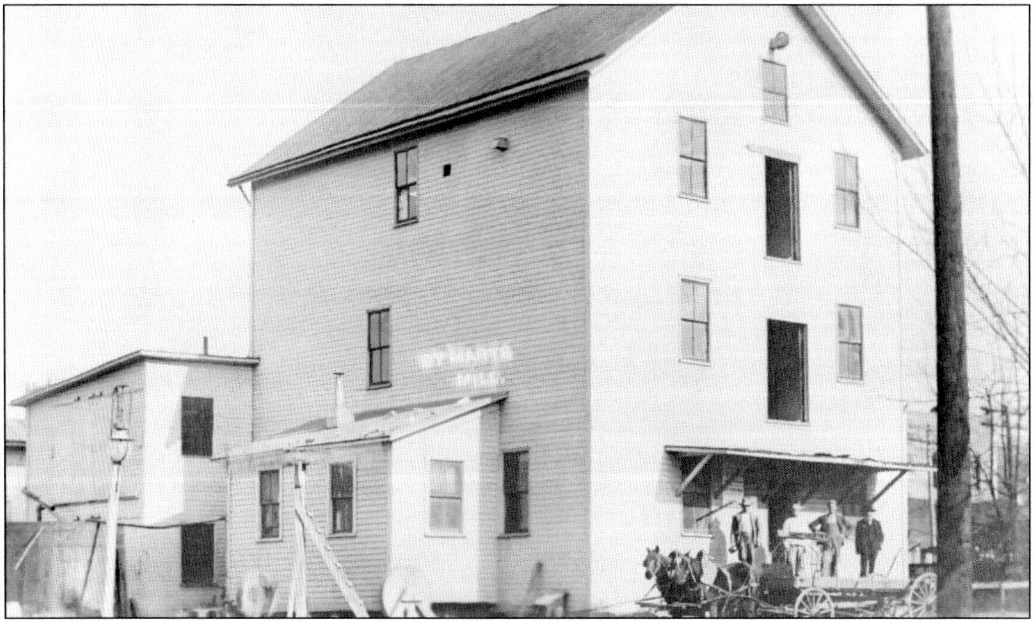

This mill at St. Marys was located near the bridge and used for many years. Later it was transformed into a service station for the Quaker State Oil Company and owned by Charles Sweeney. The first gristmill in the county, however, was the Sylvan Mill in Union District, which was erected by John and Reuben McCoy. Mills such as these ground various grains, like wheat and corn. (PCHSC, courtesy of WVDCHSA.)

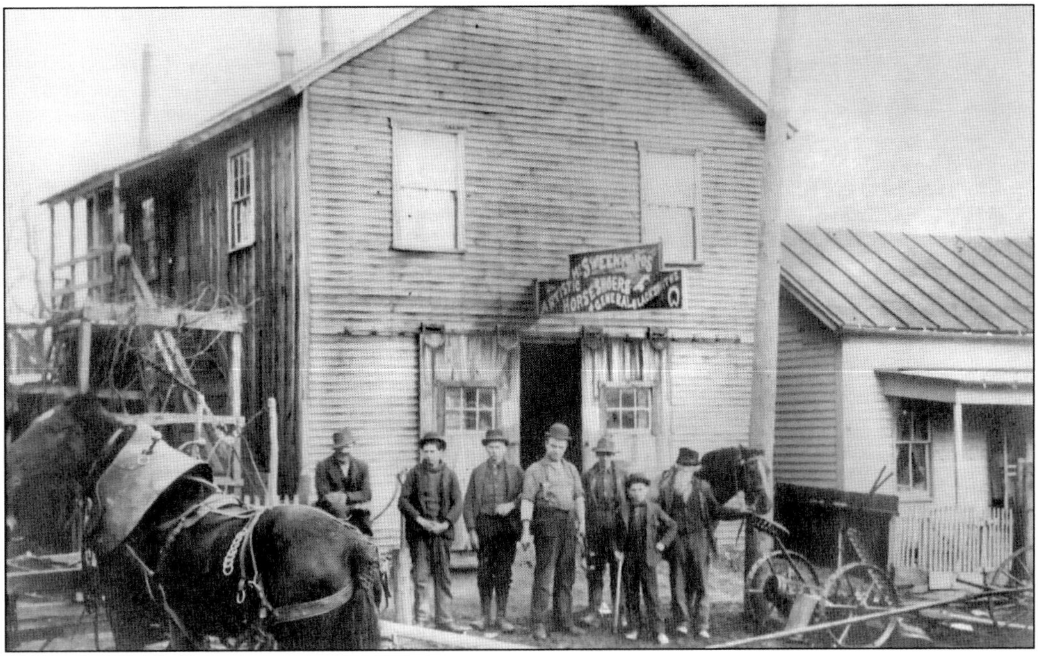

McSweeny's livery stable and blacksmith shop were owned by Theresa McSweeny Roby's grandfather. People could board their horses and have them curried, cleaned, and fed at the Livery Stable when they were in town for an extended time. If horseshoes were needed, the blacksmith shop was handy. Blacksmith shops also made tools, nails, and repaired many types of metal objects. The combined shops were located in the vicinity of the present-day Shake Shack across from the fire department. Barney Olmstead was the blacksmith, and he had a reputation for tempering steel, making his handicraft highly esteemed. He specialized in making axes, hatchets, knives, and mattocks. (Both courtesy of Joe Roby and Delno Winland.)

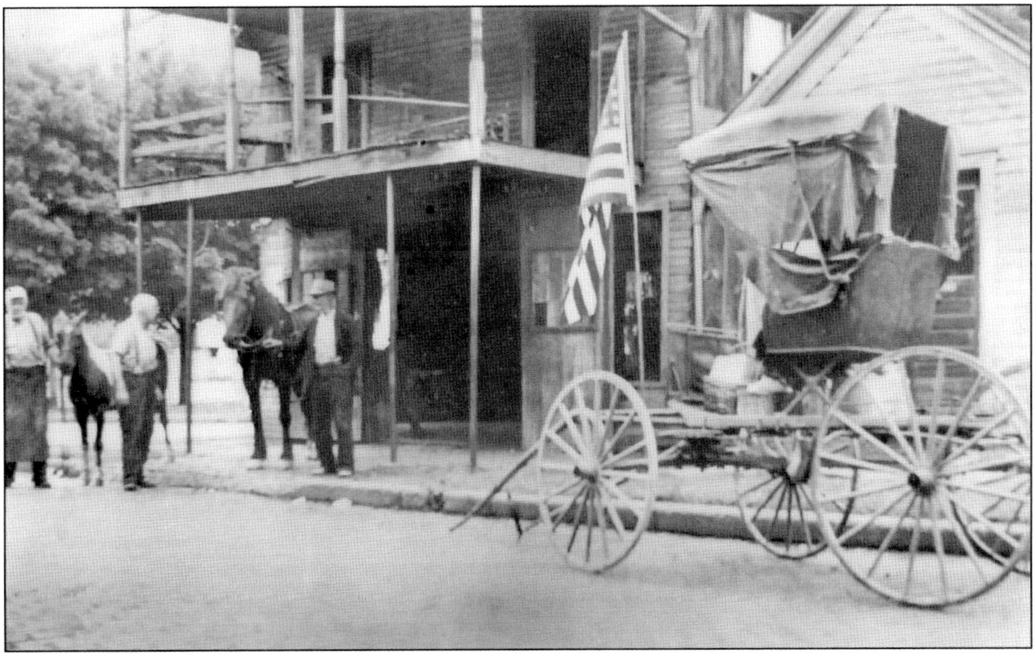

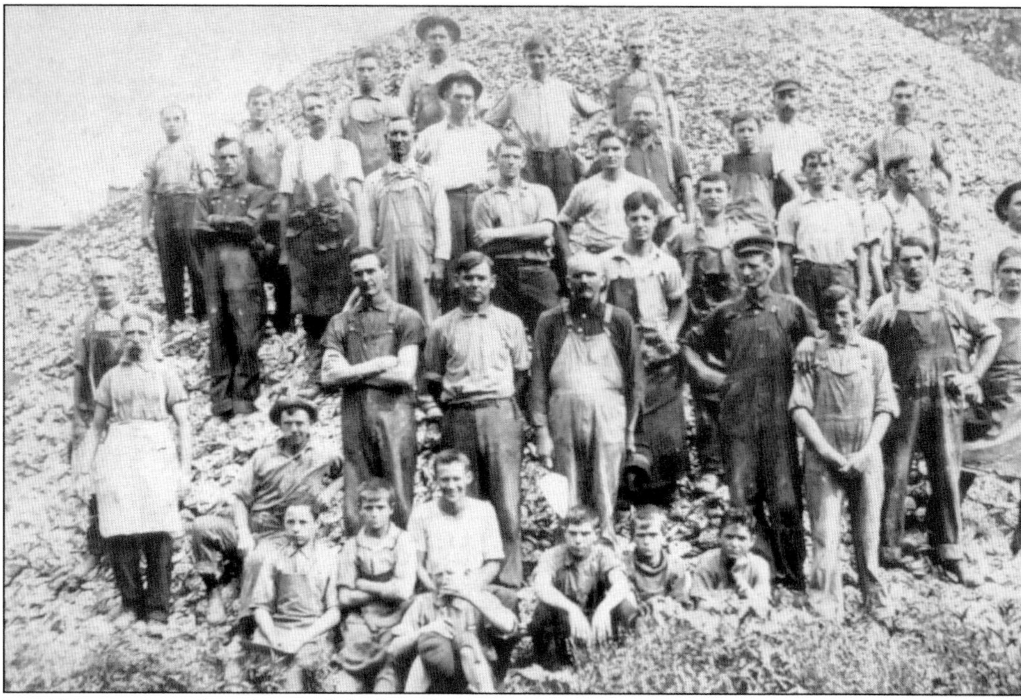

In 1909, people gathered mussel shells to be shipped to Harvey Chalmers and Sons of Amsterdam, New York, who owned factories in the Ohio Valley. Sometimes pearls valued at $150 were found. Early in 1910, a button factory was established in St. Marys, and $4,000 was donated by the citizens to purchase a site for a factory along the railroad north of the town. Between 50 and 100 men were employed to cut blanks from the mussel shells taken from the Ohio River. In the picture above, workers of all ages are standing in front of a pile of mussel shells from which the buttons were made. Below, the workers are in front of the factory. In 1928, this factory closed because the acid in the water caused the mussels to die. (Above WVDNR, courtesy of Janet Butler; below PCHSC, courtesy of WVDCHSA.)

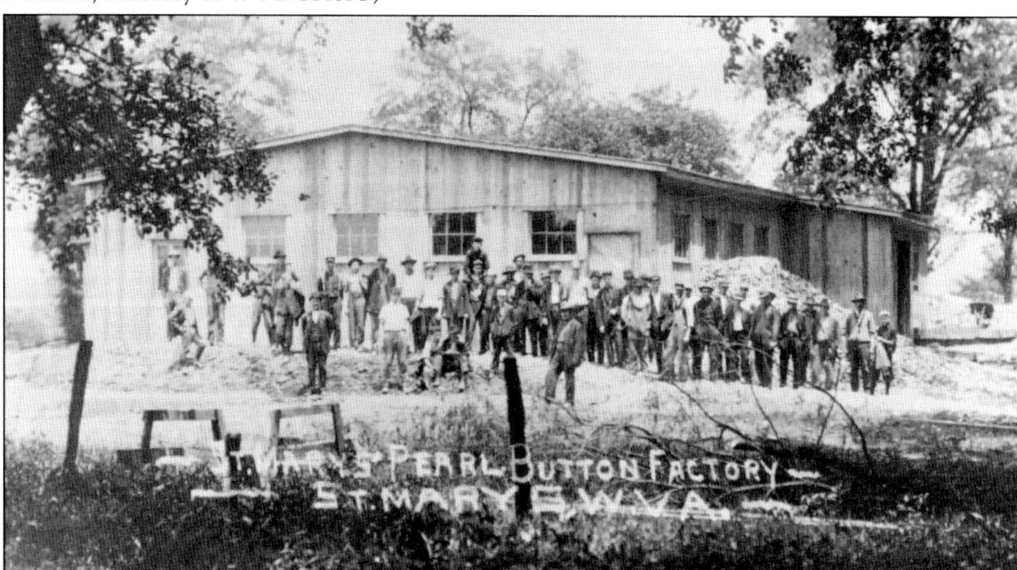

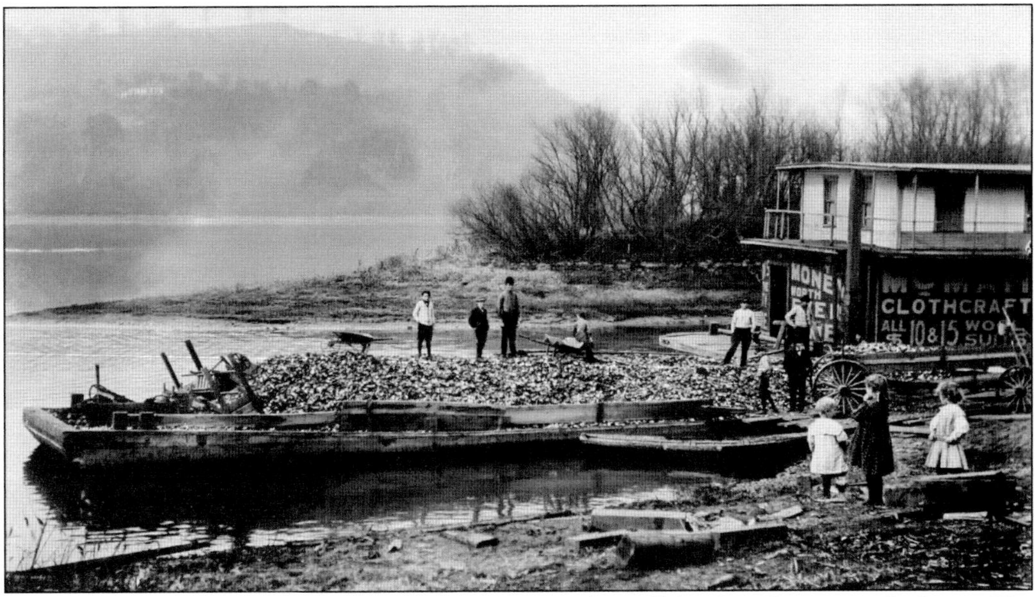

Men fished for the mussels, sometimes using lines with small hooks, often using flatboats. The mussels laid their eggs on the sandy bars where they could hatch in the sun. Deepening water covered the bars so the sun could not warm the eggs, causing the mussels to soon disappear. Acids released into the Ohio River then caused the shells to become too soft for button making. High cost prohibited the company to ship shells from western streams. The company was compelled to shut down in 1928. Later the plant burned to the ground. Below are used shells from which buttons have been made. These mother-of-pearl mussel shells were punched and peeled to create beautiful buttons of all sizes that held an elegant appeal to all. Special tools were required to make these buttons, for example, a puncher and a pincher. (Above HCWC, Mark Williams, courtesy of WVDCHSA; below WVDNR, courtesy of Janet Butler.)

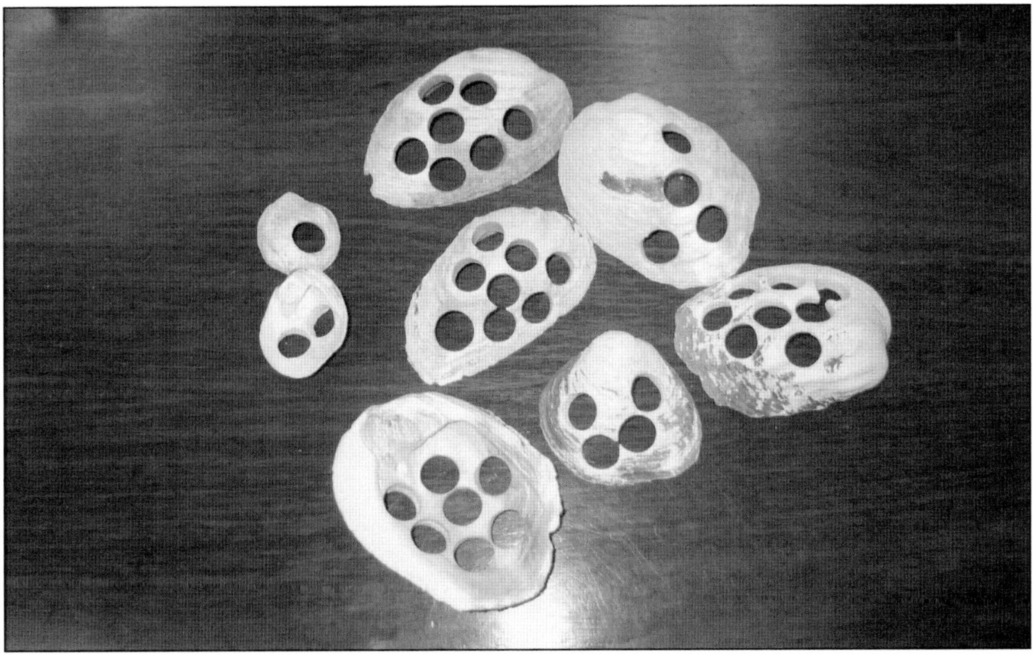

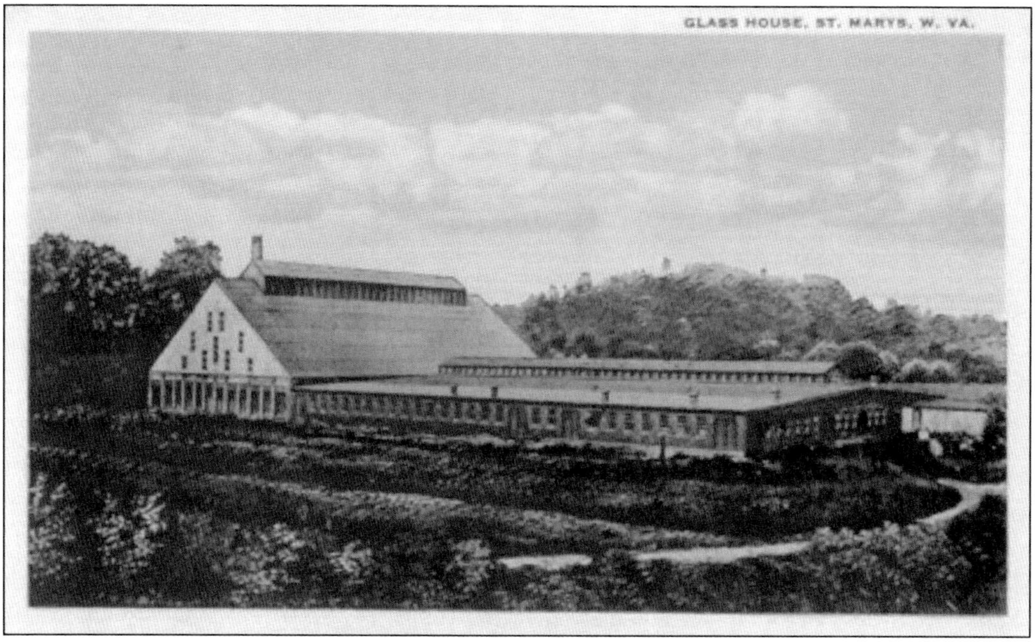

R. S. Giese of Charleroi, Pennsylvania, arrived in September 1916 to erect a plant to manufacture glassware. A site south of the Quaker State Oil refinery was purchased, and the plant was operating by 1917. Gilligan's Glass Company made various glass products, including fine art ware and electric bulbs. In September 1936, the Alley Agate Manufacturing Company purchased the building and began producing marbles and children's dishes. In 1948, they stopped the production of dishes and accelerated the production of marbles. L. E. Alley developed a marvelous machine, which produced 165 marbles per minute, and also developed a new technique for putting multiple stripes on the marbles. This boosted this industry into such high production that it is said the Alley Agate Marble factory was the largest producing marble factory in the world. (Above courtesy of Kitty Renner; below courtesy of Frank and Ruby Sellers, grandson of L. E. Alley.)

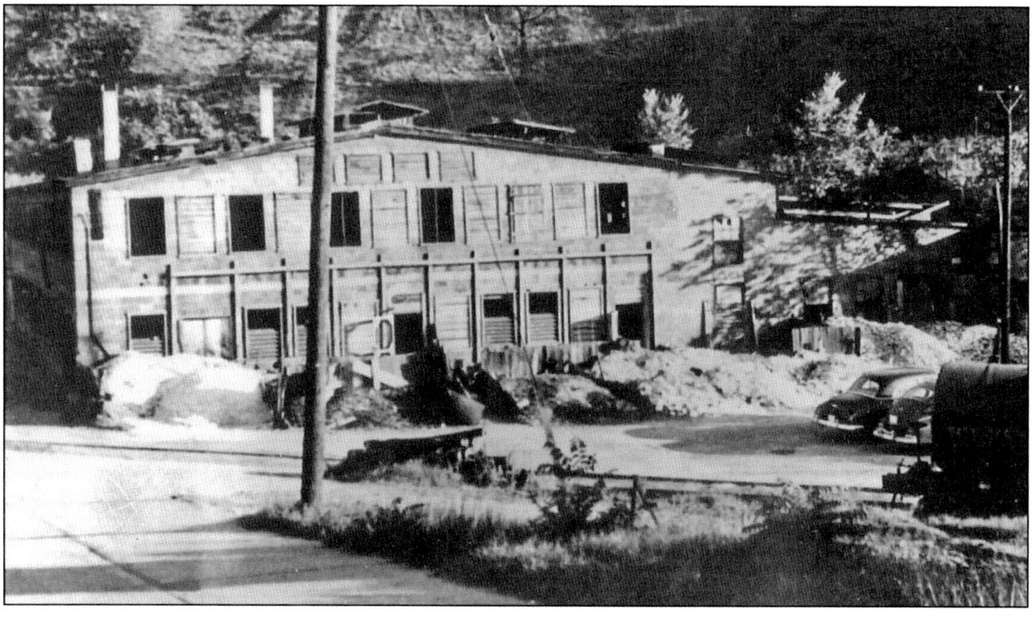

Lawrence E. Alley set up his factory in Paden City in 1929. By 1937, he relocated to St. Marys. He designed all the marble-making machines himself and produced a marble game called Hop Cuing, or Chinese checkers. He shipped 14 million Chinese checker marbles in six months. The 125 workers included batch makers, carry-in boys, machine workers, and women bagging marbles. Marbles were loaded on freight cars beside the plant. The Sylvania Electric Company asked him to produce glass tubes for radios. He succeeded, but the marbles were in so much demand that he declined. In 1949, Alley sold the business because of ill health to Berry Pink and Sellers Peltier, and they renamed it the Marble King. (Both courtesy of Frank and Ruby Sellers.)

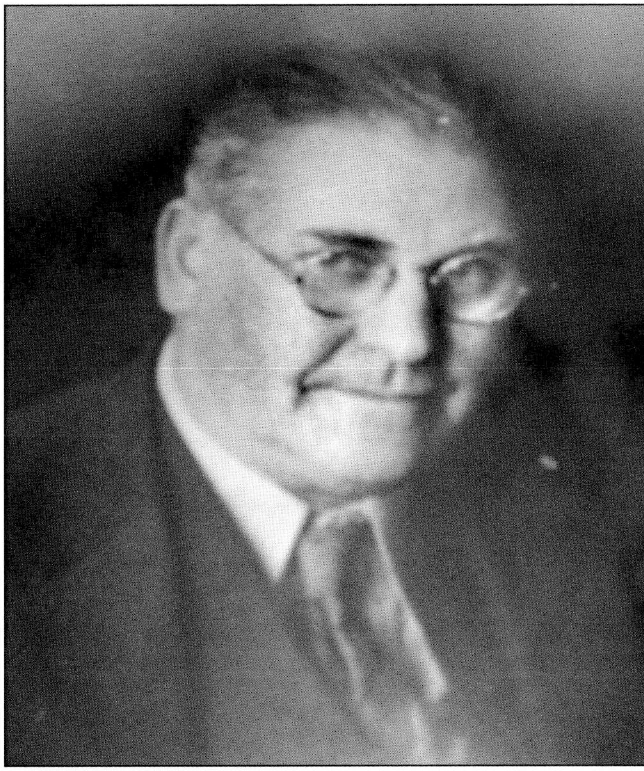

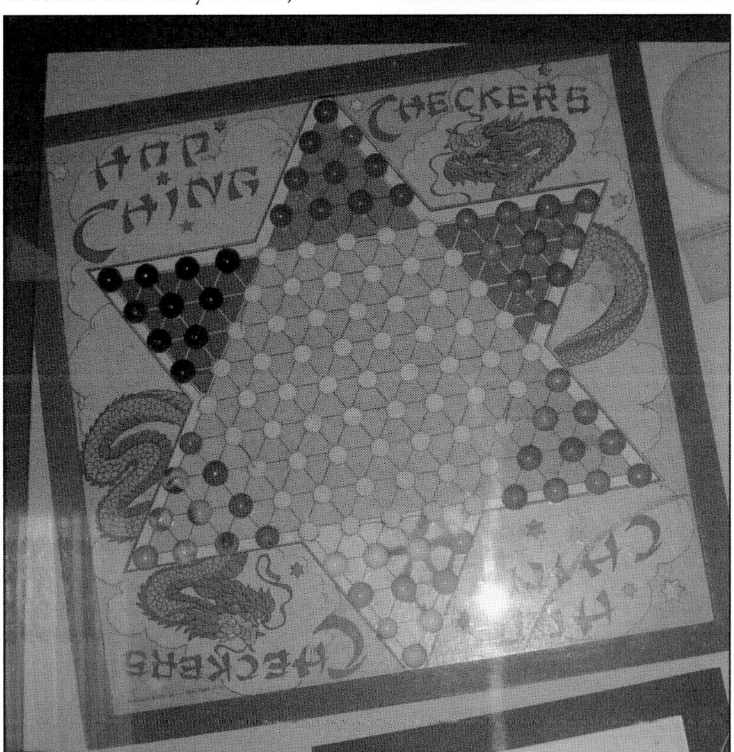

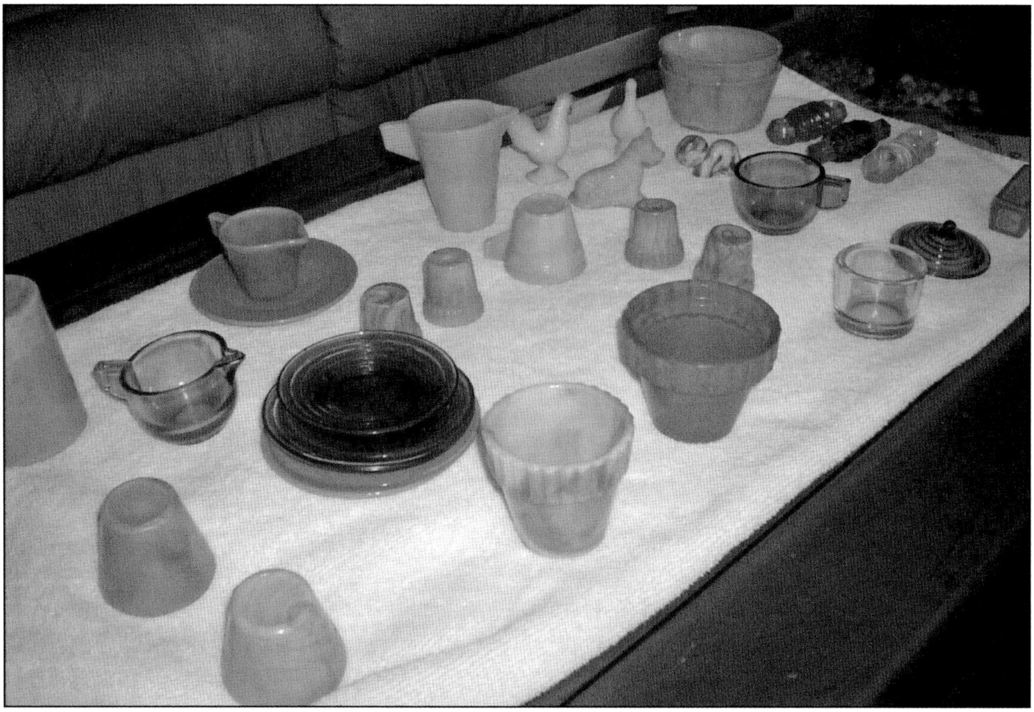

These dishes, called the Orphan Annie Children's Play Tea Sets, were made by the Alley Marble line. Alley had entered into an arrangement with J. Pressman and Company, a major New York toy company, to market all of his production. The entire outputs of toys from the St. Marys facility were distributed by Pressman in Europe. His Chinese checker marbles appeared in the *National Geographic* article on West Virginia industry in August 1940. Although L. E. Alley was the person interviewed in the St. Marys plant, he declined to be identified in the article because he was a modest person who did not like notoriety. These photographs were taken at Ruby and Frank Seller's home. (Both courtesy of Ruth Ann Dayhoff.)

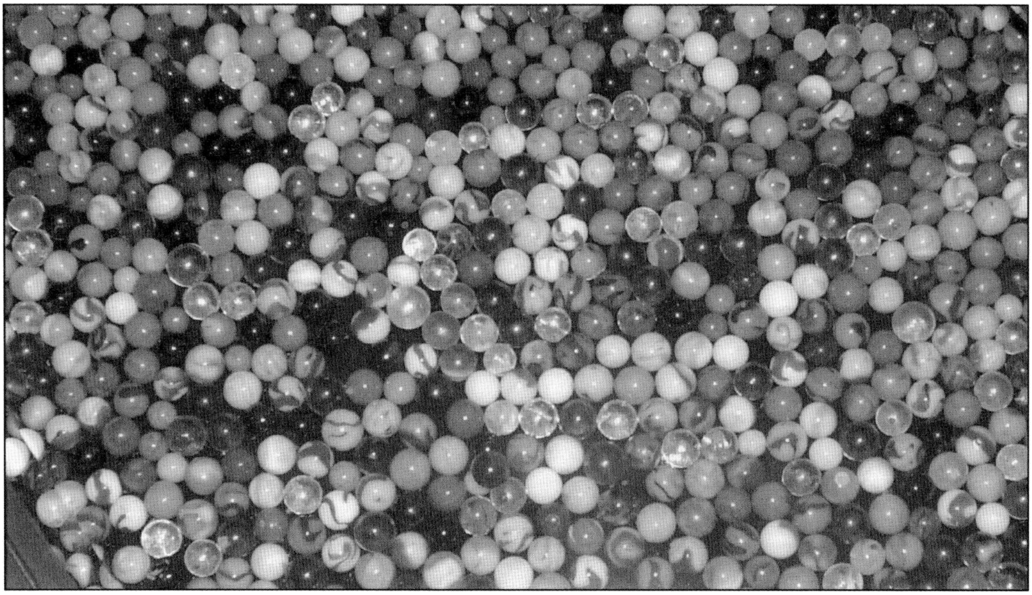

Berry Pink and Sellers Peltier purchased the factory from Alley and renamed it the Marble King in 1949. Pink traveled around the United States giving away marbles, holding marble tournaments everywhere. He earned the nickname "The Marble King." When the St. Marys factory was destroyed by fire, the company was relocated to Paden City in 1958. Today the Marble King is the country's largest maker of marbles, making West Virginia the Marble Capital of the United States. In the picture at right, Berry Pink shows an interested child his famous collection of marbles. In the photograph below, barrels of marbles are being sorted by hand. This colorful, happy factory in St. Marys was greatly missed by residents of all ages. Both photographs were taken from those on exhibit in the West Virginia Division of Culture and History State Archives in Charleston, West Virginia. (Both courtesy of Ruth Ann Dayhoff.)

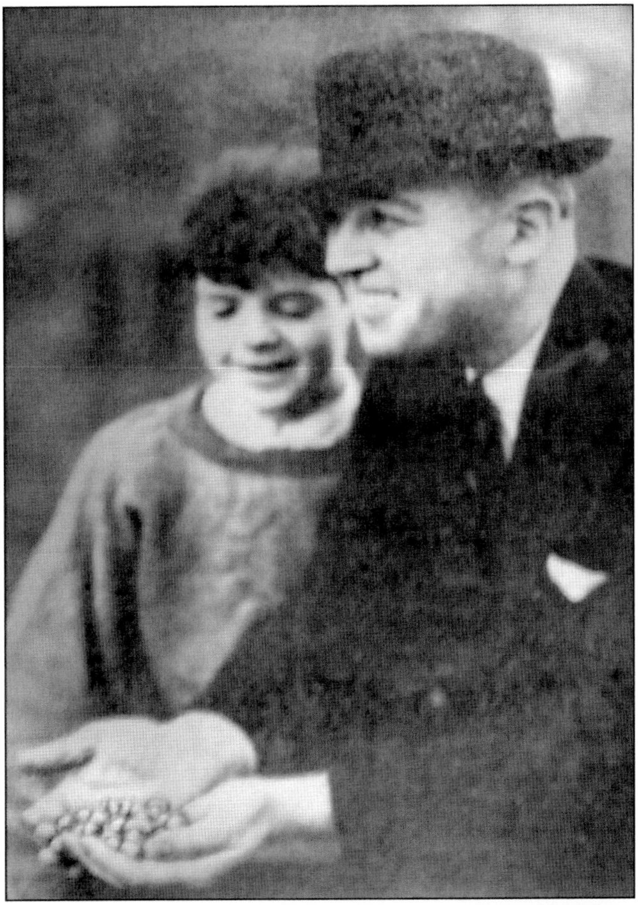

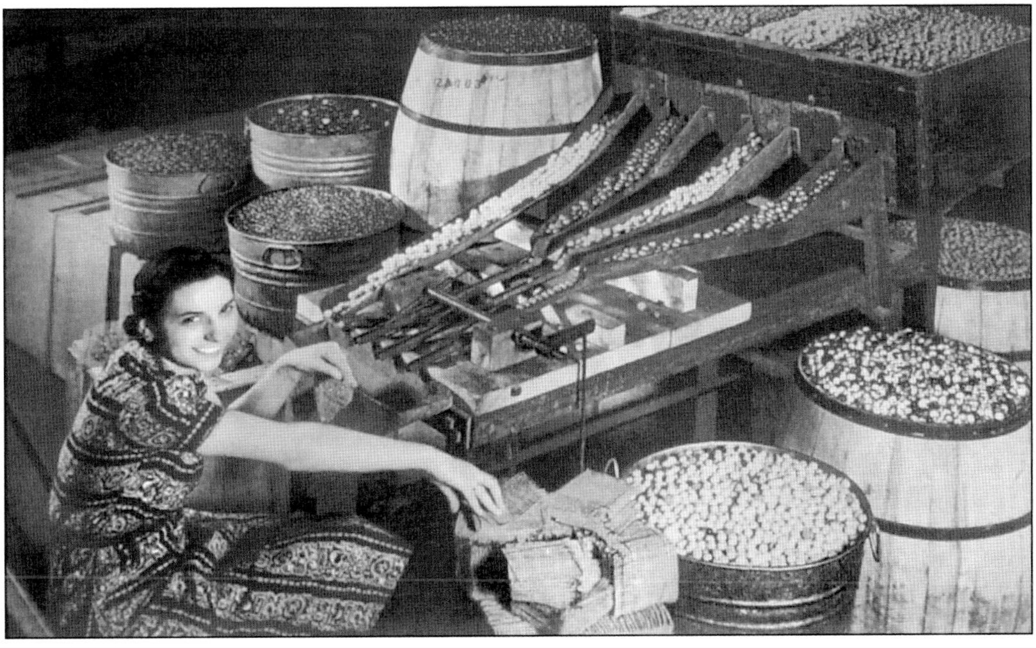

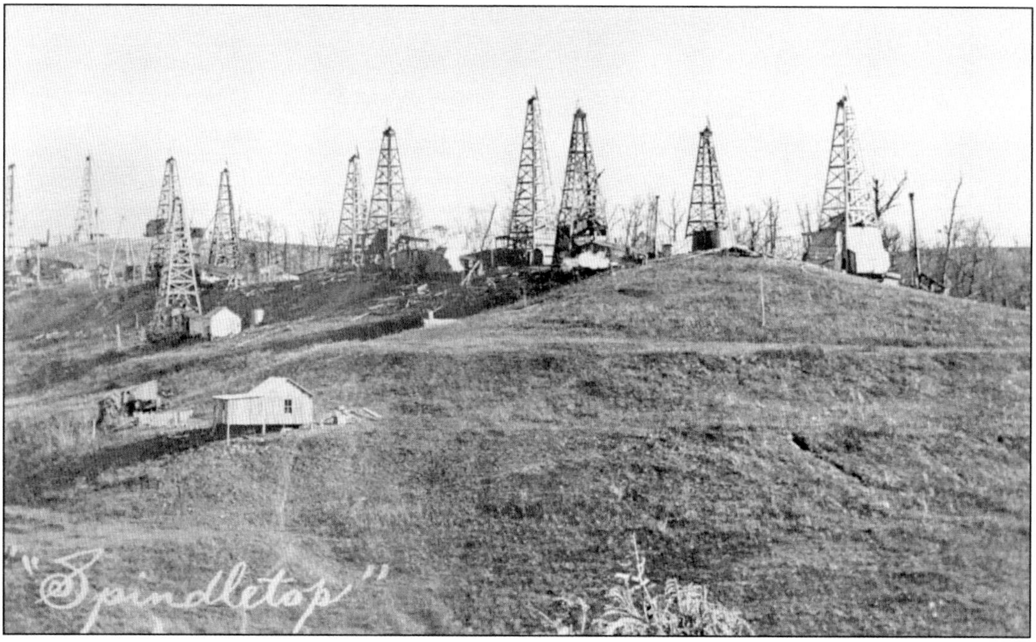

This 1905 Spindletop Oil Field started in the early 1890s as the most active field in the county. The name was an adaptation of the "spindle kopf" of the South African Boer War. Spindletop may be classed as the last of the great pools that have been developed in Pleasants County. Fields named Spindletop were developed in many states. This photograph was taken about 1905. (PCHSC, courtesy of WVDCHSA.)

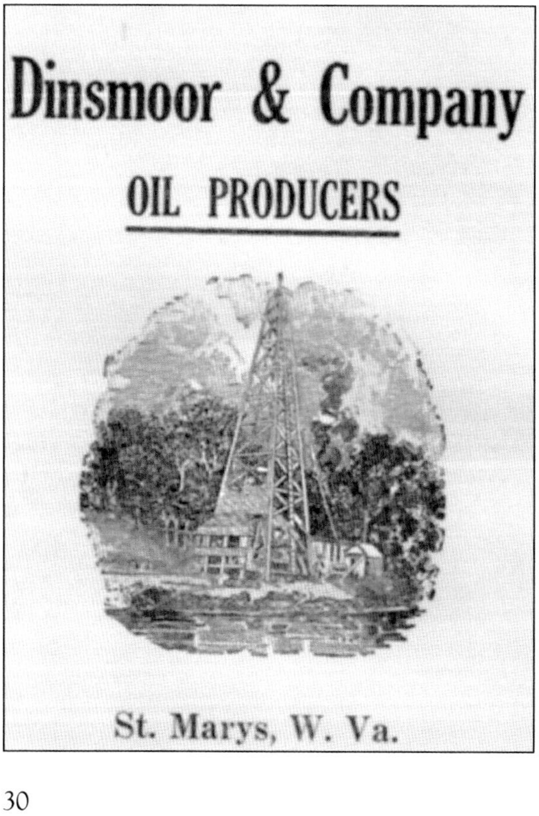

James Denton Dinsmoor came to St. Marys with the development of the oil district. No name has been more prominently identified with oil than Dinsmoor. Lyell, James, and his father, John C., owned and operated the Dinsmoor Company. Their interests also included other fields in Ohio and West Virginia. The Dinsmoor company has been considered to rank among the largest oil companies in the entire state. (Courtesy of David McCain.)

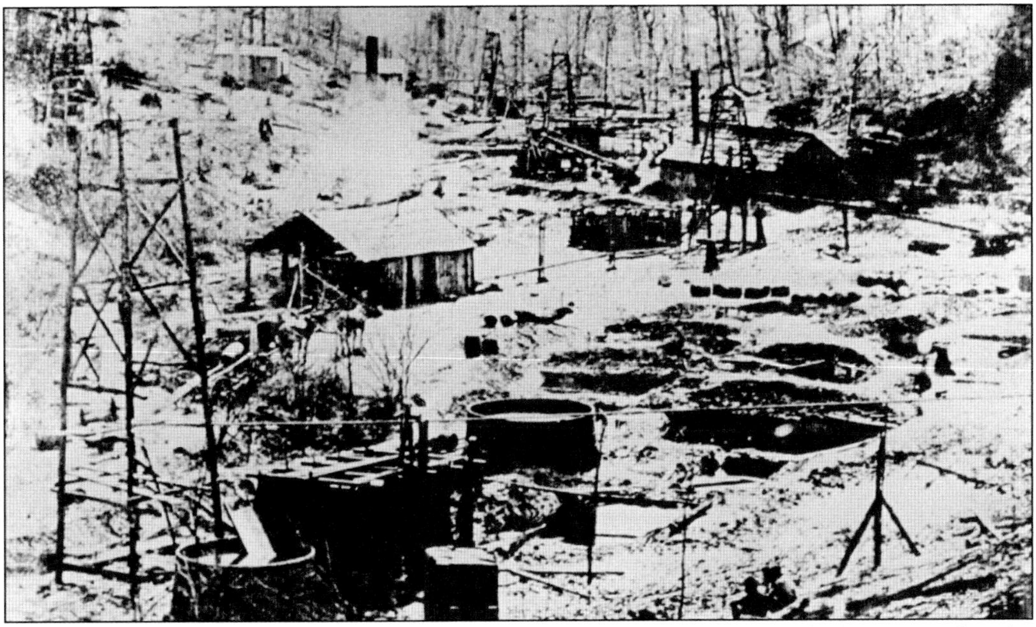

Jacob Beeson Blair and three other men from Parkersburg secured the first lease on record to the Horseneck field. Early in the 1850s, oil was seen floating in little pools in Horseneck Run. They leased the land from Jacob Hendershot and hit a gusher in April 1863 for a well that produced from 1,200 to 1,500 barrels per day. The incredible well was called Gilfillan after one of the developers. (Courtesy of WVDCHSA.)

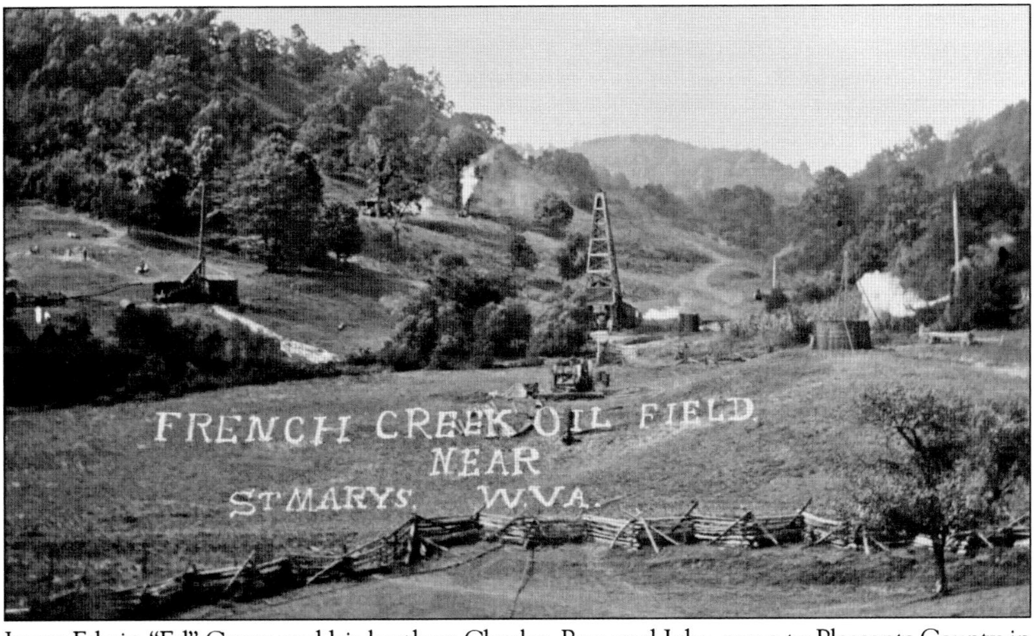

James Edwin "Ed" Green and his brothers Charles, Ray, and John came to Pleasants County in 1898. Ed Green worked at installing large engines with their network of cables to pump oil wells. The French Creek oil field had many fine wells that created much excitement. Edwin was also a serious amateur photographer, and he took many pictures of places and events in Pleasants County, including the photograph above. (JEGC, courtesy of Dale Brown.)

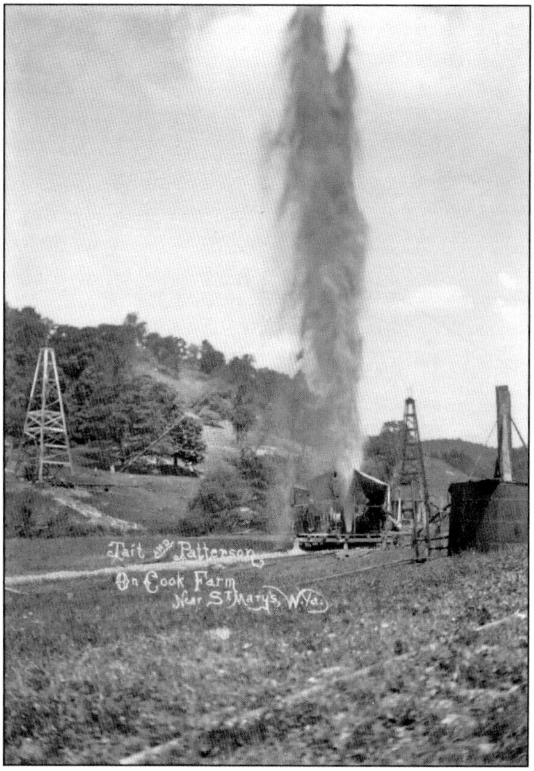

This gusher was drilled by the Tait and Patterson Company on the Cook Farm near St. Marys. It was an extremely expensive venture to drill such a well because one had to lease the land, survey it, map it, and then drill. Hugh Mearns made the statement that there was no doubt oil was in this belt, and just as sure as a blind hog could find an acorn, somebody could strike a bonanza. (JEGC, courtesy of Dale Brown.)

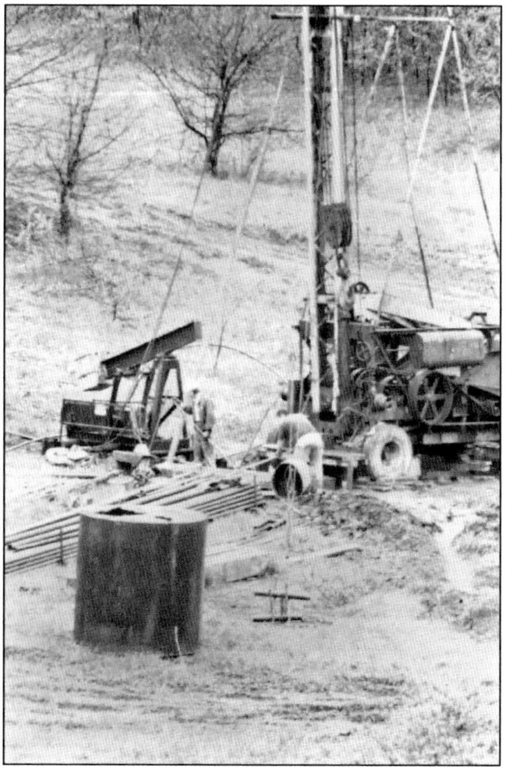

This picture is of some old oil rigs located in Pleasants County. They are a common sight around the countryside. In the Belmont and Eureka area, neighbors, side by side, often had their own small oil well. These soon ran dry, however, because surface oil soon gave out. There is plenty of oil, deep oil, but it takes much money to develop it. (Courtesy of Rev. Daniel Simmons.)

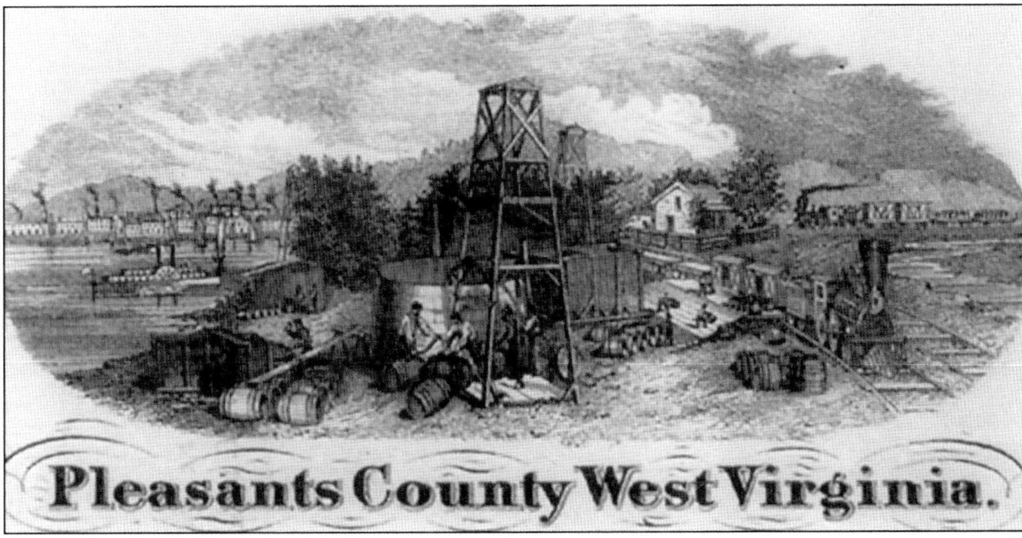

Stock certificates were sold to investors to help provide the funds to continue drilling for oil in Pleasants County. The two shown are examples of the many companies formed to drill during this wonderful oil boom. Small, unknown communities grew to enormous proportions during these exciting times. Pictures on the certificates depict various stages of the production of oil. Oil derricks pump the oil into holding tanks. Men put the oil into barrels to be shipped to refineries and processed. Eventually, this led to the establishment of the Quaker State Oil Refinery in the city of St. Marys. (Both courtesy of David McCain.)

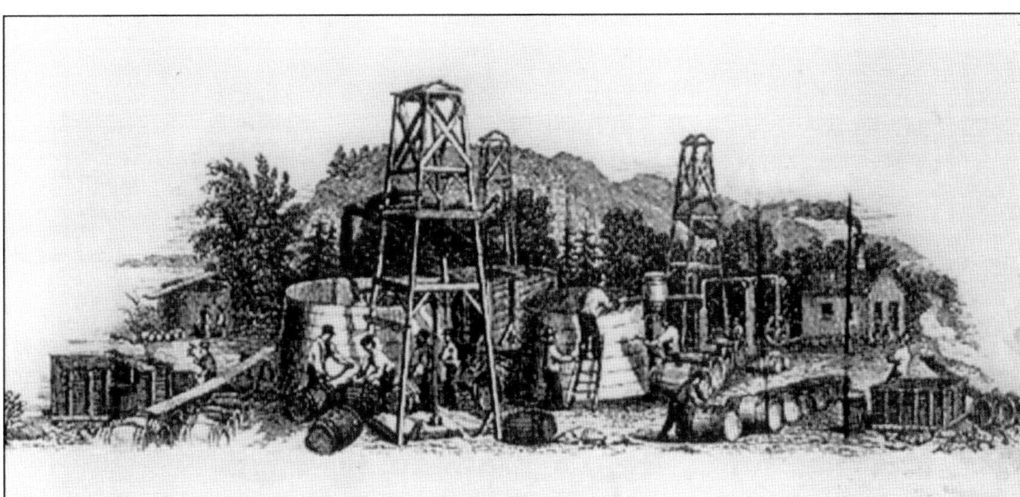

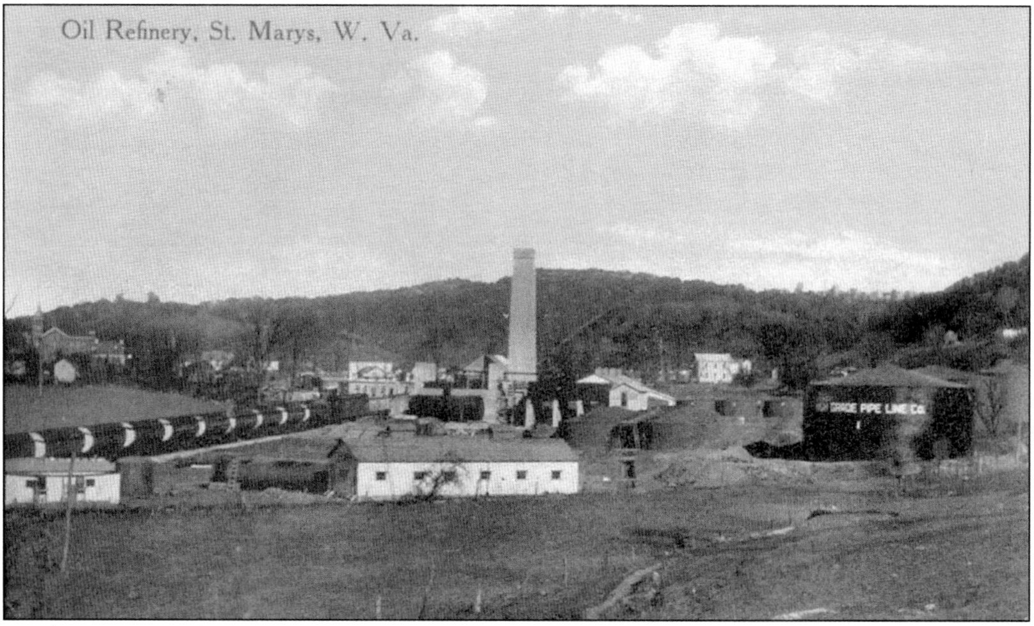

Quaker State was built by the Ohio Valley Petroleum Company in 1927 and sold to the Quaker State Oil Company in 1929. Above is a photograph showing the refinery in its earlier stages of development. Below, one can see the many oil tanks added through the years. Oil products were loaded onto boats, barges, and trains, the last of which were located in front of the plant. Quaker State products were used throughout the United States. The plant was closed in 1987. The closing of this plant was very sad for St. Marys because it had been one of the largest employers of the county. (Above courtesy of Delores Kemp; below courtesy of Rev. Daniel Simmons.)

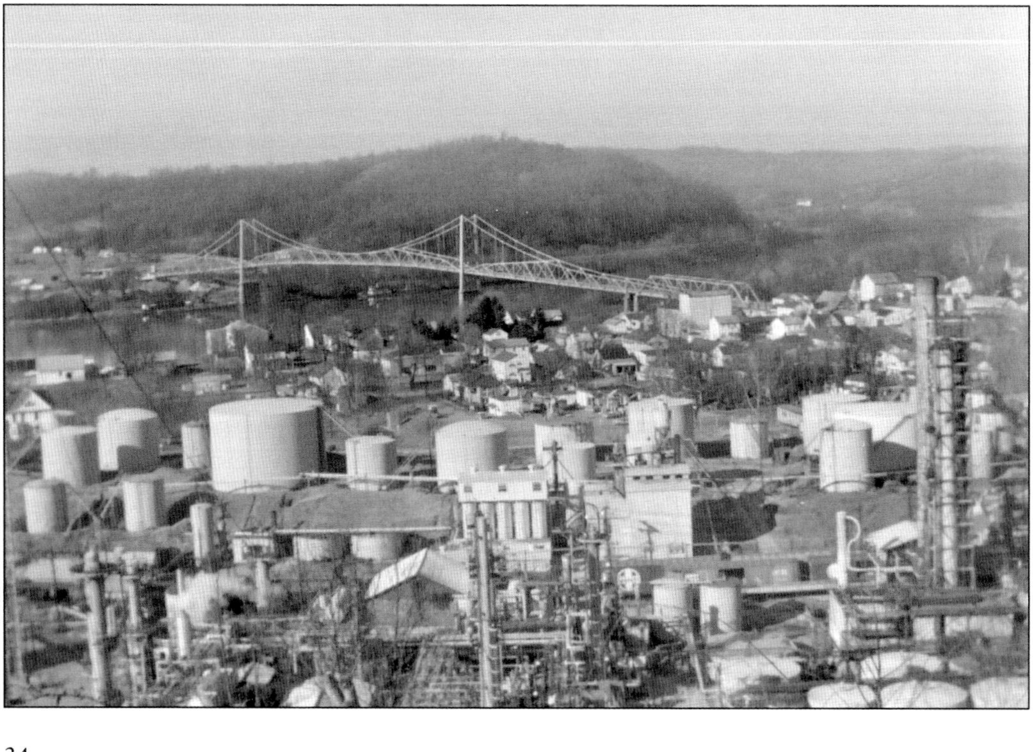

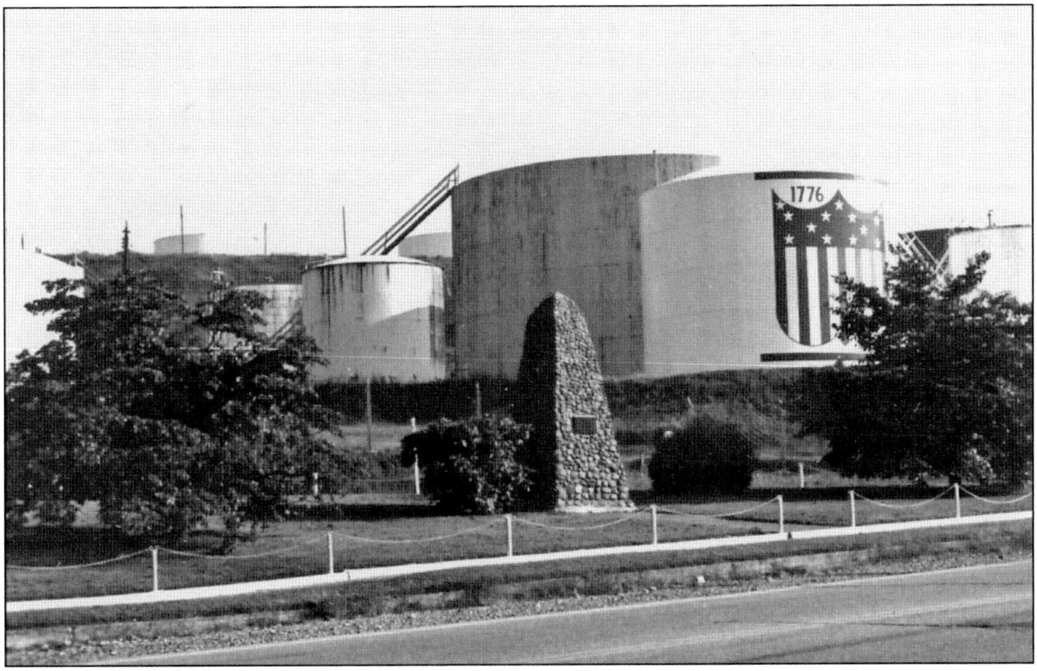

Creel Memorial Park, dedicated June 1, 1939, was created in honor of the founding of St. Marys in 1849. It was moved several yards because of the construction of the new four-lane highway through St. Marys. This photograph was taken in 1976. Notice the centennial decor on the large oil storage tank on the Quaker State Oil Refinery property located on the hill right behind this Creel Monument. Alexander Creel's brother, Bushrod, was the first major U.S. oil producer. Creel's faith in the commercial possibilities of oil was probably greater than that of anyone else of his day. West Virginia claims the honor of being the first state to commercially develop the oil and gas industry. Below are the tanks that were seen as a person entered St. Marys. (Above courtesy of Rev. Daniel Simmons; right courtesy of Teresa Reed Thompson.)

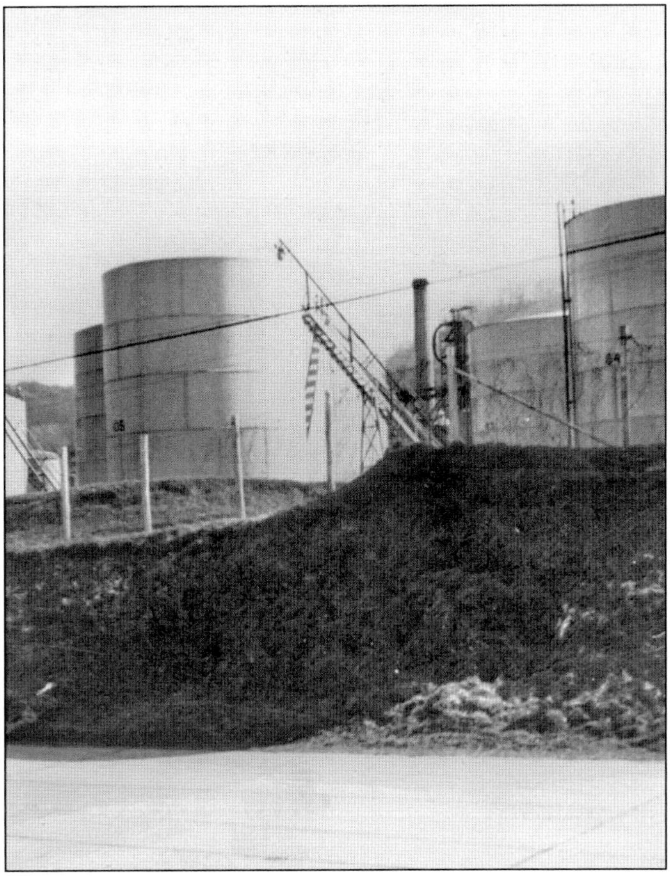

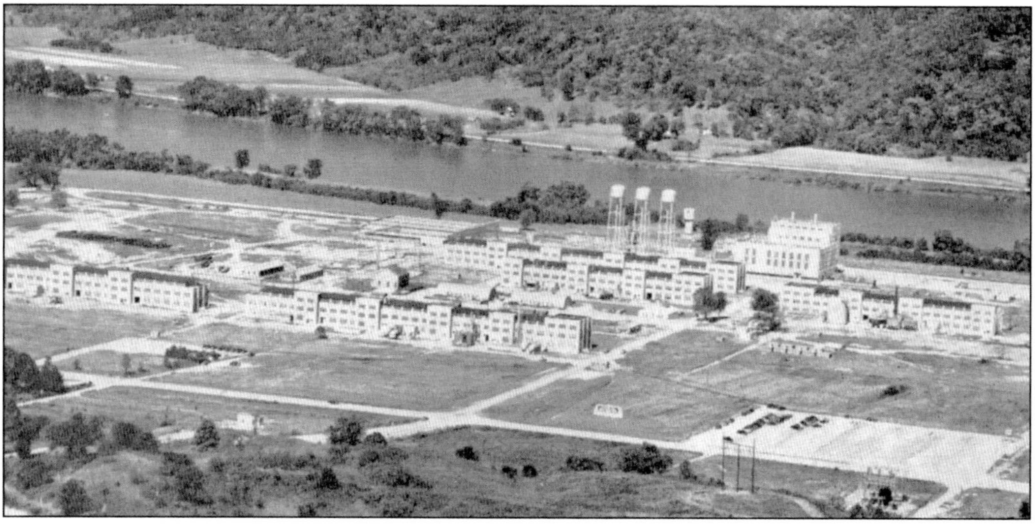

The construction work on the Willow Island Cyanamid Plant, earlier called the Calco, started in late 1945. The company purchased 1,150 acres to build the plant. Some 440 acres lie between Route 2 and the Ohio River. The remaining property is on the other side of Route 2. The plant started producing pharmaceuticals in 1947–1948. In 1948, the buildings for melamine and pigments were completed. Melamine was used in the plastic industry, and pigments were used in paints, inks, paper, and plastics. The rest of the plant was finished in 1958. Below, Charlie Dittman passes the paper for the first process to go into operation (in 1947). (Both courtesy of Mary Ellen Dittman.)

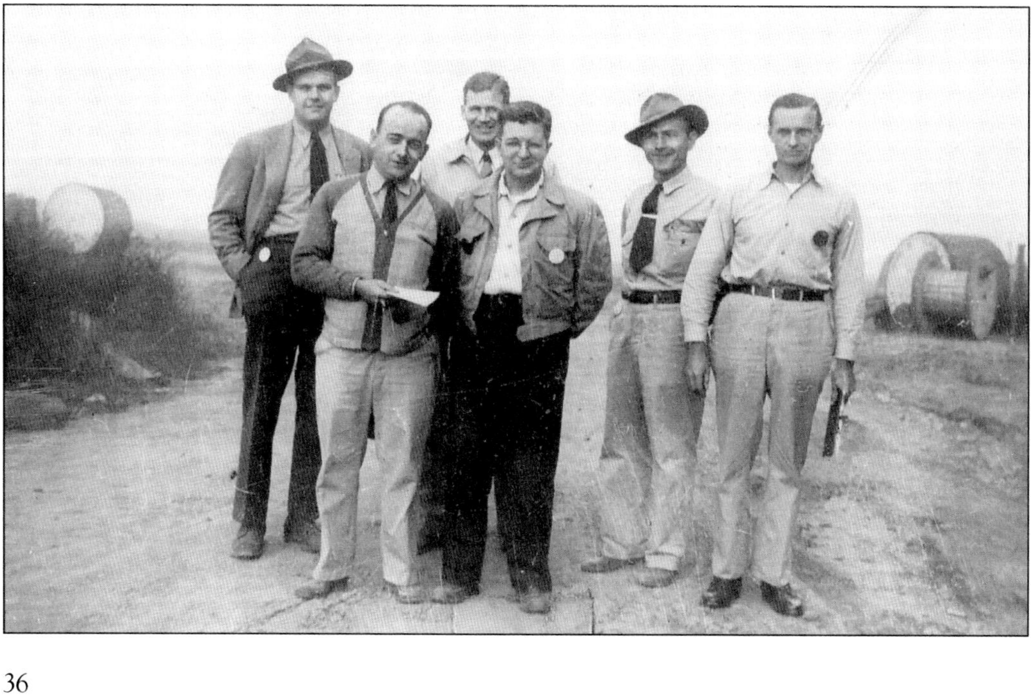

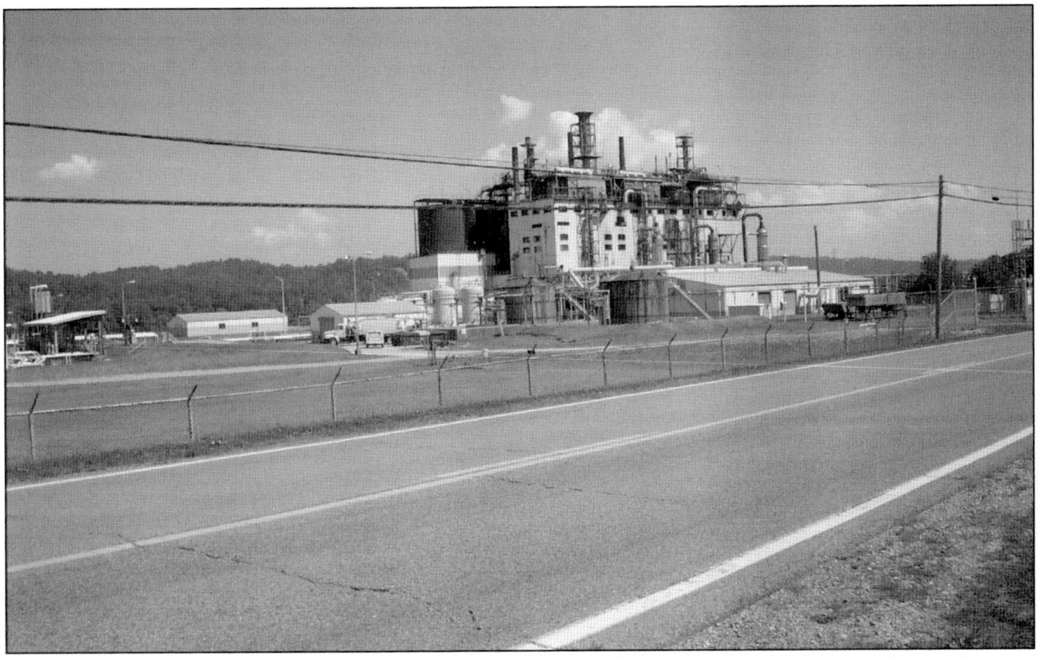

Cabot Plant of the Ohio Valley made carbon black, which was used to reinforce rubber. The tire industry was changing because the manufacturing of tires in the United States was shrinking while growing in China and other Asian countries. Cabot shut down the plant in June 2008. It was a fixture in the county for 40 years. (Courtesy of Ruth Ann Dayhoff.)

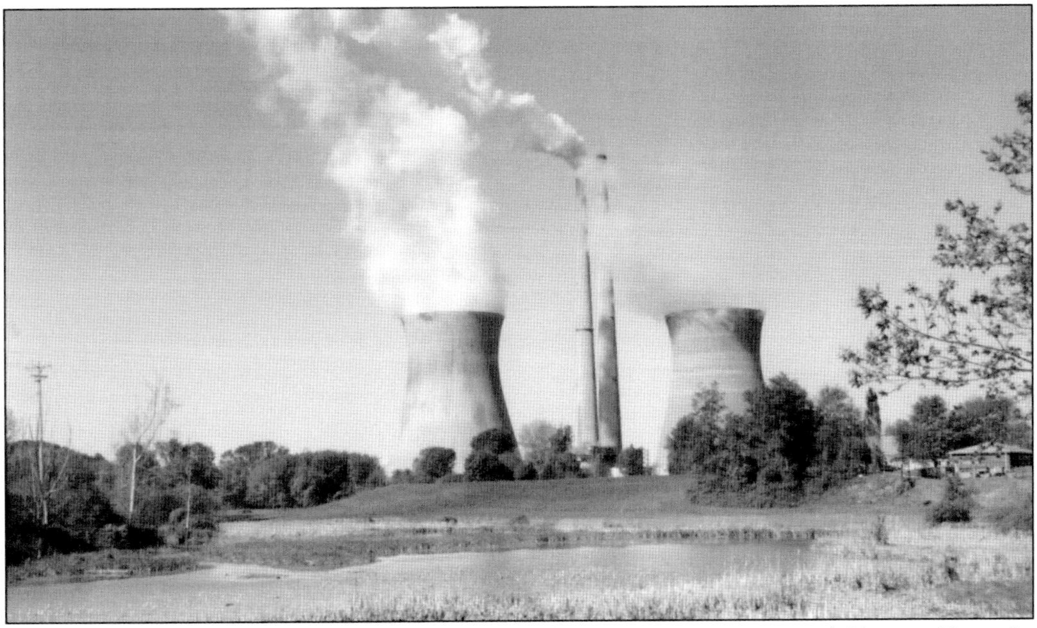

The Pleasants Power Station burns light, fluffy, hot-burning West Virginia and Ohio coal brought in by river barges. The electricity is shipped out in wires to users on the grid. In the construction of tower No. 2, fifty-one men were killed instantly when one of the cooling towers collapsed, making this the second largest construction accident in North America. When you turn on a light switch, be mindful of the people who make this possible. (Courtesy of Daniel Simmons.)

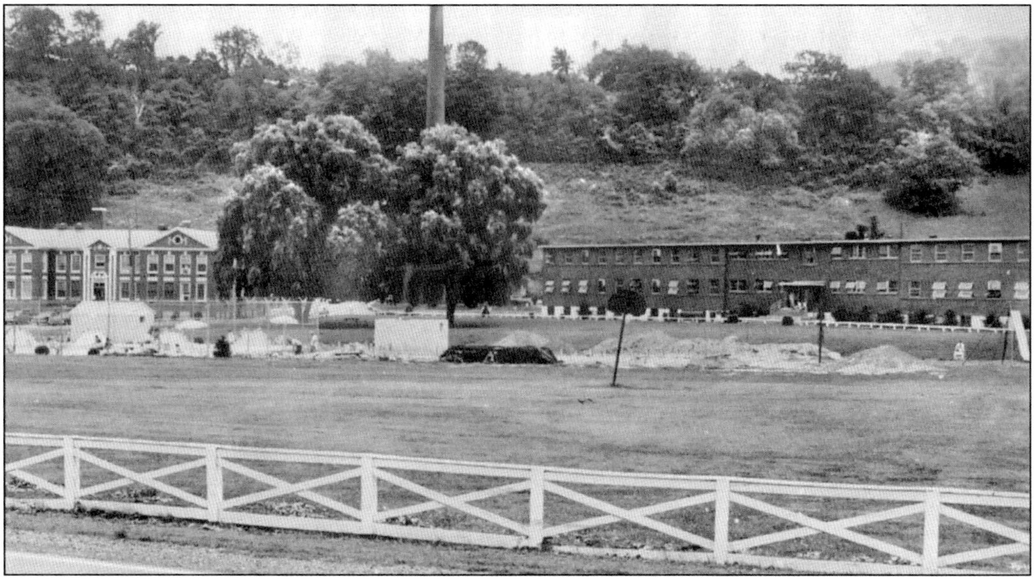

The Colin Anderson Center was established in 1921 by an act of the legislature. It was the home of many developmentally disadvantaged children. Constant improvements were made to accommodate special needs children. Thomas Browse, one of the early settlers, built a mansion, which served as the first dormitory. The Colin Anderson Center was closed in 1998 and now houses the St. Marys Correctional Facility. (Courtesy of Jennifer Efaw.)

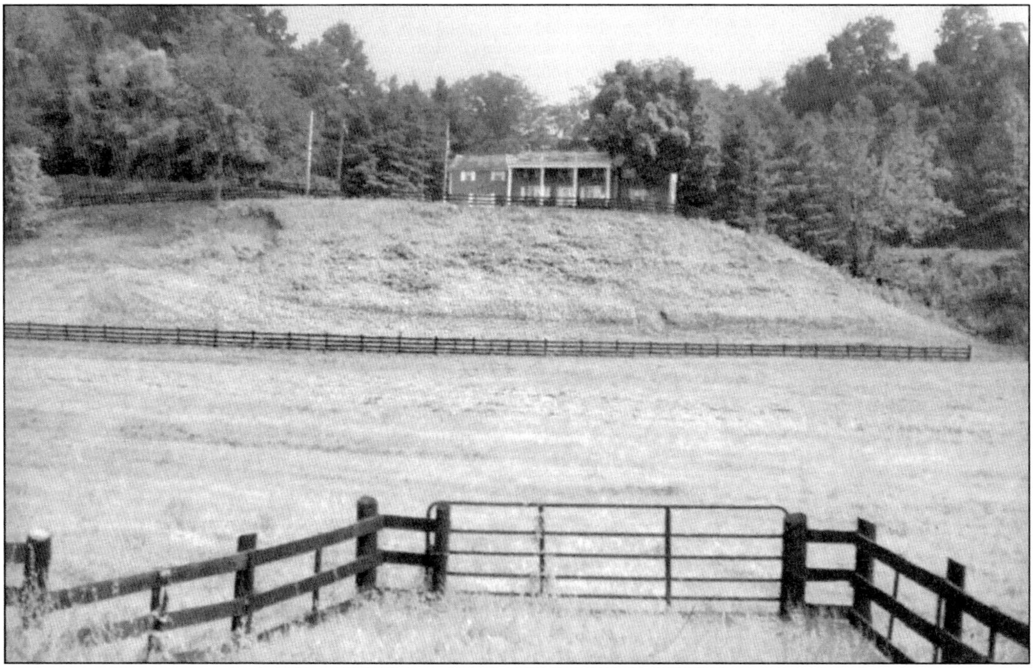

Upon entering Pleasants County from Wood County, one will pass, on the right, this beautiful home of James and Elaine Elliott. Written in slate on the roof was the date 1900, which was when the house was built. This was easily visible from the highway. Amon Adams lived in it for many years. In 1972, the Elliott family purchased and started renovating the house, which fulfilled a boyhood dream of James. (Courtesy of Elaine Elliott.)

Three

Our Town, St. Marys

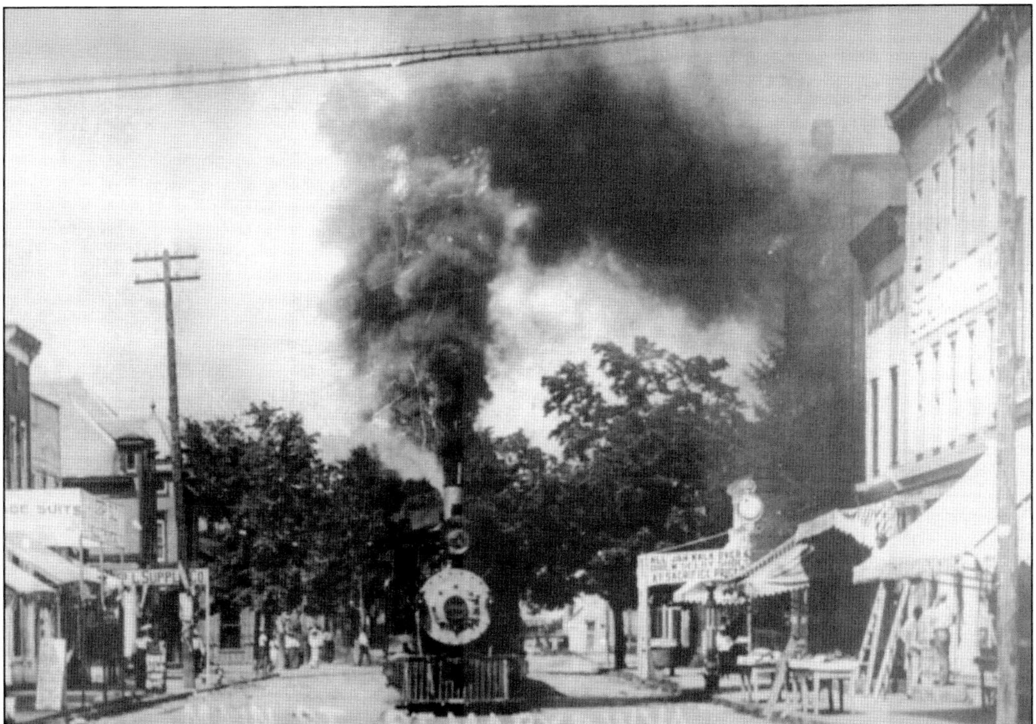

St. Marys, the busy county seat of Pleasants County, has a unique claim. Down the middle of Main Street runs a railroad track. Before automobiles and highways, train travel was the way to transport both people and products. Several passenger and many freight trains daily came through town. This made Main Street even more busy because many banks, hotels, and businesses were located there. (Courtesy of the City of St. Marys.)

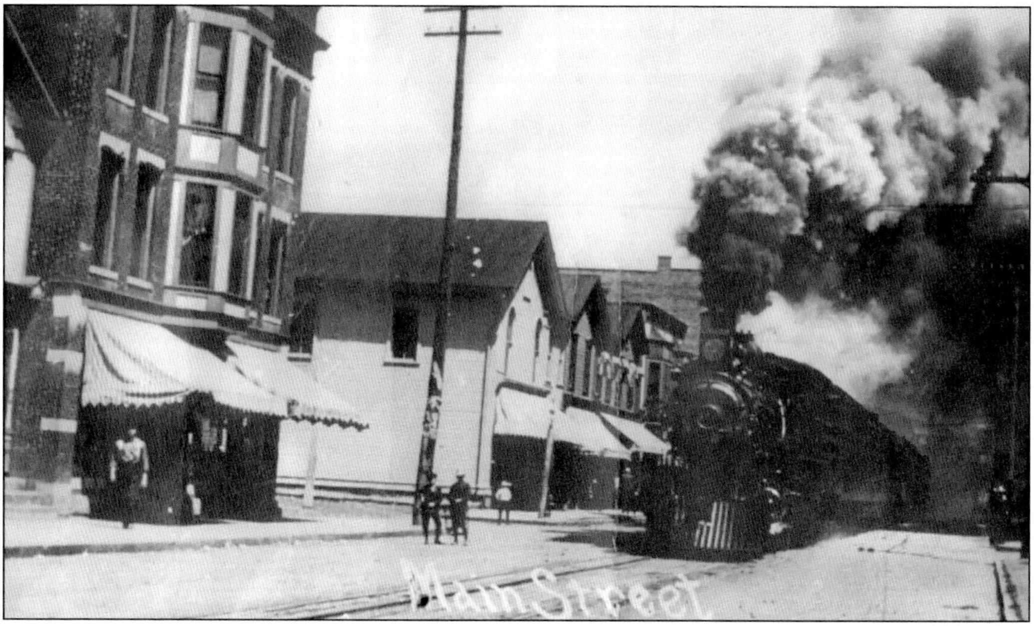

In 1882, the county leaders met to discuss bringing a train from Wheeling to Parkersburg through St. Marys. Much passionate discussion was made as to where the tracks should be built. Finally, it was decided to split the town in two by putting the track straight through the center of town. Final tracks were laid on November 27, 1883, and the line was completed in June 1884. (Courtesy of the City of St. Marys.)

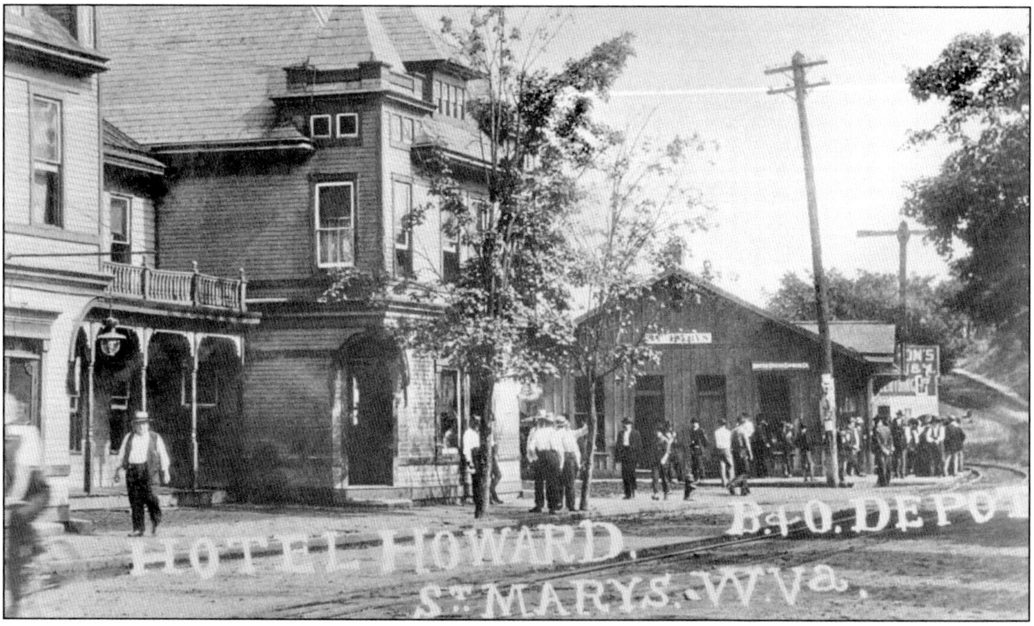

The Howard Hotel and depot were located on Main Street in St. Marys. This hotel was very elegant, and people coming to town for business or just visiting families could sleep in style and eat in a high-class restaurant. The people in front of the depot were waiting for one of the many passenger trains coming through town daily. The hotel was located where the Food Giant stands today. (PCHSC, courtesy of WVDCHSA.)

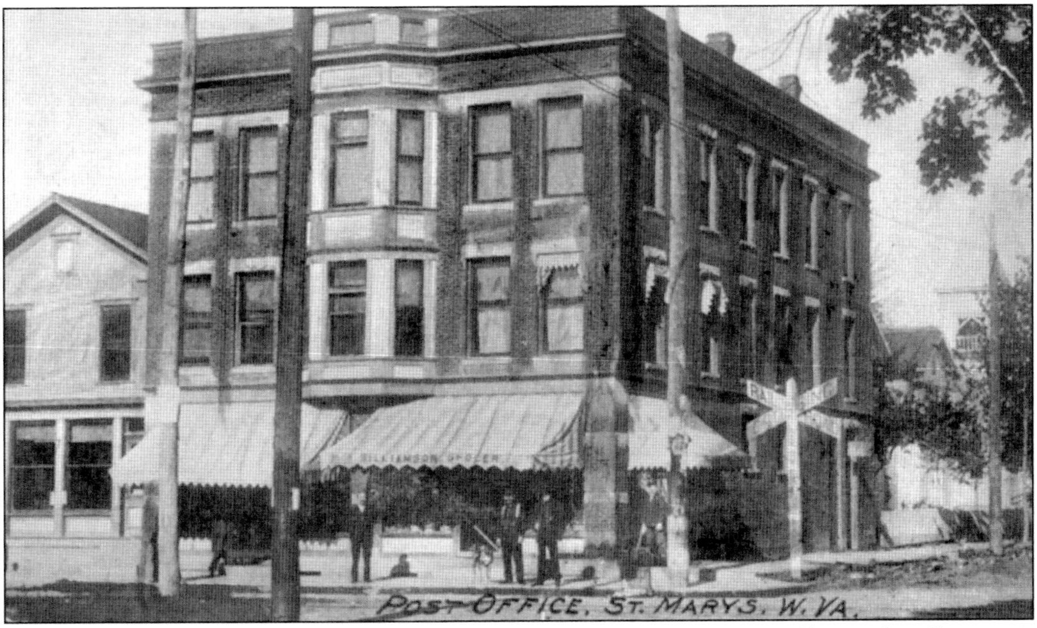

In 1909, on the corner of Main and George Streets stood this first post office and Williamson's Grocery. After a fire destroyed a city block nearby, a permanent post office was built on that location. This grocery store later became Gerber's Grocery. The large building still stands and well serves the community. (PCHSC, courtesy of WVDCHSA and Delores Kemp.)

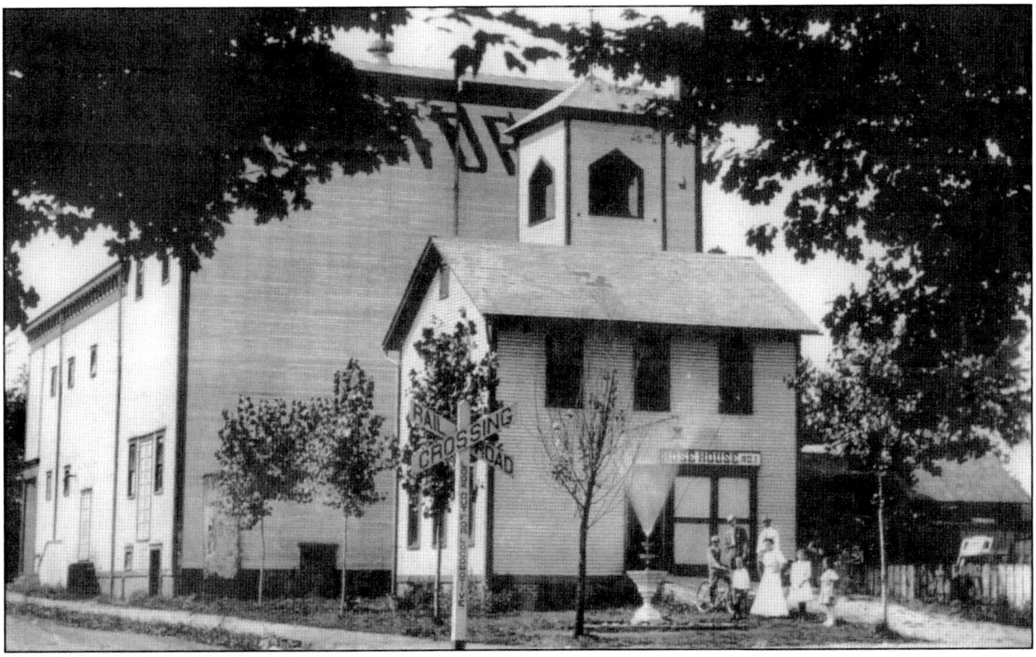

The public library provided this picture of the first library, which was originally in the old auditorium. (Notice the word "Auditorium" written on the large building.) The auditorium later became the Robey Theater, proudly presenting "talking" movies to the public. The first city building and fire station was located in the smaller building in front. (PCPLC, courtesy of Eleanor Poling.)

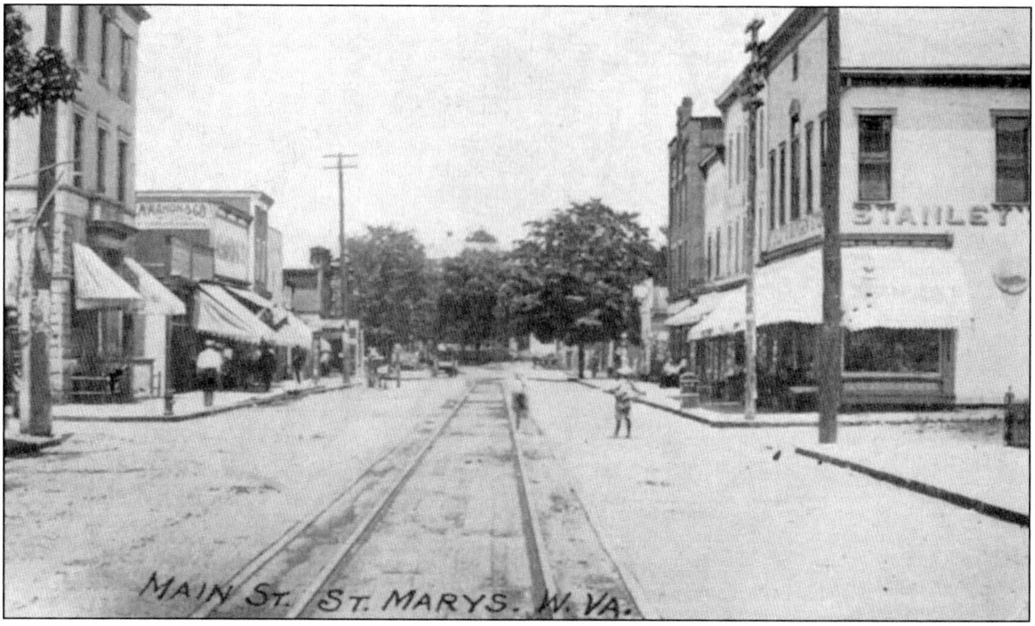

Notice Stanley's Store on the right, which is directly across from the First National Bank. Stanley's Store, the Ruttencutter building, and the F. M. Gardner Grocery burned to the ground in 1936. Stanley's was moved to a new location on Washington Street. A new post office was erected in 1938 on the corner of Washington and Second (or Main) Streets, where Stanley's once stood. (Courtesy of Delores Kemp.)

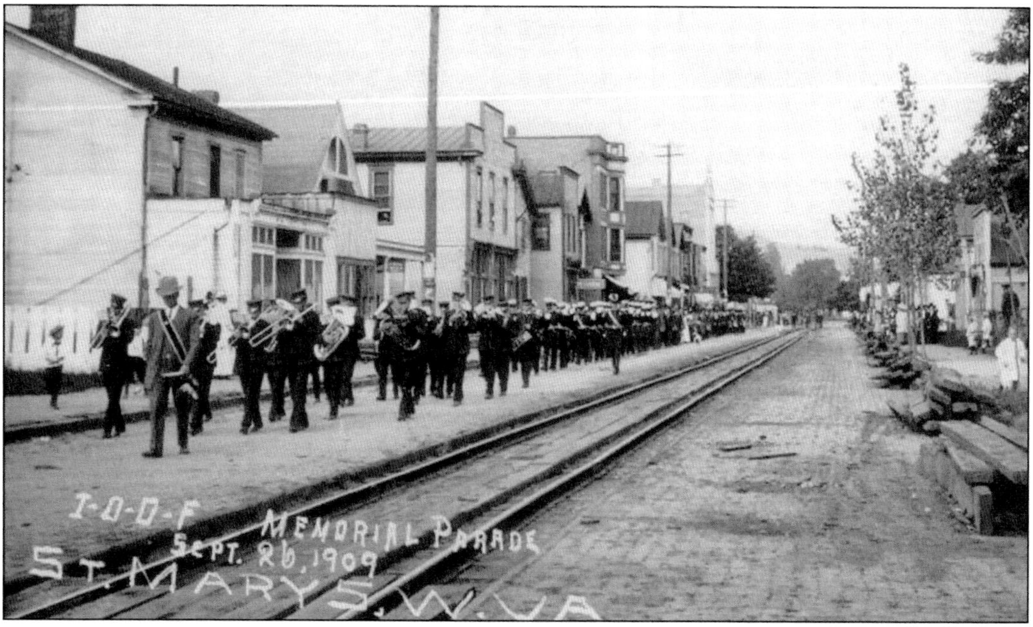

In September 1909, a band plays as it marches down lower Main Street of St. Marys in the IOOF (Independent Order of Odd Fellows) Memorial Parade. Notice the brick street and the crude wooden benches that line the lower end of town. Bands played for fairs, parades, and various celebrations. They performed on stage at the local auditorium. The first high school band was formed in 1928. (Courtesy of Delores Kemp.)

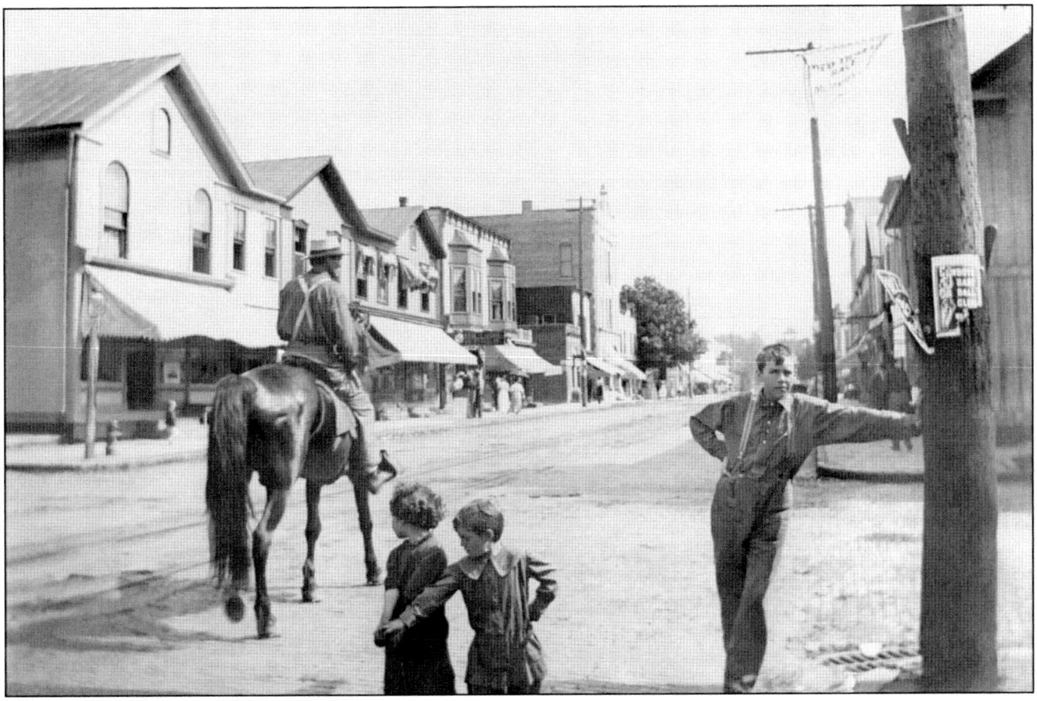

The two young boys standing on the street are Julian Stanley (left) and Crandall Strickling (right) in the year 1909. Both of these boys grew up to become prominent citizens and businessmen of the town. The light pole the young man is leaning against has a flyer promoting the Cowboy's Baseball Club. Below, readers can view the stores on Main Street a little closer. The third store up is a clothing store and has dresses exhibited in the window. Almost all of the stores have cloth awnings as was the custom of the day. (Above PCHSC, courtesy of WVDCHSA; below courtesy of Delores Kemp.)

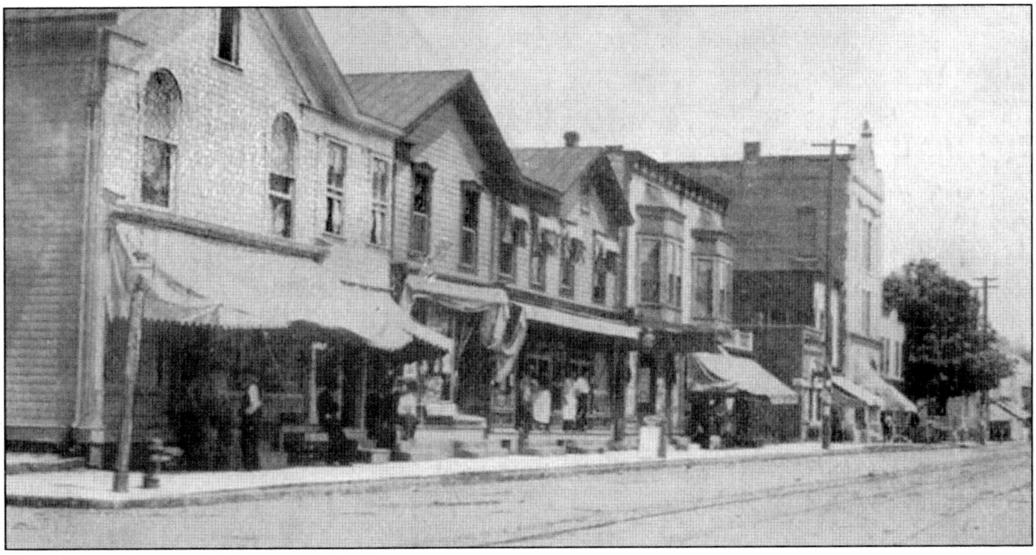

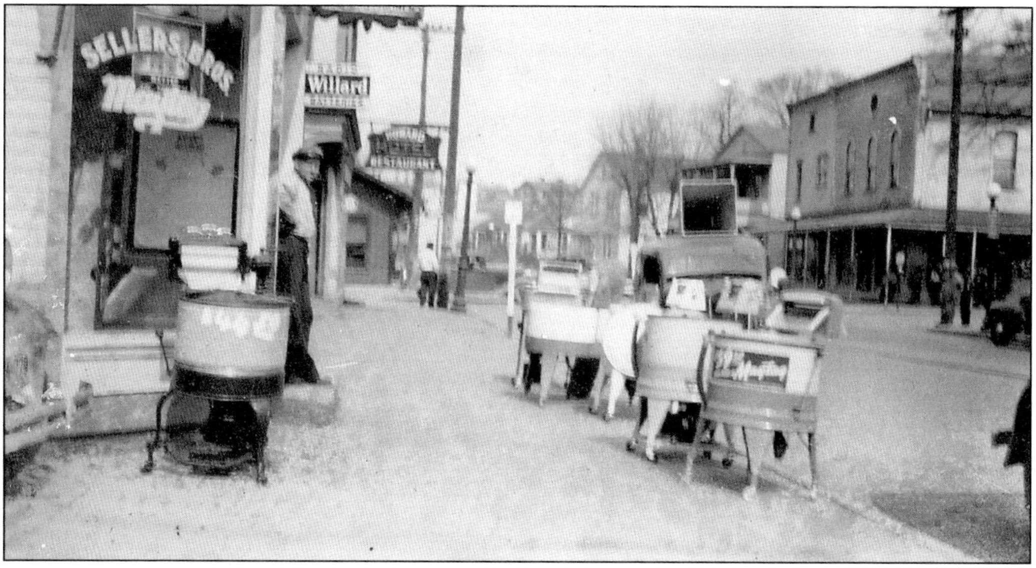

The Sellers brothers, Kramer and Frank Jr., owned and operated an appliance store that sold Maytag washers and Willard radios. The store was located on Main Street very near the Howard Hotel, which their father owned. To advertise, they placed on the sidewalk some samples of their ringer washing machines. Below, they even invited some musicians to entertain potential customers. Frank Jr. and Kramer together built the Main Theater in 1949. In 1956, they converted it into the Food Giant. Their father was a partner with the Dinsmoor Oil Company and later purchased the Browse mansion and farm to pursue his farming interests. However, the aforementioned sons were more interested in business. Residents should be happy they gave St. Marys such a boost with their contributions to the community. (Both courtesy of Frank and Ruby Sellers.)

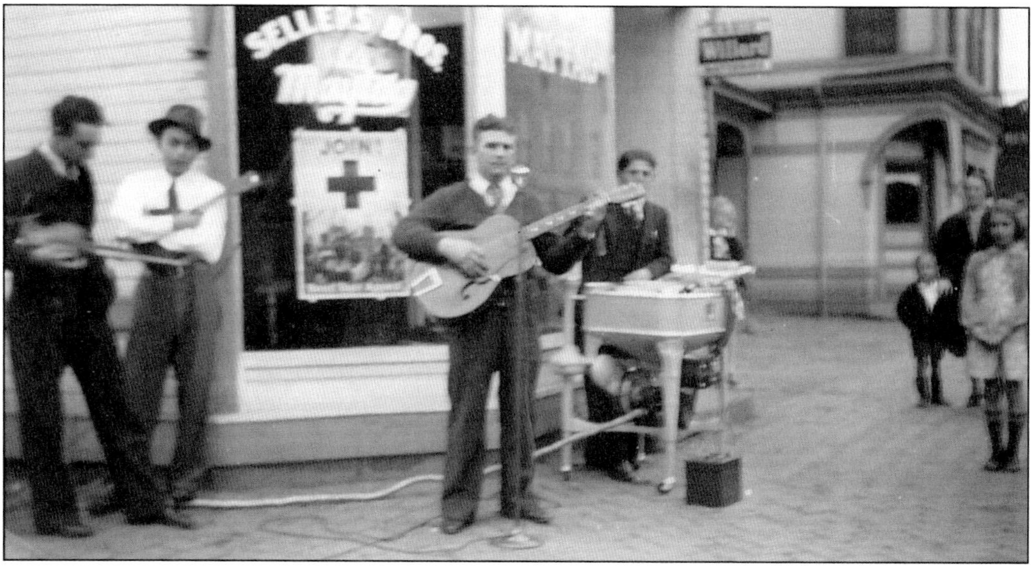

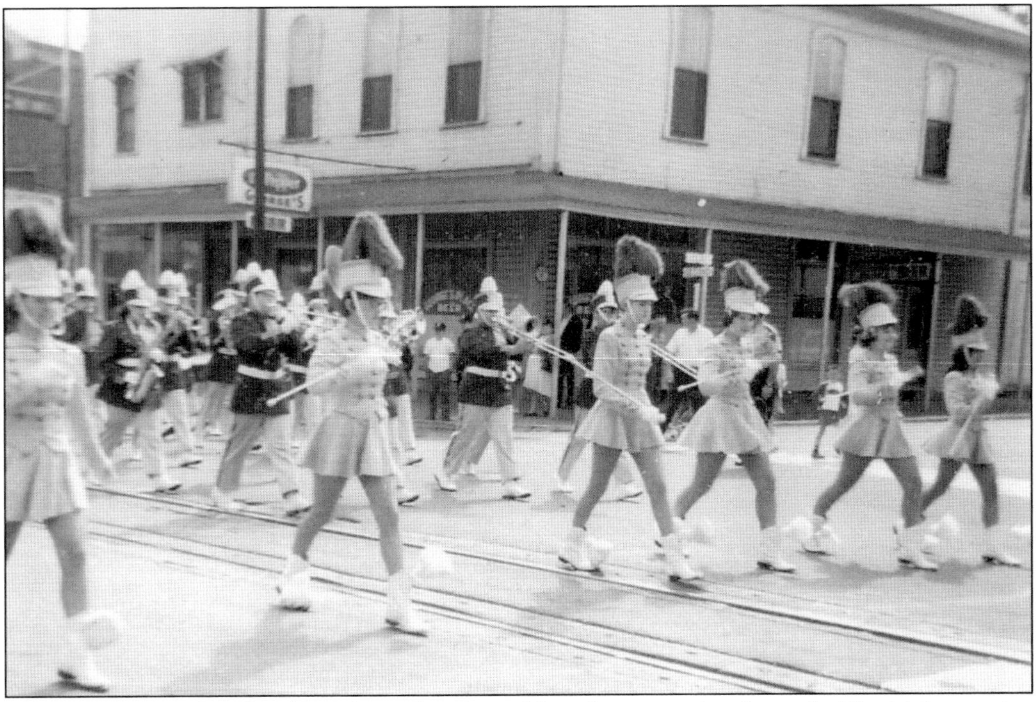

The St. Marys High School Band marches down Main Street in a local parade. The high-stepping majorettes lead the band past the City Confectionery, which was owned by Moses Coram and his nephews, George Joseph and John Habeeb from Lebanon. It was the first ice cream parlor opened in the city. Next door, Crosser's Five and Dime Store was run by R. F. Crosser, often referred to as the "Old Man of the Mountains" because of the beard he grew for the 1949 Centennial Celebration. Crosser's was a favorite store because it sold everything imaginable. Children loved the store (as the authors both keenly remember) because of the ice cream, candy, and toys. Adults enjoyed the variety of goods and wonderful atmosphere. (Above courtesy of John and Dorothy Evans; below courtesy of Frank and Ruby Sellers.)

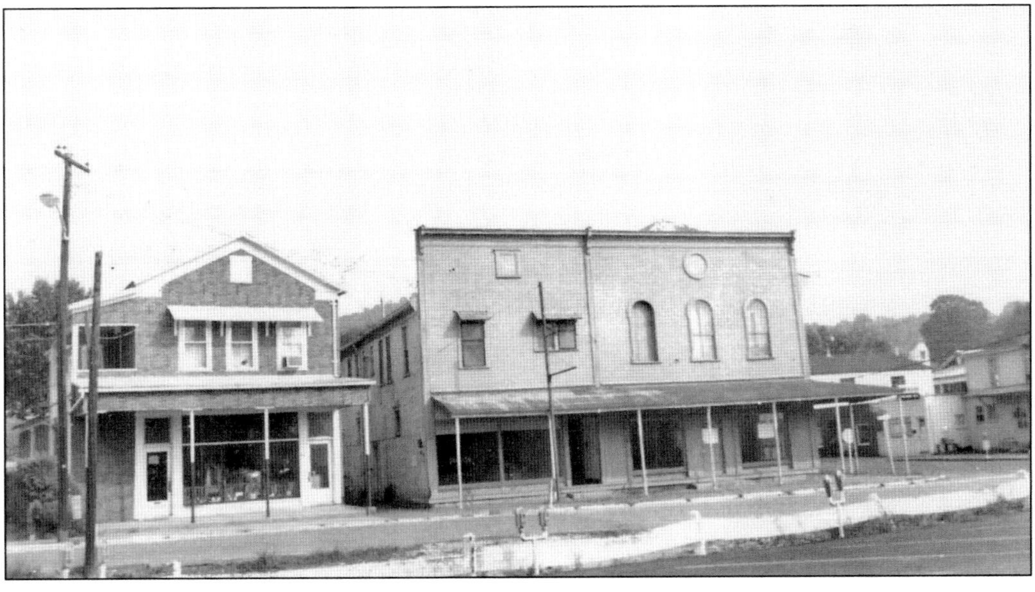

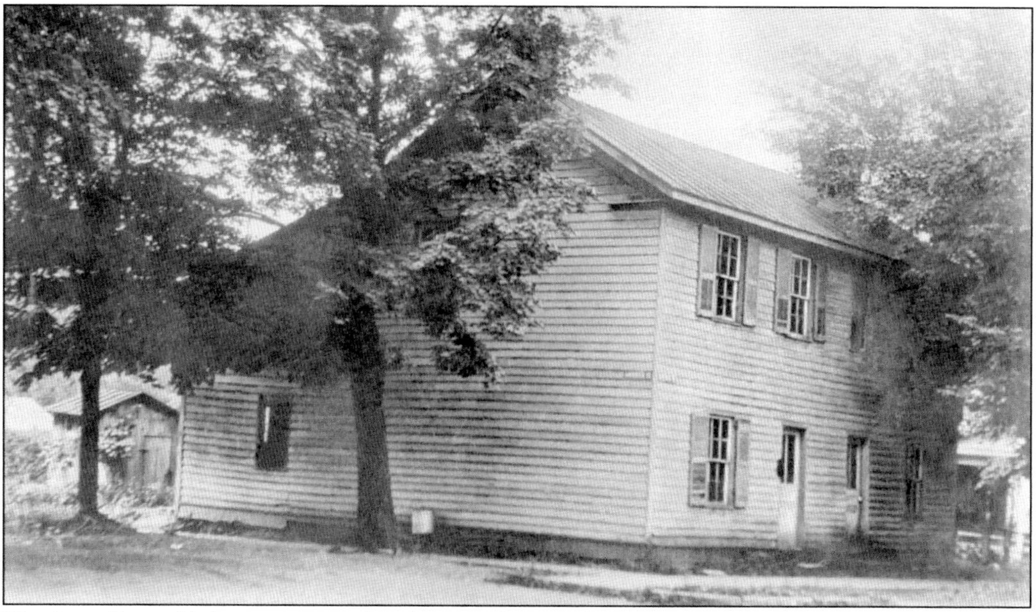

The Isaac Reynolds house was used as the courthouse while an authentic one was being built. The committee for selecting the site for the new building was composed of Alexander Creel, Thomas Browse, John Stewart, Joseph Taylor, and John Widderfield in 1854. This new courthouse building appears in the picture below behind the Grimm Hospital. In 1923, the courthouse below was struck by lightning and declared to be unsafe. In 1925, it was replaced by the present structure. The Grimm Hospital was established in 1860 by Dr. A. S. Grimm. The large house below served as a family residence and the county's only hospital. It discontinued operation in 1930. In 1970, the building was demolished to make way for a new St. John's Catholic church. (Both PCHSC, courtesy of WVDSHSA.)

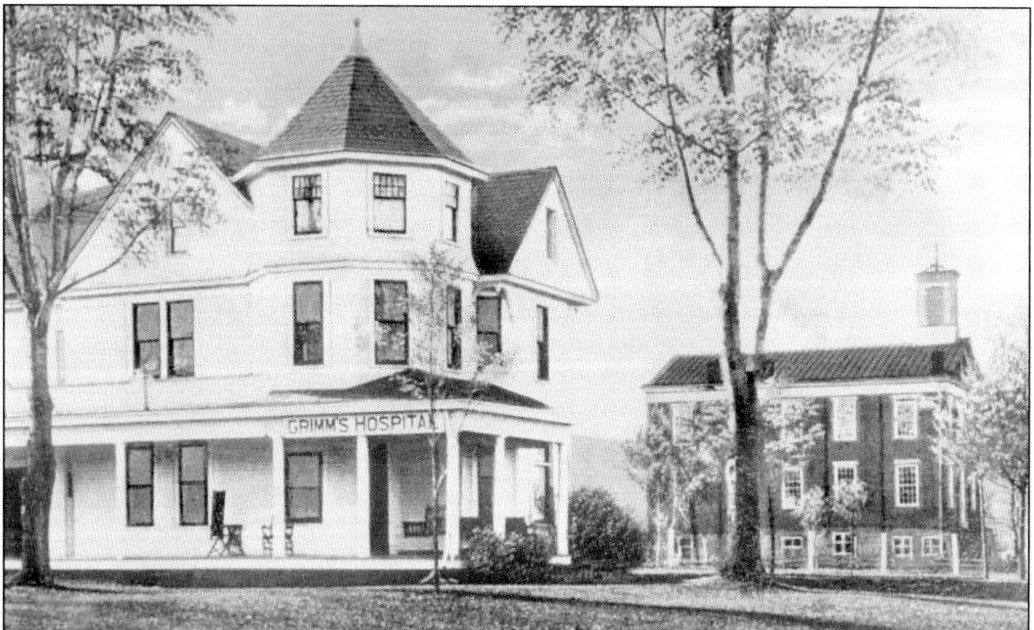

Yesterday's Stroll

by Denzil Locke

Come go with me to St. Marys
Some thirty or forty years back,
Which in itself is quite unique
For down Main Street runs the RR Track.
On the corner was the M. P. Church
On Sunday its bells would toll,
Next door was Triplett's Hardware
Who sold most anything but a post hole.
Upstairs was Dr. Hamilton's office
Where you could go for an exam,
Next door behind the green front
Was R. N. Ogden's Five and Ten.
Next door was Histy's Restaurant
A real good place to eat
Who had some completion
From Mrs. Ben Coen across the street.
Wilma had her beauty shop
Where ladies got their hair curled and cut.
Then go next door to Sadie's
And buy a hat to cover it up!
Joe Procopio had his shoe shop
Carl Severn a pool hall.
Harry Michael, the cleaning and pressing
And Santa Claus was Paul.
There was Les Morgan's Dairy Lunch
As well as East and Creek produce.
Dr. Woodward and Uncle Pud Tucker
Who could pull and fix a tooth.
Mose and George had a Confectionery
Where you could buy a good five-cent cigar.
There was the Howard and the Haddox Hotels
And the Howard was destroyed by fire.
At Winer's Department Store
Where Sam always had your size
Or you could go upstairs
Delno Webb would check your eyes.
Virgie Everly sold women's apparel
A department store was run by Mr. and Mrs. Guth.
And the Monongahelia Power office
Managed by C. A. Ruckman and Ruth.
Stanley's Department Store, with Oakey and Katie,
Lucy and Iris who sold china.
F. M. Gardner's meat market
Bob and Edna had a little diner
There was the A & P and Pete Gerber
Coleman McCullough's cash store.
Bill Core had a shoe shop
And fixed our shoes during the war.

There was H. A. Carpenter's office
Electric repair shop with Memme and Earl
Phillip's and Central Drug Store
Where a boy could treat his girl.
The Sellers boys, Junior and Cramer,
Ran a little appliance store
Where there had been other businesses
So many other times before.
With lawyers, Frank Barron and J. C. Powell
To defend you and me if we had to appear before Dippie Walker
Who was then the J. P.
There was the Post Office on the corner
The Pleasants County and the First National Banks.
Bernard Riggs ran the city,
City Manager was his rank.
There were others who had their businesses
Down Main Street from time to time.
But these were just a few
Who were here when Mail Pouch was a dime.
(Courtesy of Mrs. Denzil Locke.)

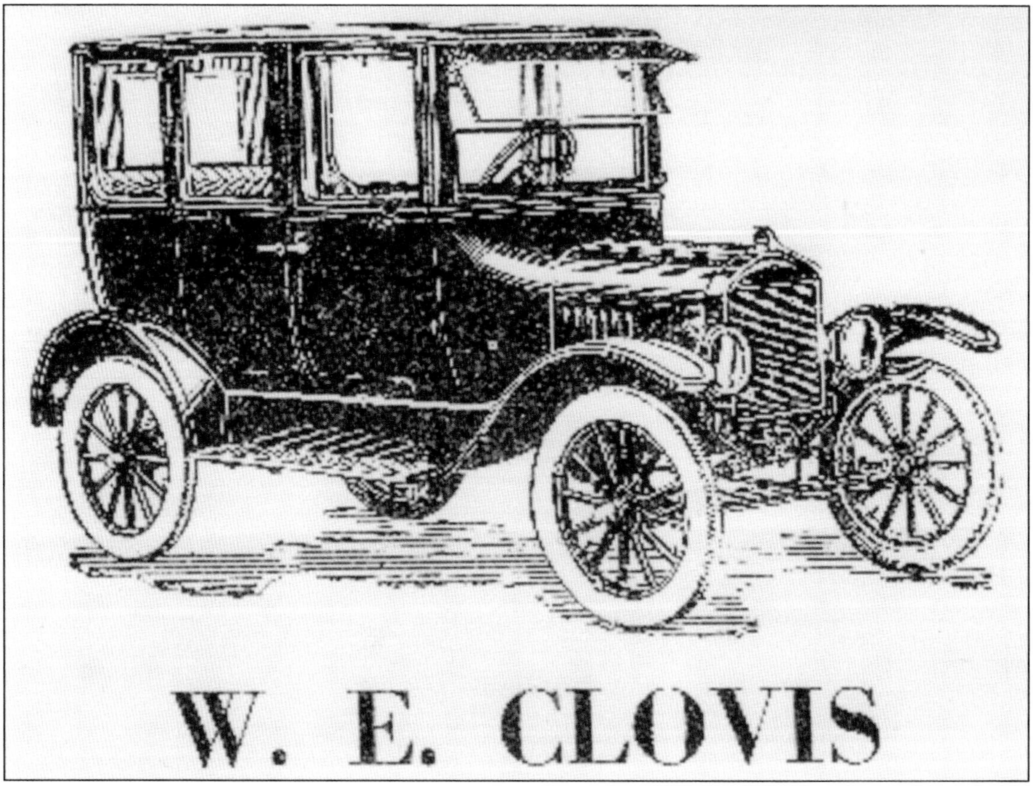

When the Clovis Motor Company started its business in the early 1900s, this advertisement was used to depict the wonderful new models of automobiles that were available for sale. Their Ford vehicle business became a permanent town fixture throughout the century. (PCPLC, courtesy of Eleanor Poling.)

Four

DISASTERS AND FLOODS

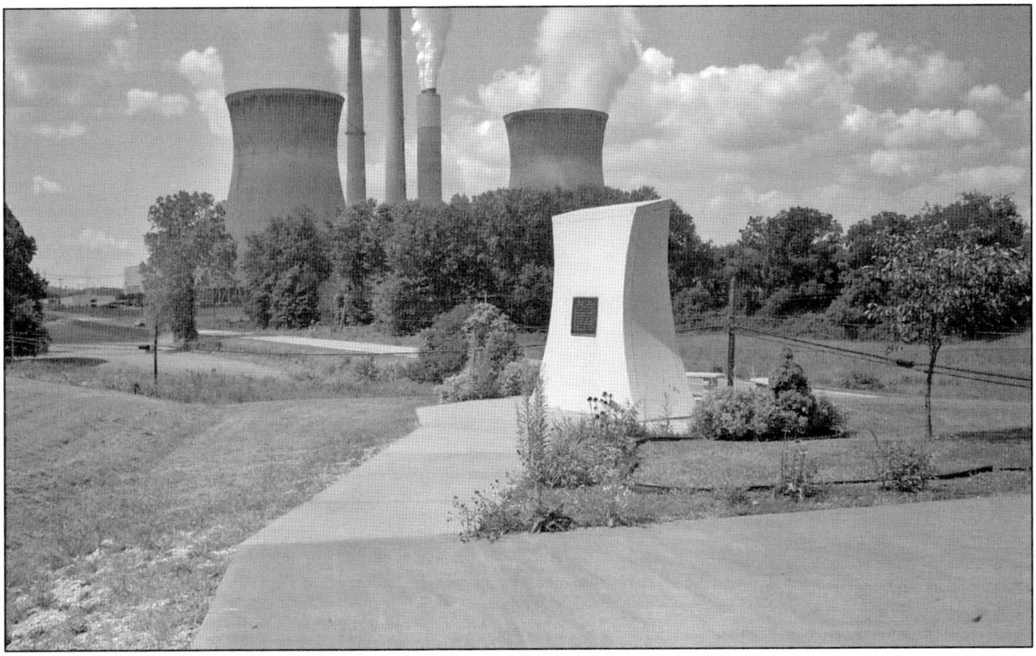

April 27, 1978, was a day of great tragedy for Pleasants County. Fifty-one men were working on No. 2 cooling tower at the Pleasants Power Station when the scaffolding and one lift of concrete fell to the floor of the tower, 170 feet below. This is a memorial to remember the men who died here. In the background, one can view the completed towers as they stand today. (Courtesy of Ruth Ann Dayhoff.)

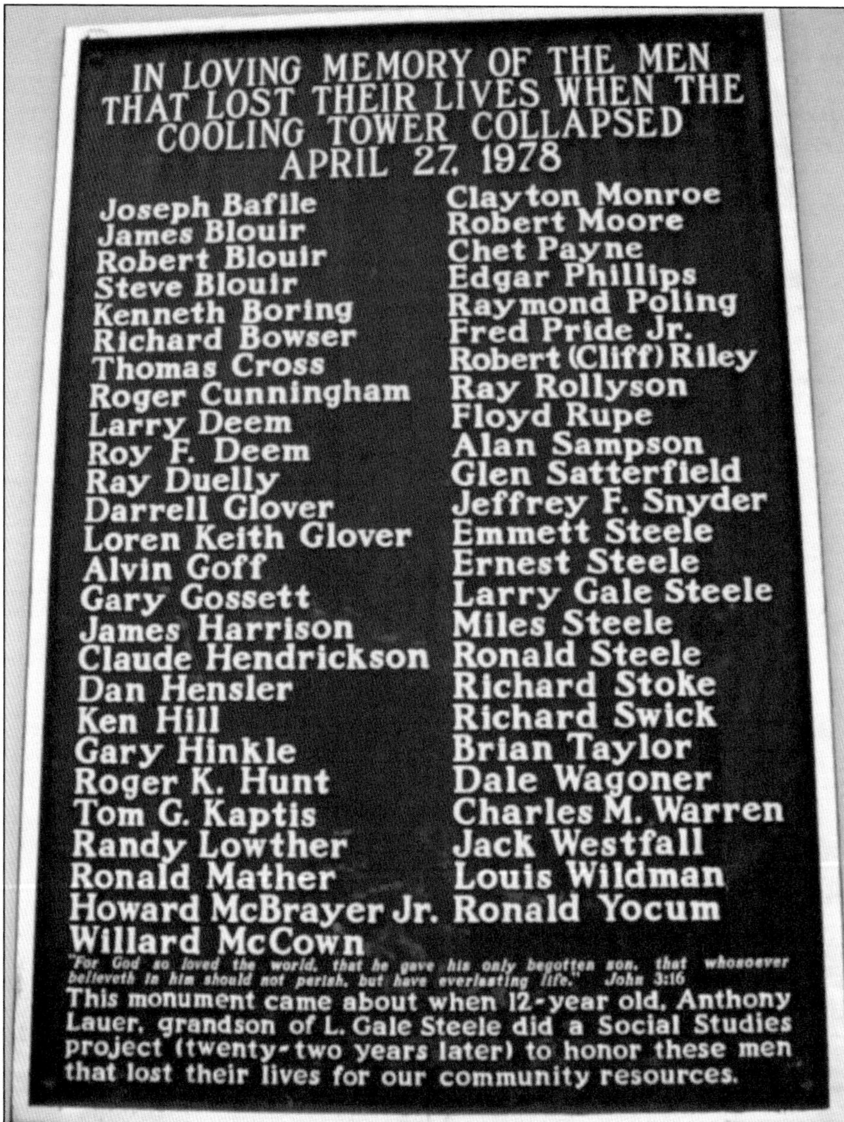

This memorial is in loving memory of the men who lost their lives when the cooling tower collapsed on April 27, 1978. On the Pleasants Power Memorial, one can view the names of these men. They were not only from Pleasants County but from many other counties and several states. The names are as follows: Joseph Bafile, James Blouir, Robert Blouir, Steve Blouir, Kenneth Boring, Richard Bowser, Thomas Cross, Roger Cunningham, Larry Deem, Ray Duelly, Darrell Glover, Loren Glover, Alvin Goff, Gary Gossett, James Harrison, Claude Hendrickson, Dan Hensler, Ken Hill, Gary Hinkle, Roger Hunt, Tom Kaptis, Randy Lowther, Ronald Mather, Howard McBrayer Jr., Willard McCown, Clayton Monroe, Robert Moore, Chet Payne, Edgar Phillips, Raymond Poling, Fred Pride Jr., Robert "Cliff" Riley, Ray Rollyson, Floyd Rupe, Alan Sampson, Glen Satterfield, Jeffery Snyder, Emmett Steele, Ernest Steele, Larry Gale Steele, Miles Steele, Ronald Steel, Richard Stoke, Richard Swick, Brian Taylor, Dale Wagoner, Charles Warren, Jack Westfall, Louis Wildman, and Ronald Yocum. Five members of the Steele family and three members of the Blouir family were lost in this tragedy. An earlier tragedy took place on January 9, 1975, when Claude R. Wilson fell to his death from a different tower. (Courtesy of Ruth Ann Dayhoff.)

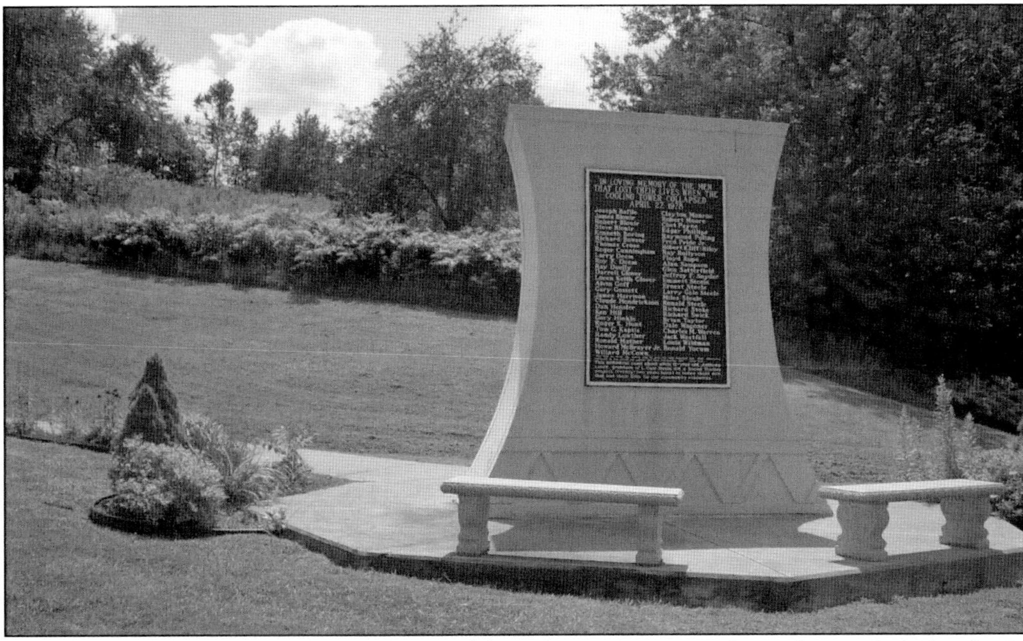

This monument came about when 12-year-old Anthony Lauer, grandson of Larry Gale Steele, did a social studies project 22 years later to honor these men who lost their lives for our community resources. When Anthony was in the third grade, he asked his teacher, Ruth Ann Dayhoff, why something had not been done to honor his grandfather and those who died with him. Four years later, this inspired young man collected contributions from all over the county and the state to make his dream come true. Young dreamers should never be ignored. Thank you, Anthony, for your hard work and perseverance. (Courtesy of Ruth Ann Dayhoff.)

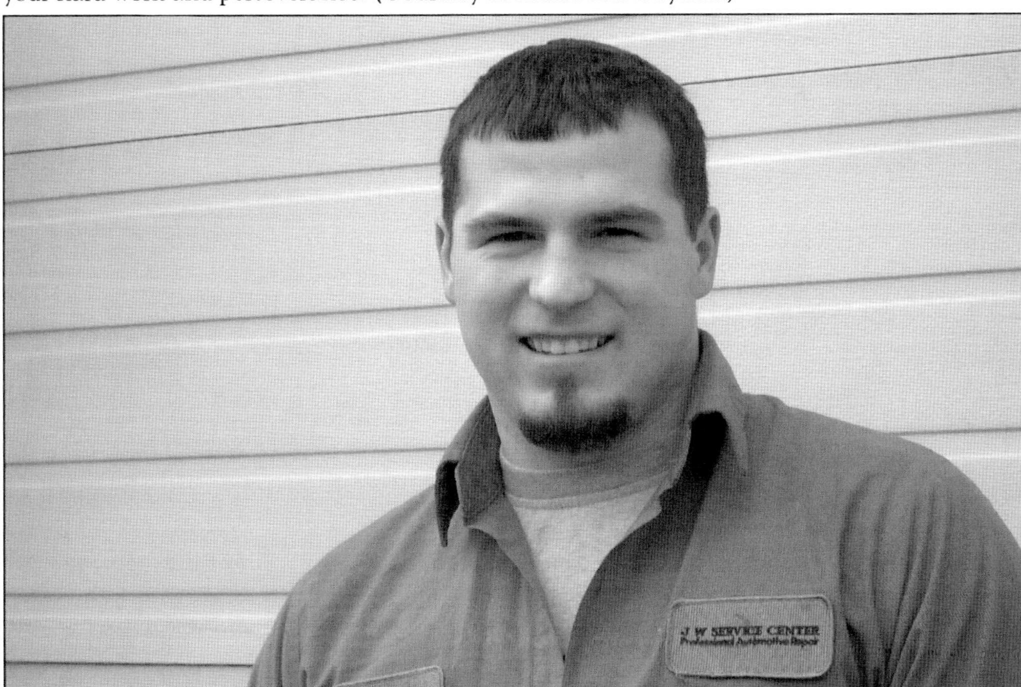

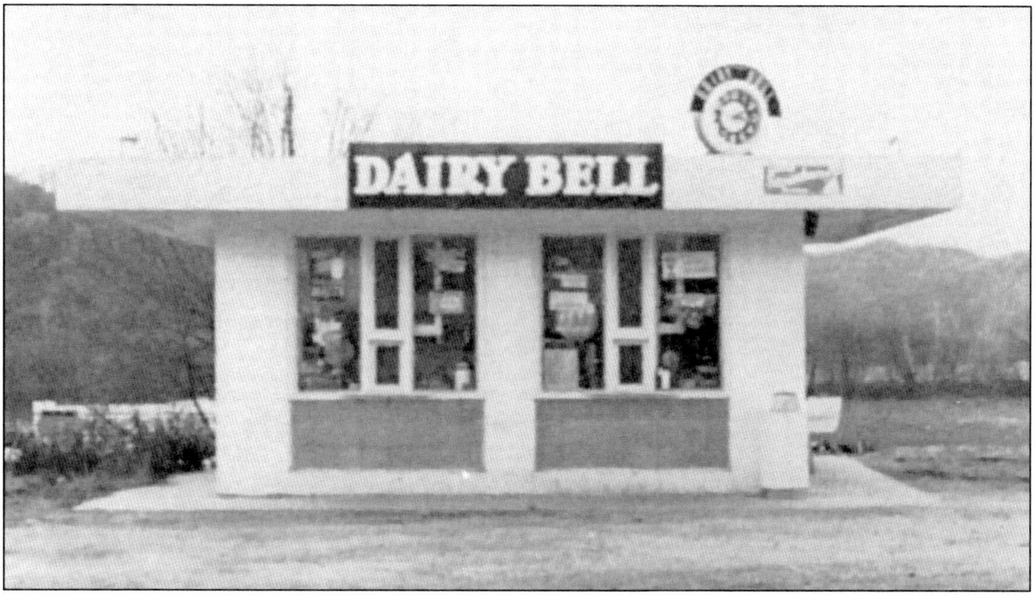

This popular Dairy Bell was located in an area where disaster was almost inevitable. Directly across from the St. Marys High School, many young people regularly purchased their lunch here. Unfortunately, it was at the bottom of a nearly mile-long hill at the end of Route 16. Huge trucks sometimes lost their brakes. Below is a photograph of one such truck. Through the years, several truckers lost their lives in this manner. Nothing could stop a truck from going directly over the steep embankment, and any dangerous swerve to miss this building would cause a vehicle to tip over or jackknife. We are all thankful that when the inevitable really did happen, the Dairy Bell was demolished but nobody was badly hurt. Many youth could easily have died here. (Above courtesy of PCPLC; below courtesy of Eleanor Poling.)

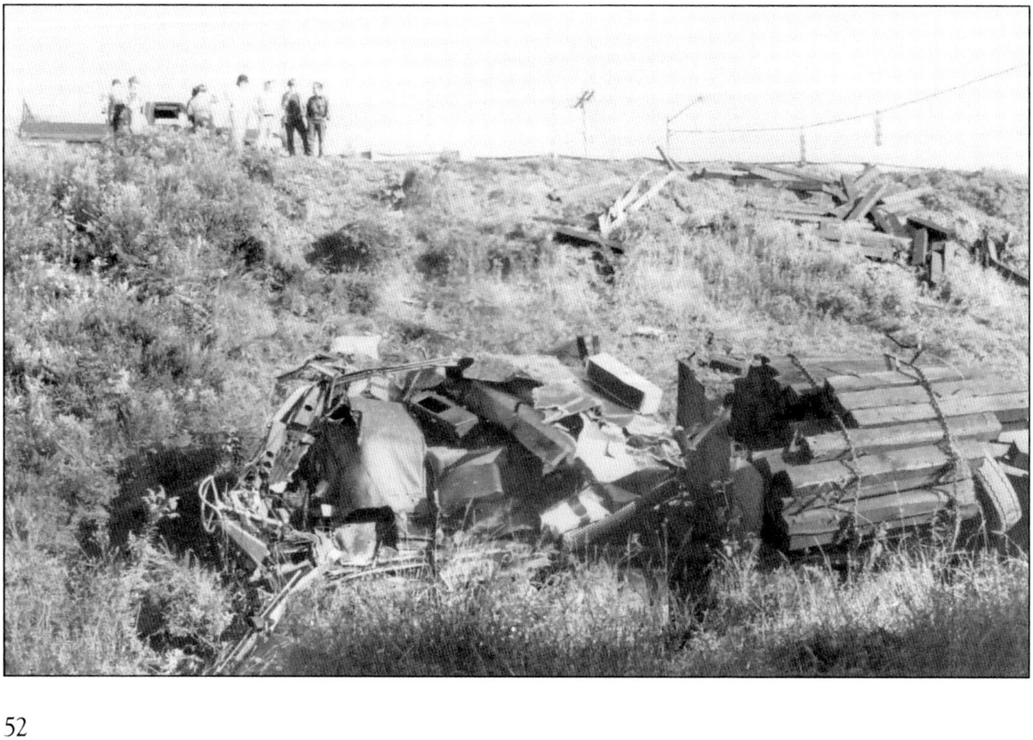

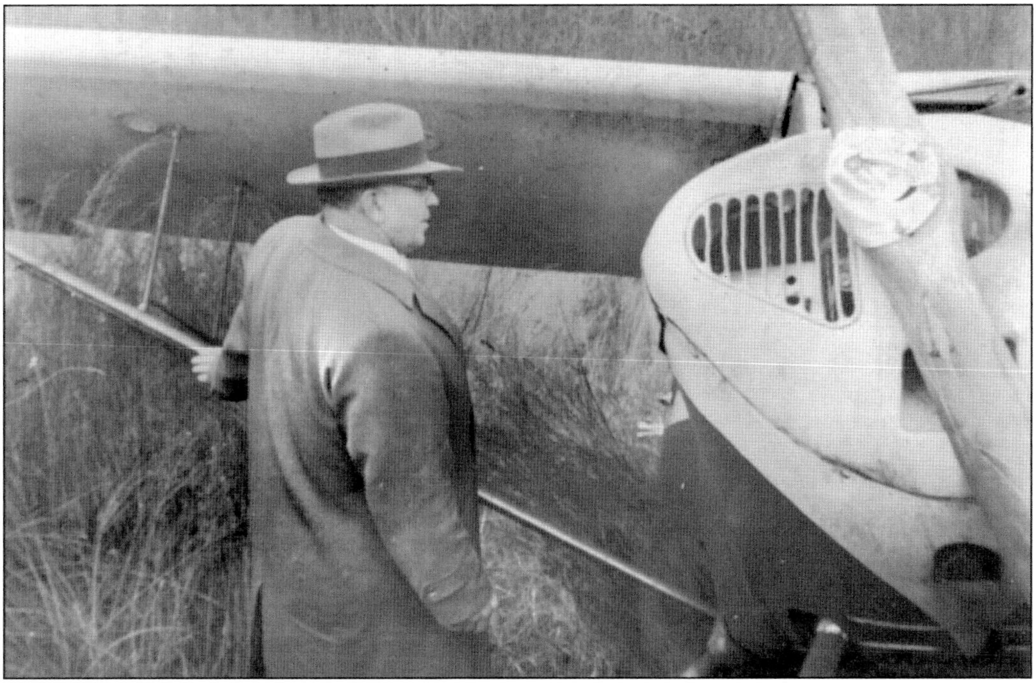

After hearing the news of a small airplane crashing on its way to the Wood County Airport, Rev. C. S. Dayhoff investigates the scene of this tragedy. Airplane crashes are very rare in this area. Below is another picture of an unusual airplane crash. While flying too low over St. Marys, the pilot collided with Mildred Bills's chimney. It then crashed into Chester Bills's roof, landed in a tree, and then fell out of the tree into a field near the houses. Mildred's is located near the intersection of Route 2 and Alternate Route 16 across from where the high school stands. The house is now a gift shop called Mildred's owned by her daughter, Mary Sue Ross. (Above courtesy of Ruth Ann Dayhoff; below courtesy of Mary Sue Ross.)

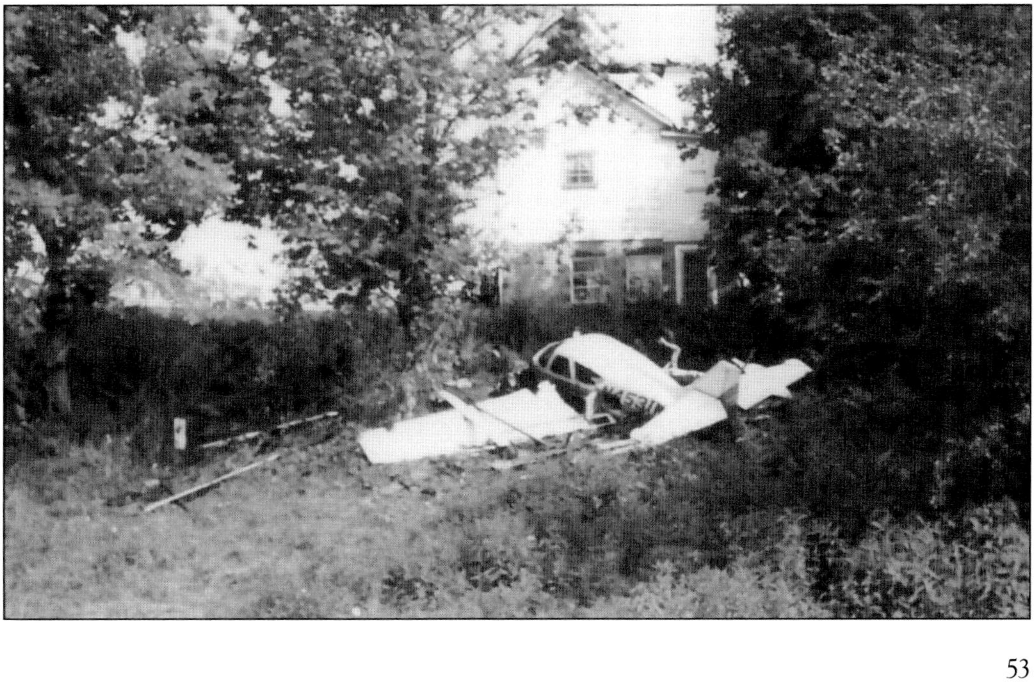

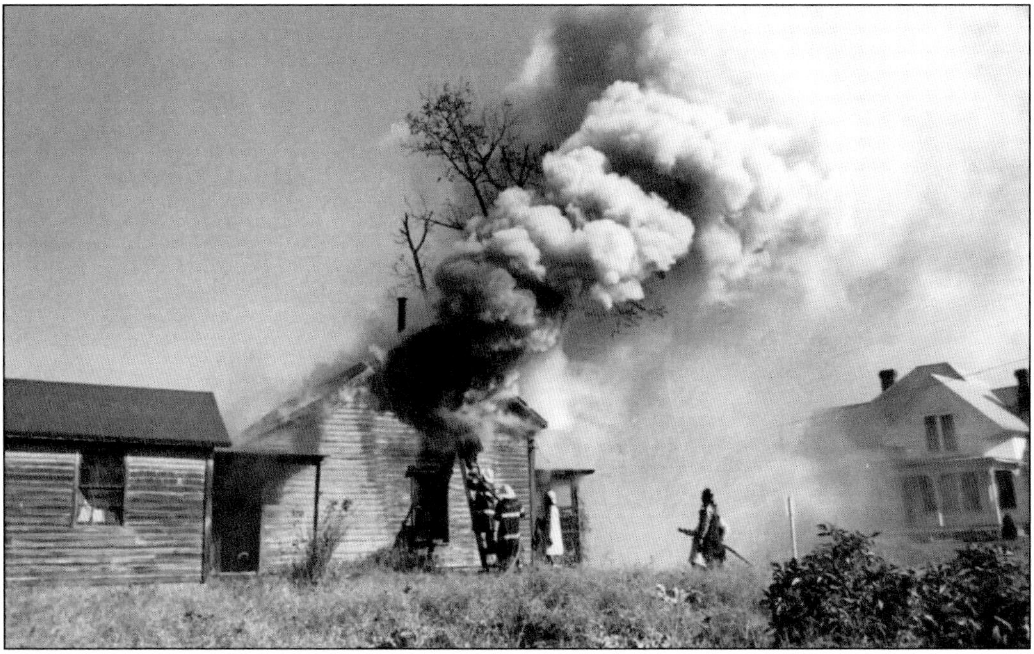

This fire in Belmont brought both the St. Marys Volunteer Fire Department and the Belmont Volunteer Fire Department to the scene. The two departments often work closely together, and sometimes they work with the fire department in Newport, Ohio. Pleasants County can be sure that help will arrive soon after the need is reported. (Courtesy of Rev. Daniel Simmons.)

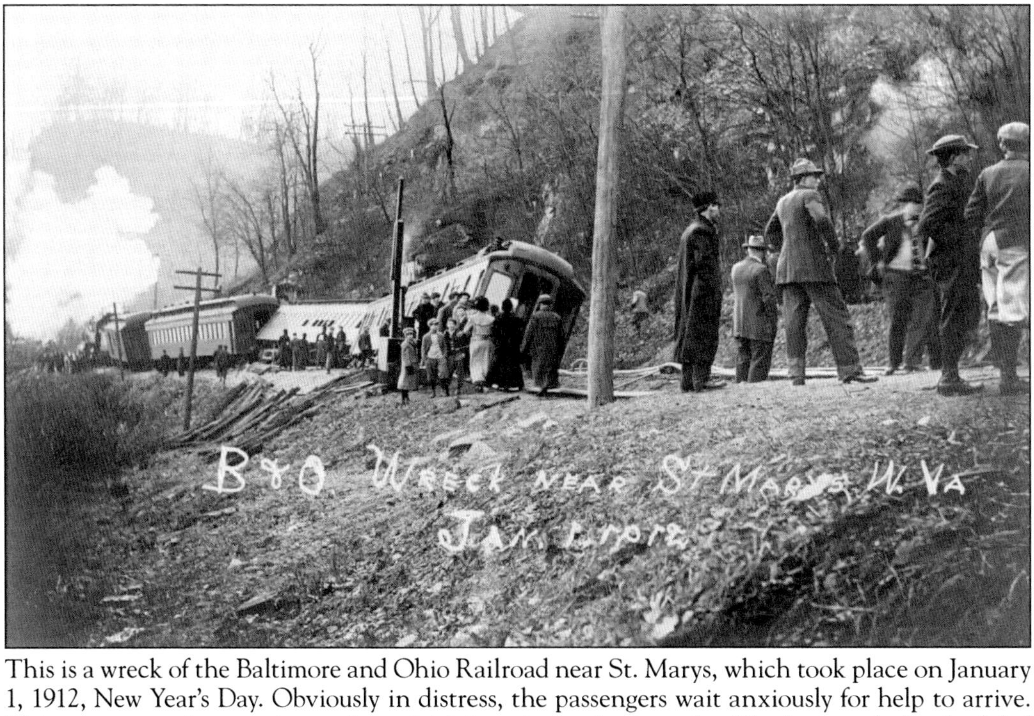

This is a wreck of the Baltimore and Ohio Railroad near St. Marys, which took place on January 1, 1912, New Year's Day. Obviously in distress, the passengers wait anxiously for help to arrive. This was a steam locomotive engine, which is no longer in use today. The last regularly scheduled steam locomotive ran in the mid-1950s. (Courtesy of WVDCHSA.)

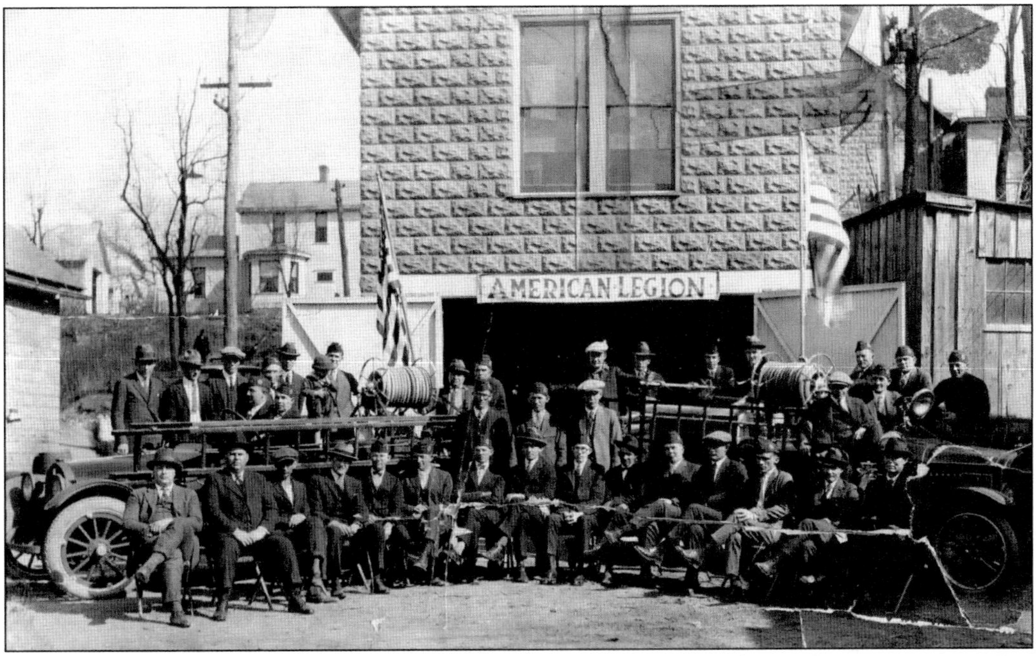

The Pleasants Post 79 American Legion Fire Department was started on February 22, 1920. Cap Russell was the first fire chief. These men braved disastrous conditions fighting fires with very little equipment. With the support of the business community, they were gradually able to purchase updated equipment and materials to build the above fire station. In 2006, the local fire department was 70 years old. They annually give back to the community a wonderful event called the Ice Cream Social. This event includes rides for children on the red fire truck as well as fun, food, and games. Men who serve with this organization are very proud to be members of the department. They go through rigorous training to be able to save lives. They also come into the public schools to teach fire safety to the children. (Both courtesy of fire department chief Lee Ogdin.)

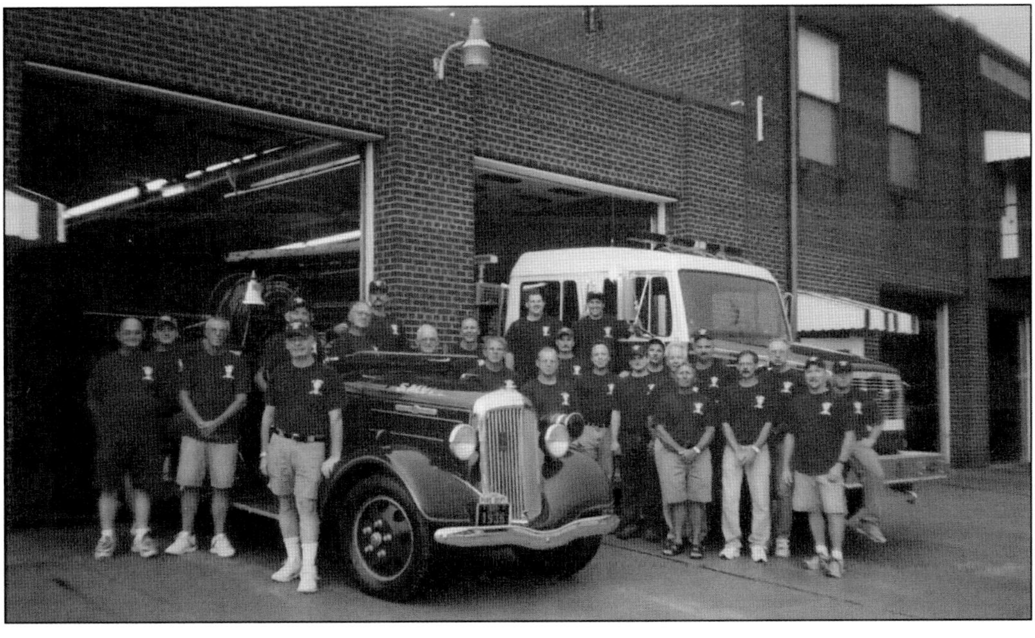

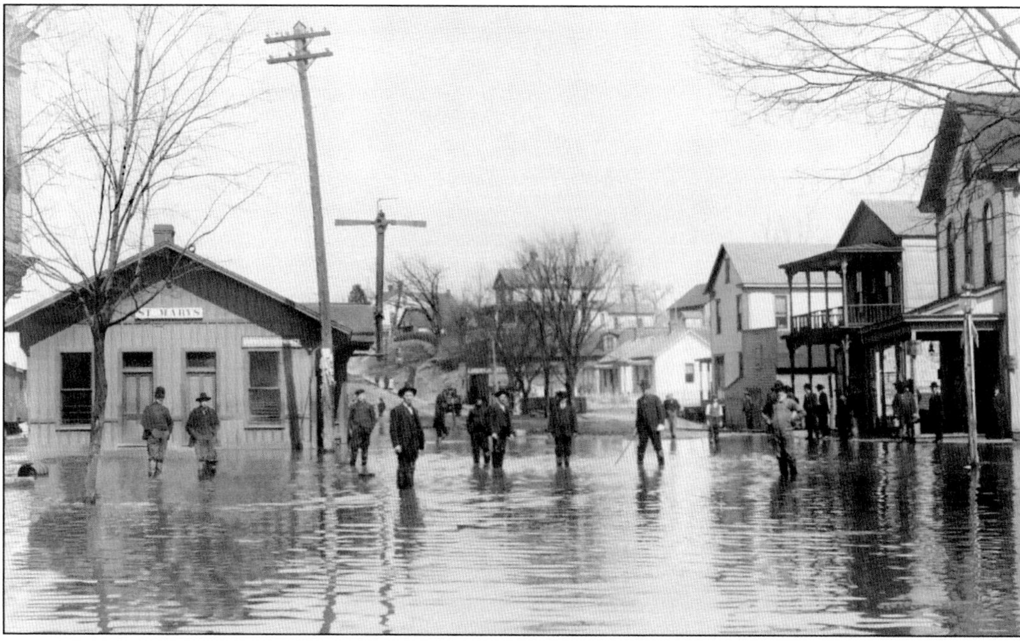

A disastrous flood occurred in 1913 that affected the entire county. The photograph above of the train depot shows the water first coming onto the downtown area. The men are checking out the height of the water as it rises, affecting business property as well as homes. In the photograph below, the water has risen so high that boats are becoming necessary in order to move safely about on the streets. The trains can no longer get through. March 29, 1913, was a very cold, snowy, wet, and unhappy day. In 1852, there was a flood that wiped out the entire city of Vaucluse, very near St. Marys. (Above HCWC, courtesy of WVDCHSA; below PMC, courtesy of Daniel Pitts.)

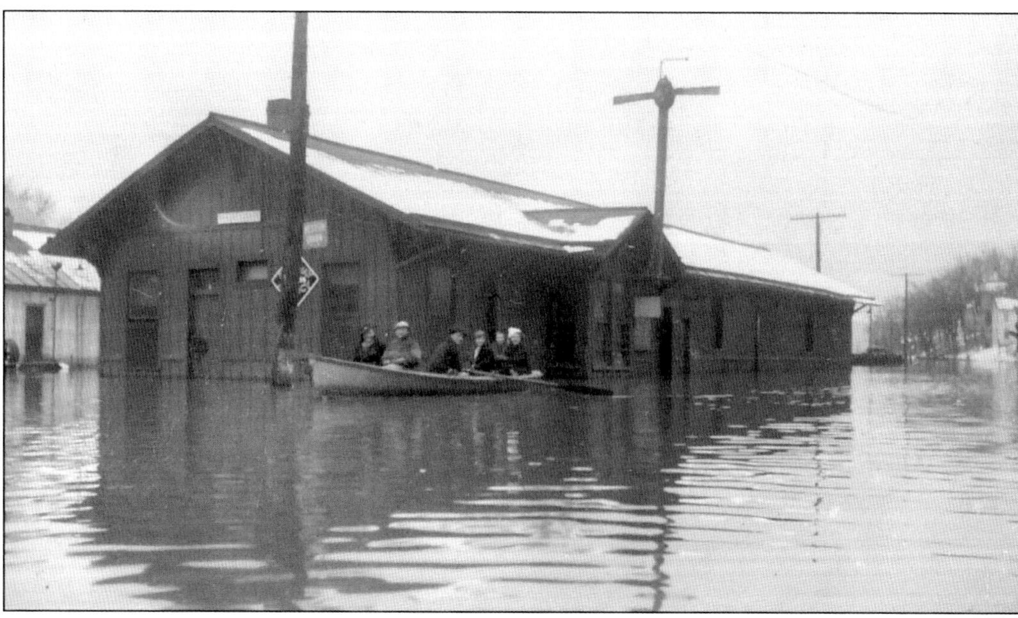

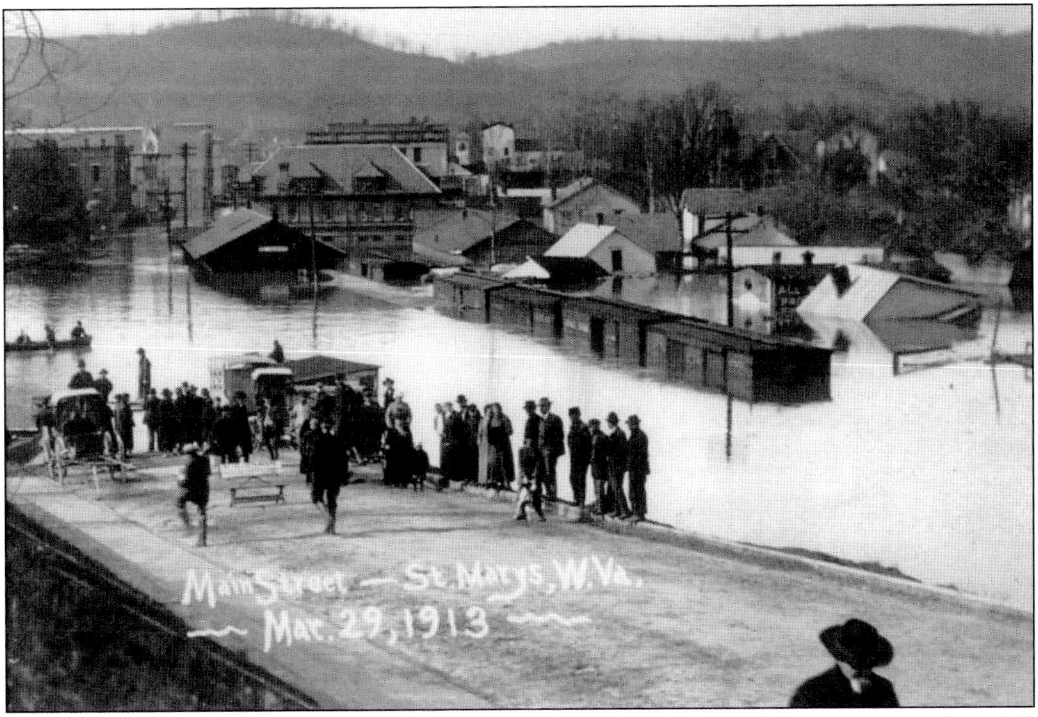

Look at the depot now. Can you find the train? It is almost completely underwater. This 1913 flood was disastrous. The hill where people are standing is the upper part of Main Street. How helpless they must feel. Follow the water down the street and imagine what would be flooded if this were to happen today. Below, one can see how far the water has risen. It is above the roofs of several houses. Landmarks are disappearing until one can hardly recognize this as St. Marys. Residents should very much appreciate the dams that have been built that help keep the mighty Ohio River in control. (Both courtesy of Delores Kemp.)

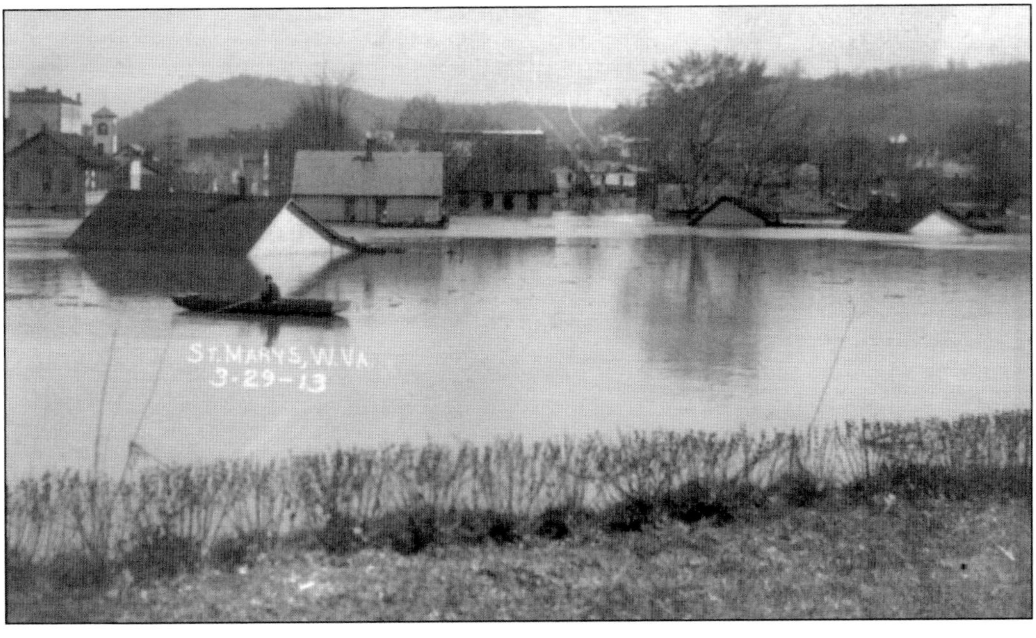

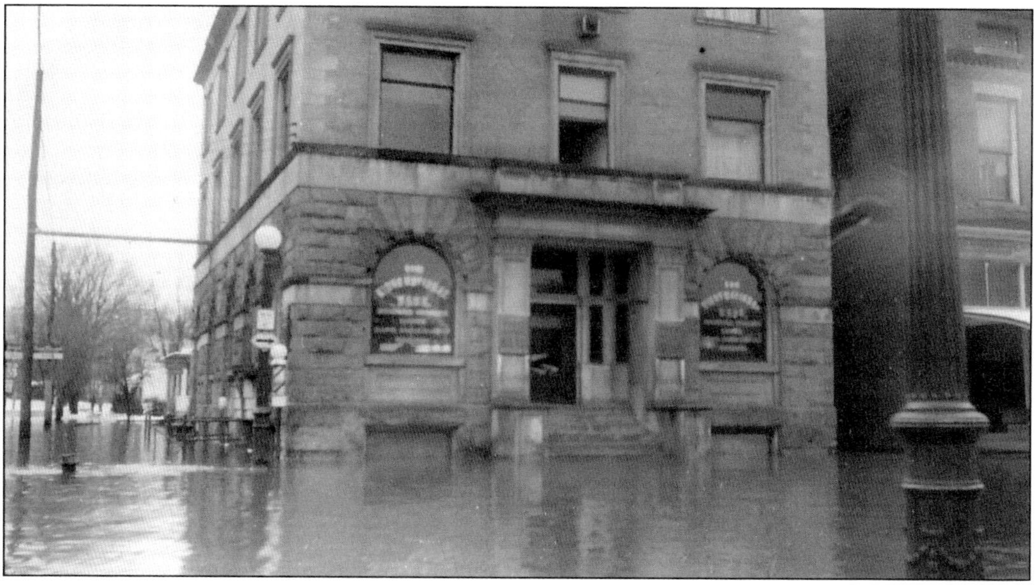

The 1937 flood crested at 52 feet. The center of town was underwater. The current on Main Street was so swift that a fire truck on a barge was anchored on lower Main Street for emergency use, if needed. Within days of this picture, the water had risen above the door of the bank. Scenes like these motivated people to find ways to control the river. (Both PMC, courtesy of Daniel Pitts.)

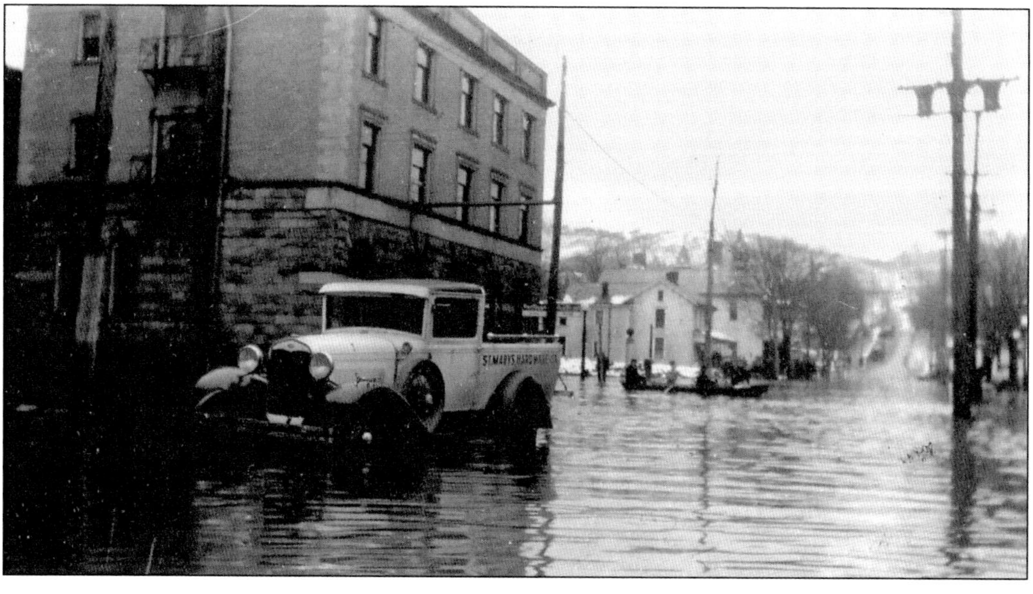

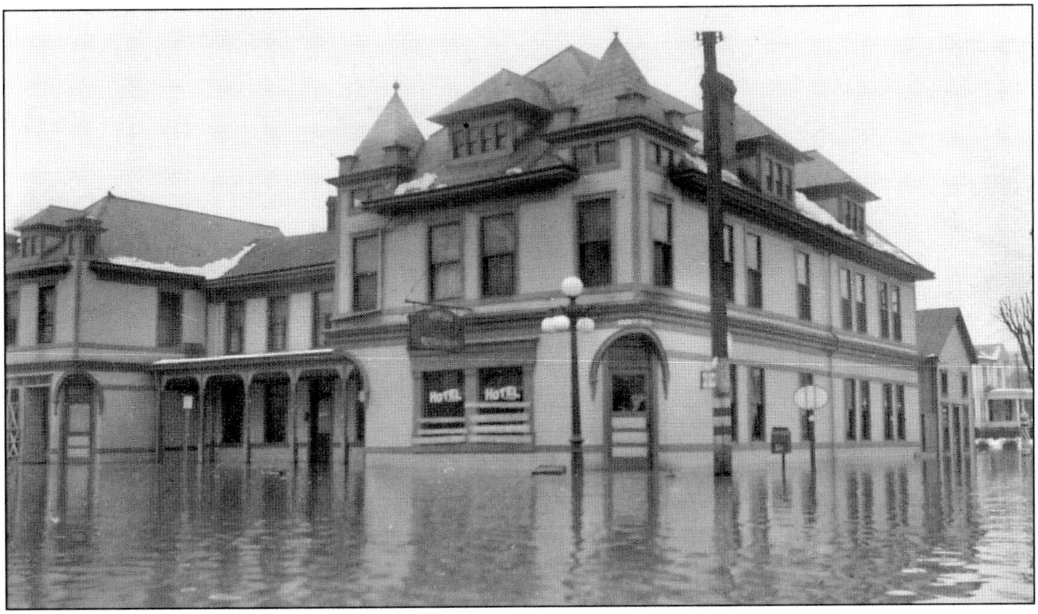

No meals are being served today at the Howard Hotel Restaurant. In fact, the windows and doors are boarded up, but this did not keep out the water. This flood of almost 100 years ago nearly destroyed the town. Some of Pleasants County's ancestors were being challenged beyond belief. Below, in the 1937 flood, it is hard to believe that school was still in session. We know this because of the picture below. Louise Pitts is in the rowboat on her way to teach school at St. Marys Elementary School, about two blocks away. Much of the town was above the water level, so those children were still required to attend, as was their teacher, in spite of the rising waters. This picture is crooked because the photograph was taken from a rocking boat. (Both PMC, courtesy of Daniel Pitts.)

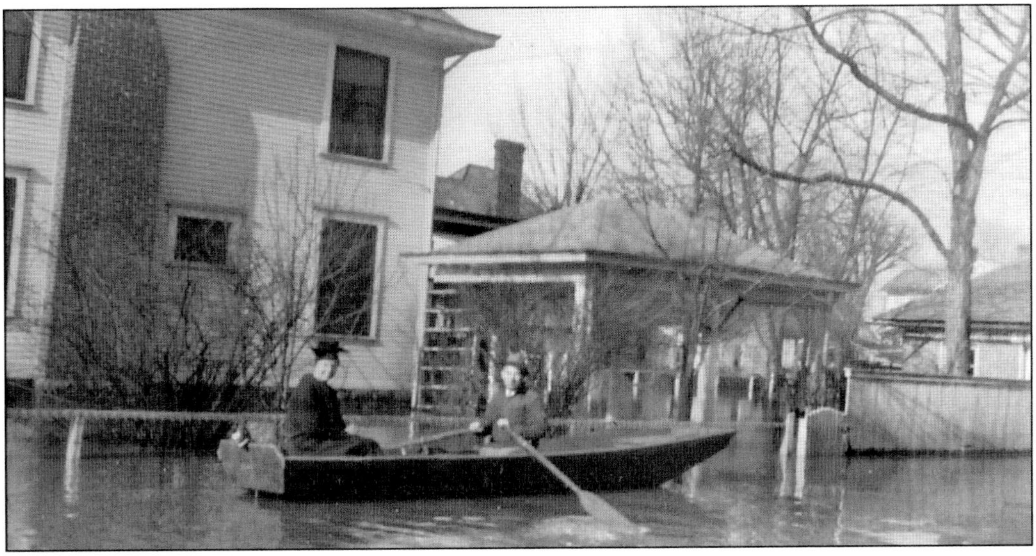

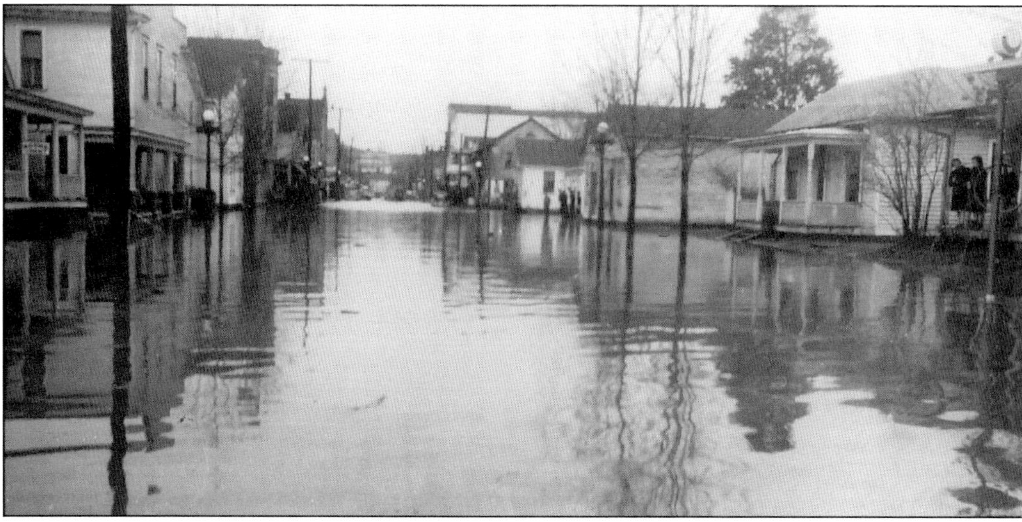

This March 29, 1913, flood rose to its height as the greatest flood within memory. It was immediately preceded by a terrible storm, and approximately 11 inches fell within 24 hours. As bad as this was, there had been worse floods. In 1877, the road from the Cain House through the Narrows had been completely washed away by flooding. A nearby town of Vaucluse had already been destroyed by earlier floodwaters. On May 12, 1885, there was such a violent electrical and rain storm that the water in French Creek rose 25 feet in one day. As the water was rising, people prepared to abandon their homes. In the 1937 picture below, Dr. James Riley McCollum (left) assesses the situation with a friend. (Both PMC, courtesy of Daniel Pitts.)

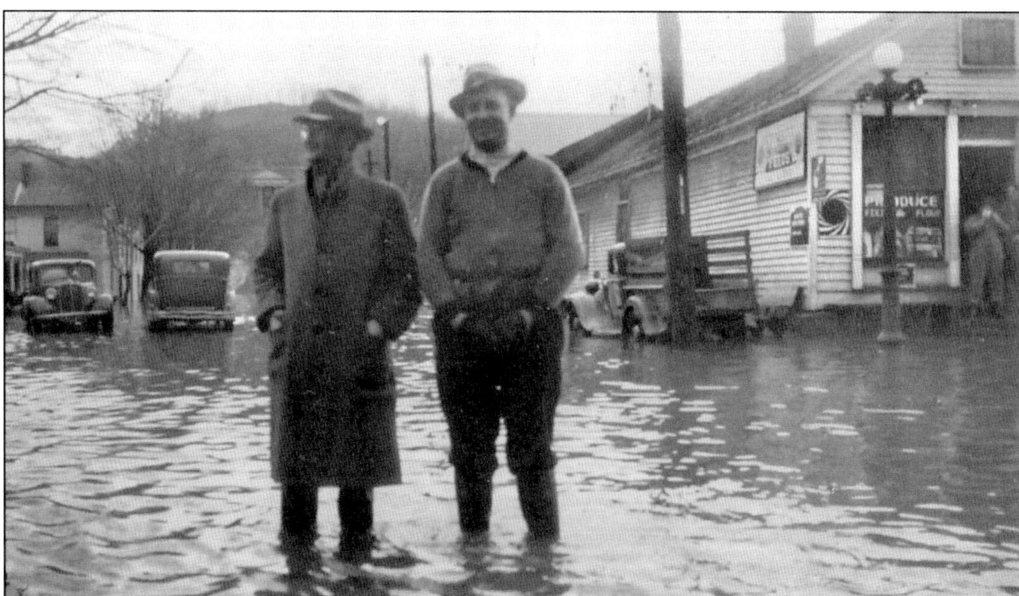

Five

River and Land Transportation

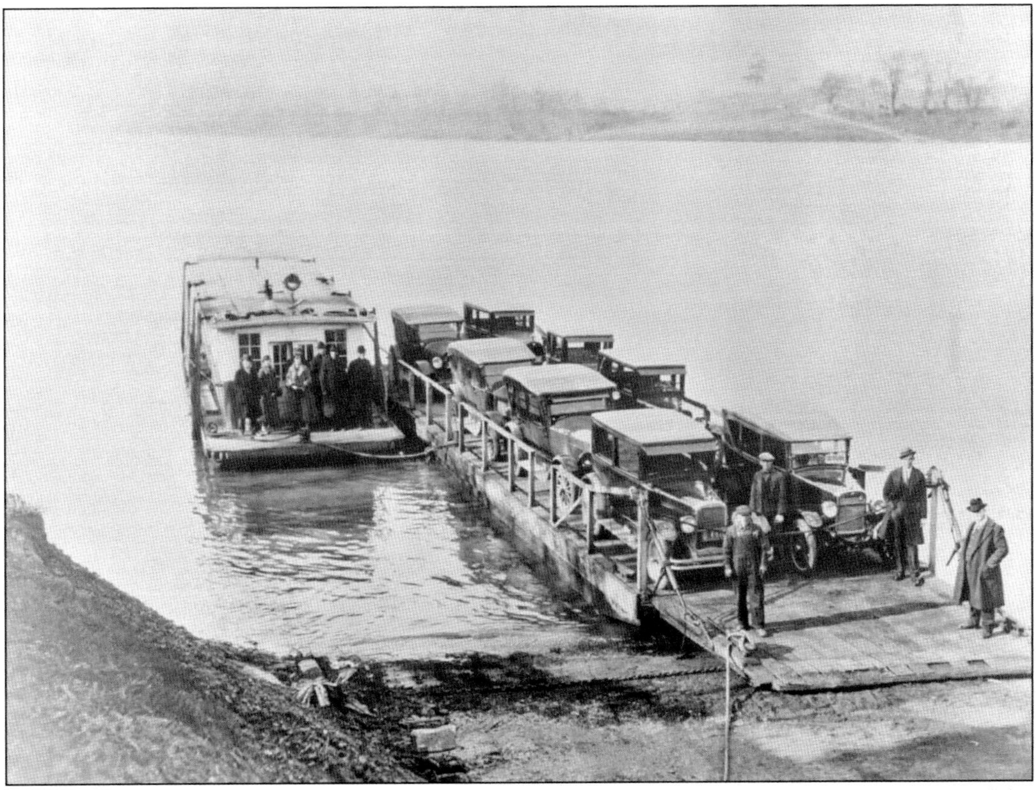

This picture shows the St. Marys ferry in 1925 with a load of eight brand-new modern cars of the day. All of the cars are Willys Knight-Overland cars that were being delivered from Toledo, Ohio. Standing from left to right on the ferry is Gilbert Duffy, Bob Walton, auto dealer Kenneth Weber, and George Phillips of the Phillips Drug Store. (PCHSC, courtesy of WVDCHSA.)

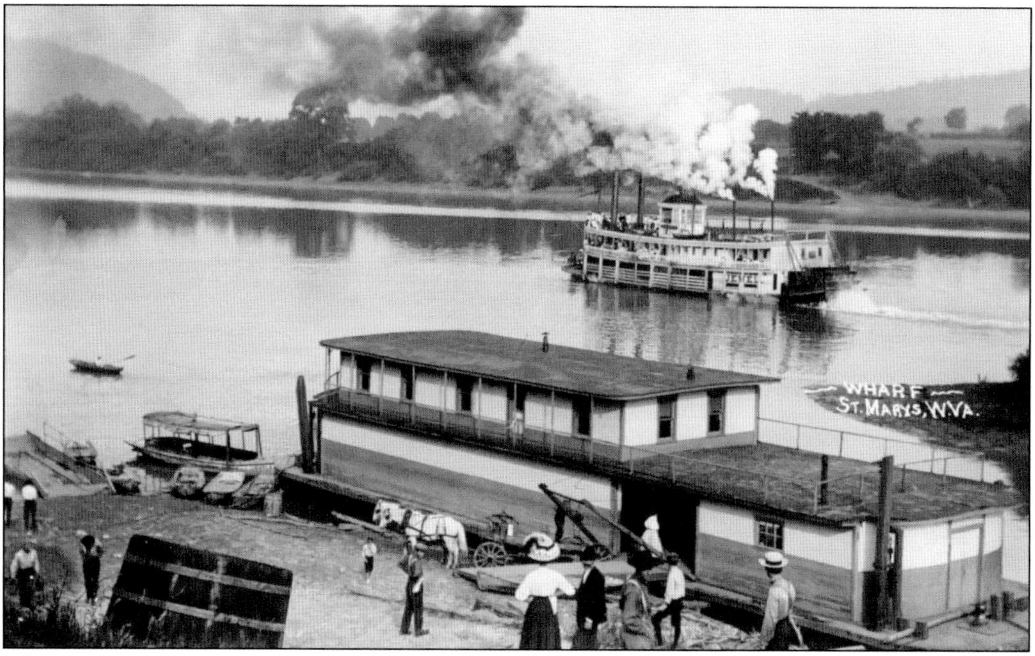

This is a view of the St. Marys wharf in the early 1900s. The steamer *Jewel* is passing by in the background. Notice the old-fashioned styles of clothing. The lady is standing on the landing where the cars go down to drive onto the ferry. After all, there was no bridge available at this time. (HCWC, courtesy of WVDCHSA.)

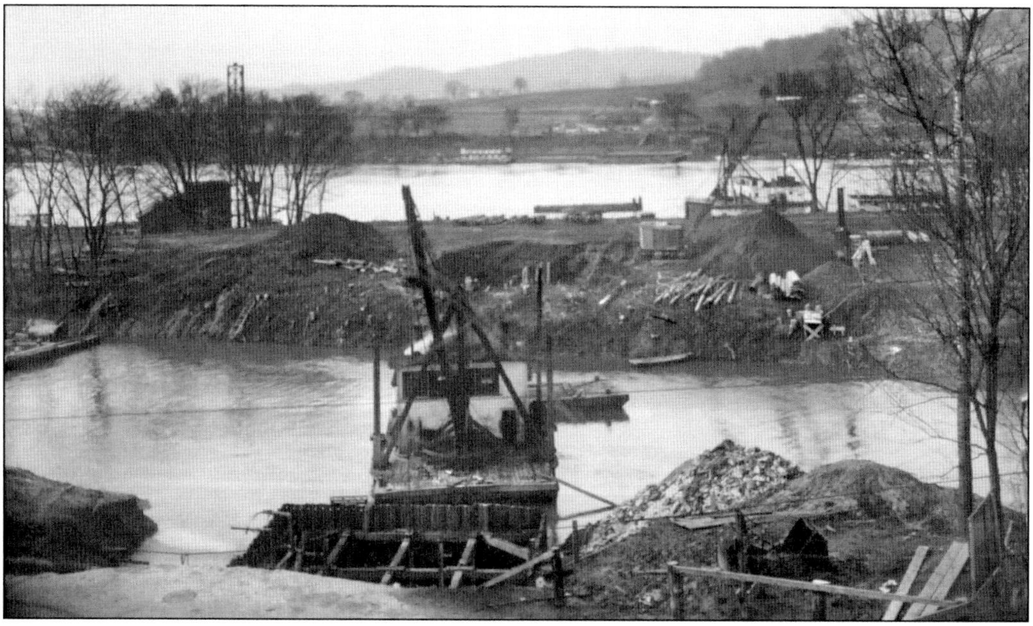

Good news traveled through the community. A bridge was finally going to be built from St. Marys, West Virginia, to Newport, Ohio. This picture shows an early construction phase of the Clarksburg-Columbus Short Route bridge over the Ohio River. It was built in 1927 and served us well until 1971. Because of its unusual I-beam construction, it was dismantled after a similar bridge in Point Pleasant, West Virginia, collapsed in 1967. (Courtesy of WVDCHSA.)

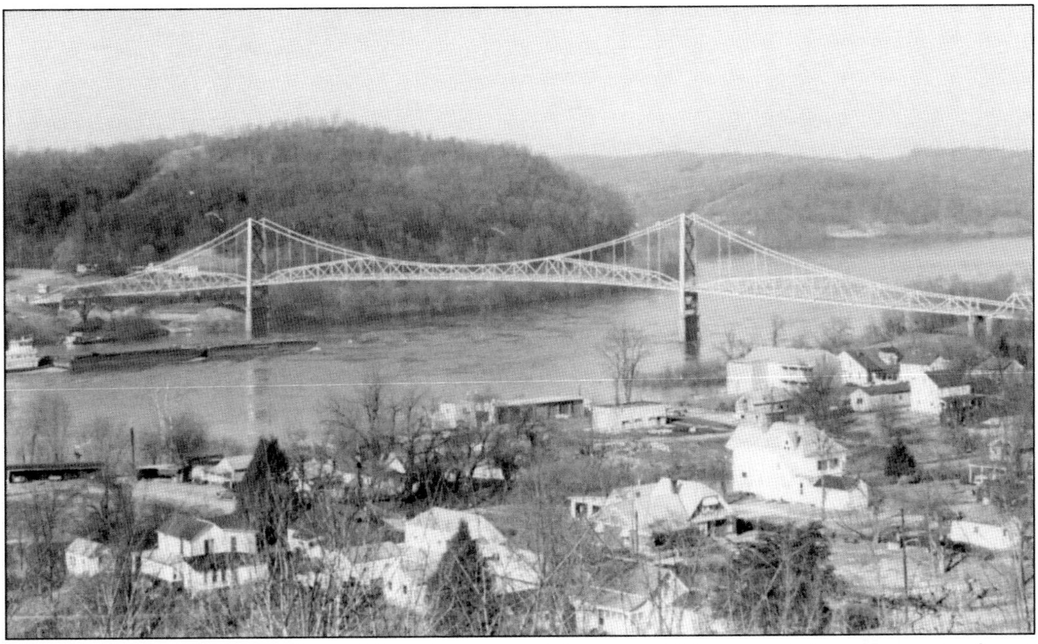

This first bridge from St. Marys, West Virginia, to Newport, Ohio, served the community for 44 years. It was built through the efforts of Hiram Alexander Carpenter, first as a toll bridge. Later on, its operation was taken over by the state of West Virginia. (Courtesy of Rev. Daniel Simmons.)

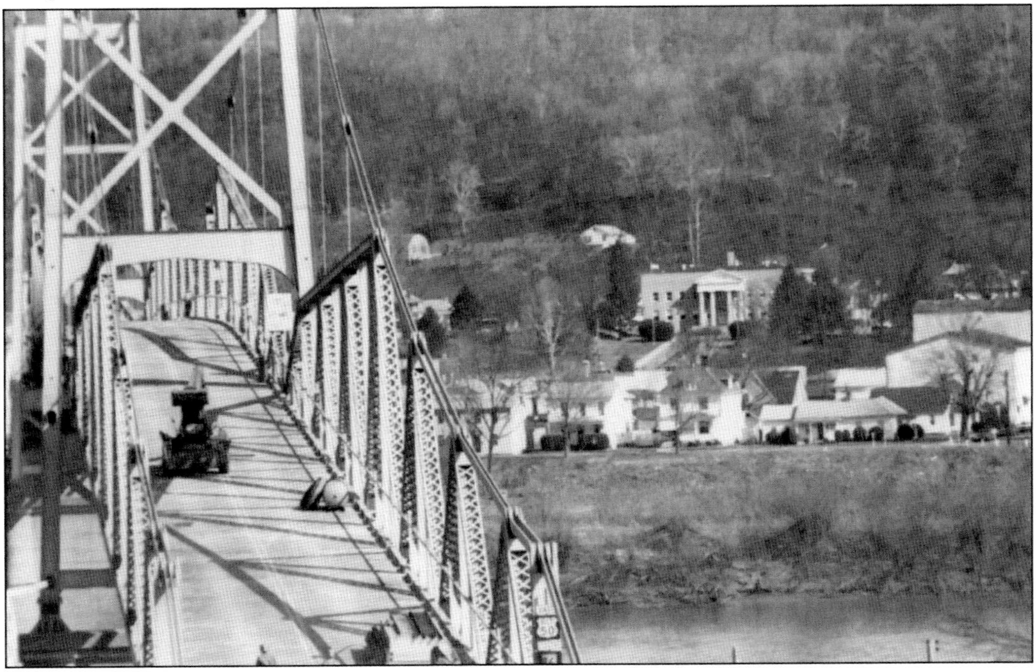

As a person drove across this two-lane bridge from Ohio, he would find himself entering into St. Marys on Riverside Drive. The beautiful St. Marys Courthouse stands upon the hill overlooking the city. Both Newport and St. Marys grieved when they learned their beloved bridge must be dismantled. The Silver Bridge in Point Pleasant had fallen, and this bridge was built much like it. (Courtesy of Rev. Daniel Simmons.)

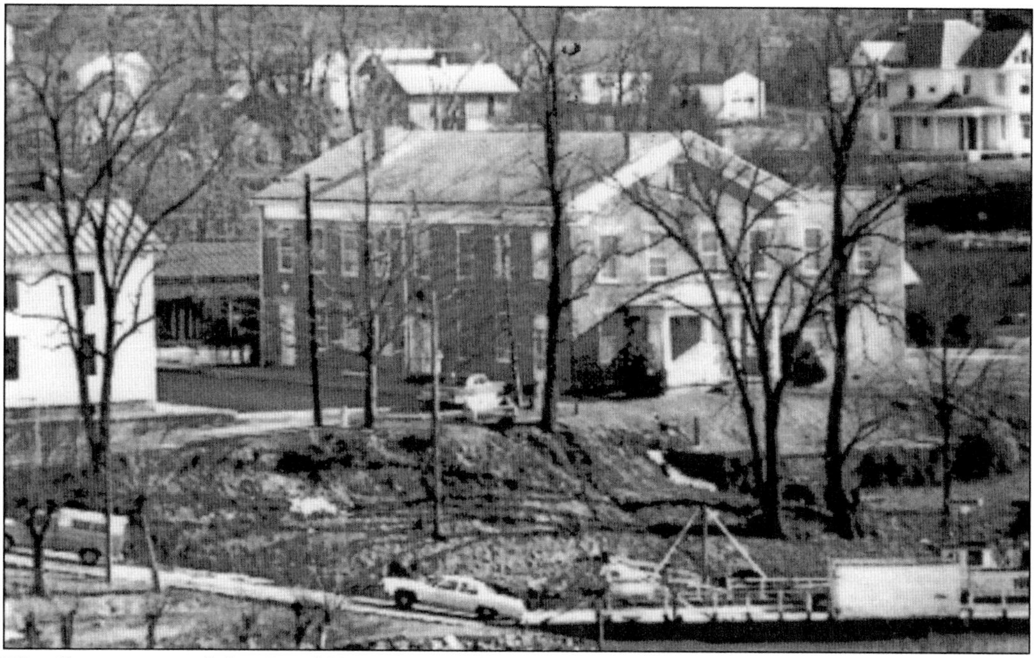

The Carpenter and the Creel Houses were the first two homes built in St. Marys by the Logan brothers for Alexander Creel. The Creel House is listed in the National Register of Historical Places. Both houses were used for businesses as well as family dwellings. Pictured to the left of the Creel House is the wharf, and vehicles are ascending from the ferry. In the distance to the right is a large white house over 100 years old. The town still has many beautiful old homes still in use. Below, the ferry is crossing to the Ohio side of the river. The ferry was necessary after the bridge was dismantled. The ferry is carrying seven vehicles. (Both courtesy of Rev. Daniel Simmons.)

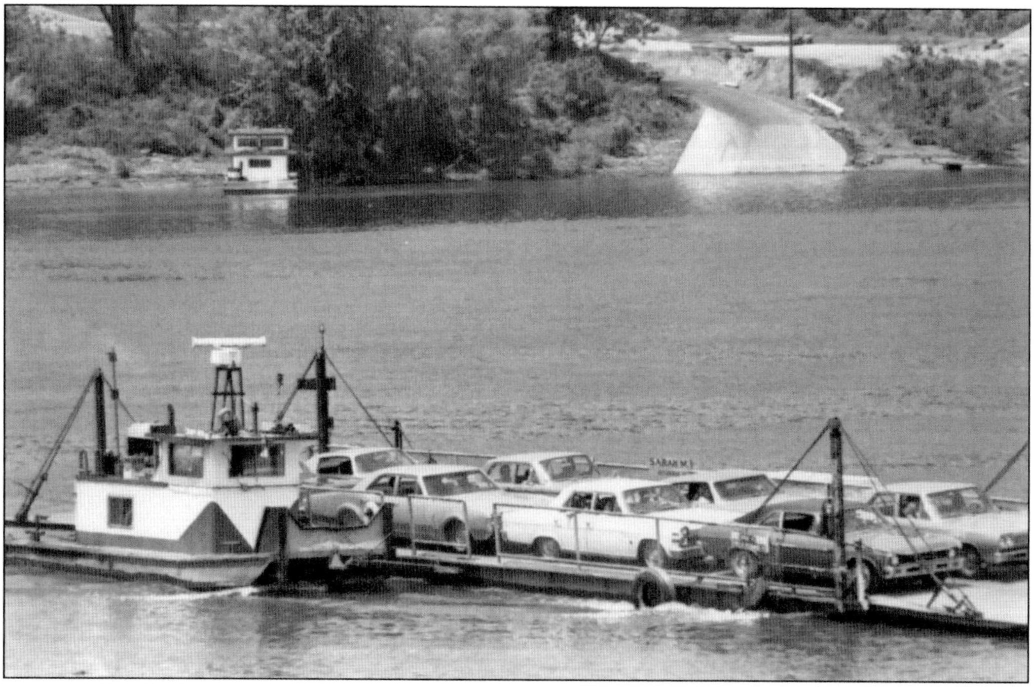

Cars are loading onto the ferry to travel to the Ohio side from the wharf in front of the Creel House. The ferry made many trips to and from West Virginia to Ohio daily. This is the usual peaceful scene seen by travelers, but the ferry traveled in bad weather also. As seen in the picture below, the bridge is almost completely dismantled. Although this bridge had a sister bridge at Point Pleasant that collapsed in December 1967, another sister bridge in South America is still in use. (Both courtesy of Rev. Daniel Simmons.)

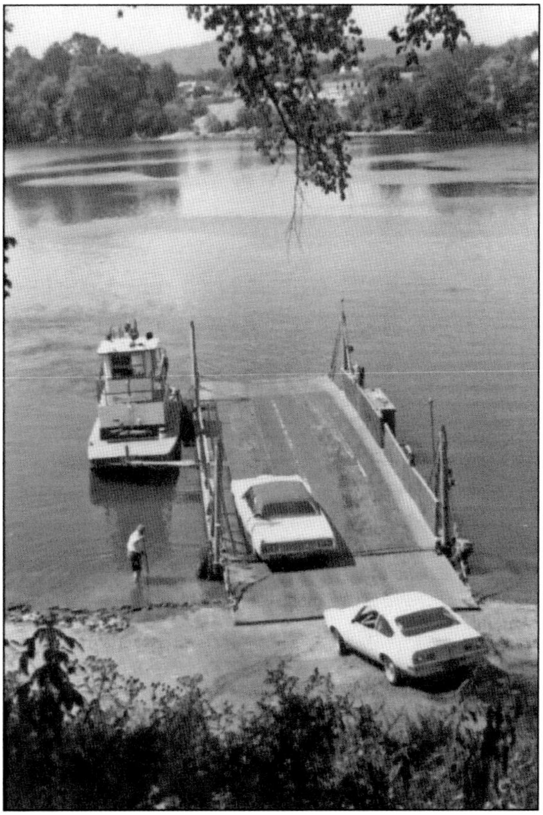

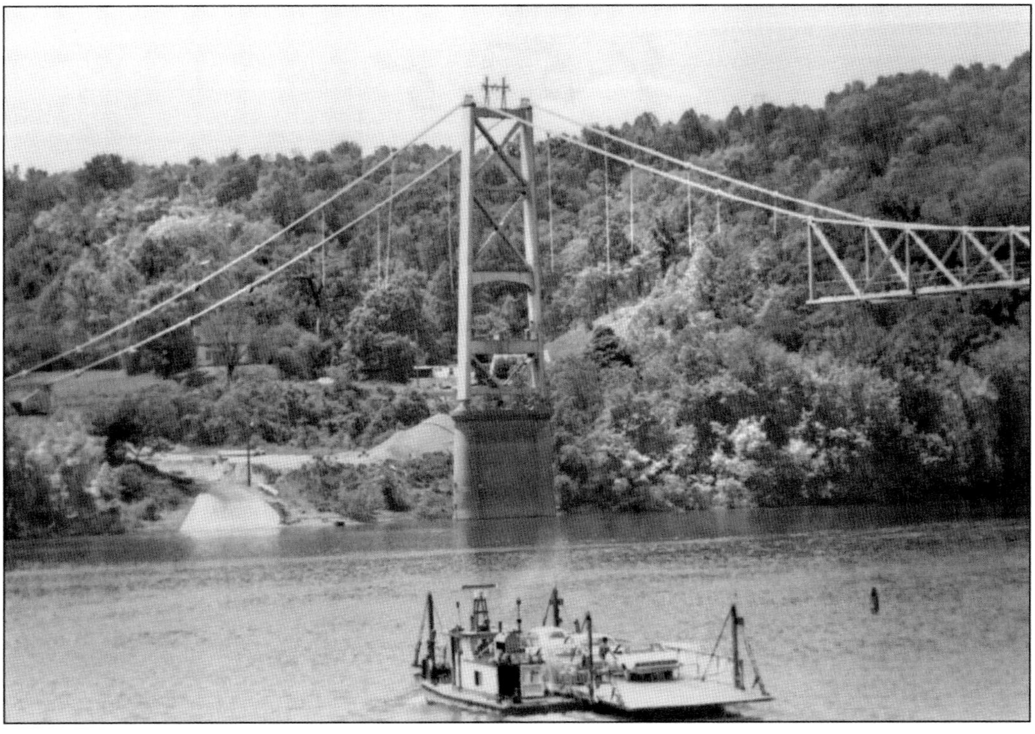

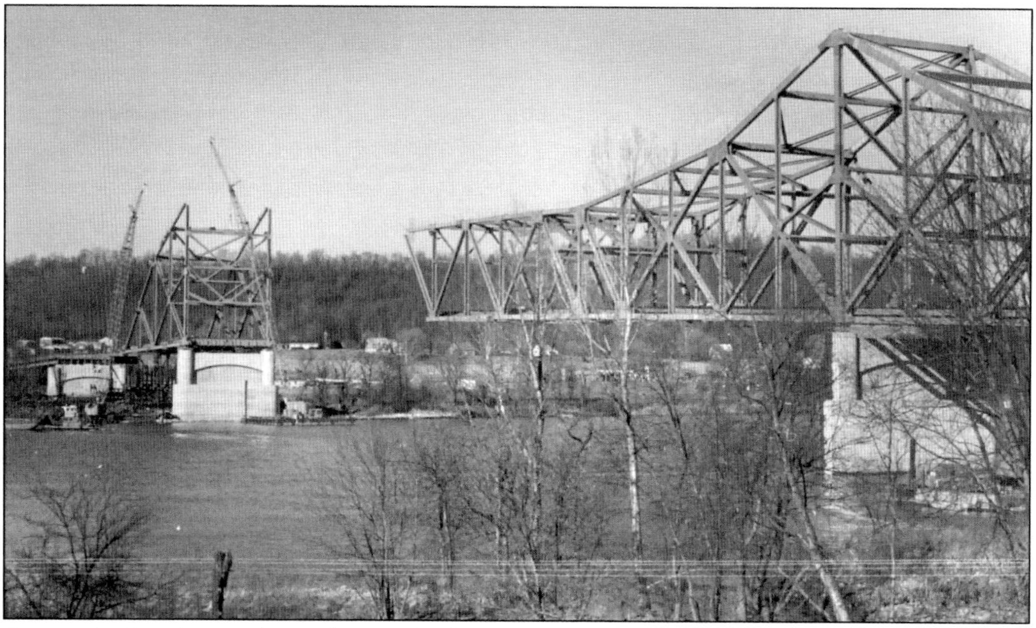

As seen in the picture above, the new bridge is coming together. It has taken a lot of hard work to build a bridge of this magnitude. Below, the bridge has been completed, and the band prepares to play as the dedication takes place for the new Hi Carpenter Bridge joining St. Marys, West Virginia, and Newport, Ohio. The twin daughters of Hi Carpenter, Barbara Ann Topper and Helen Mary Hewitt, as small girls, cut the ribbon for the first bridge 49 years before. They also cut the ribbon for the new bridge. In 1928, at the first dedication, they were 22 months old and loosened the bow knot; another sister, Rebecca, broke a bottle and christened the structure the Short Route Bridge. There were over 3,000 people attending the first dedication. (Both courtesy of Rev. Daniel Simmons.)

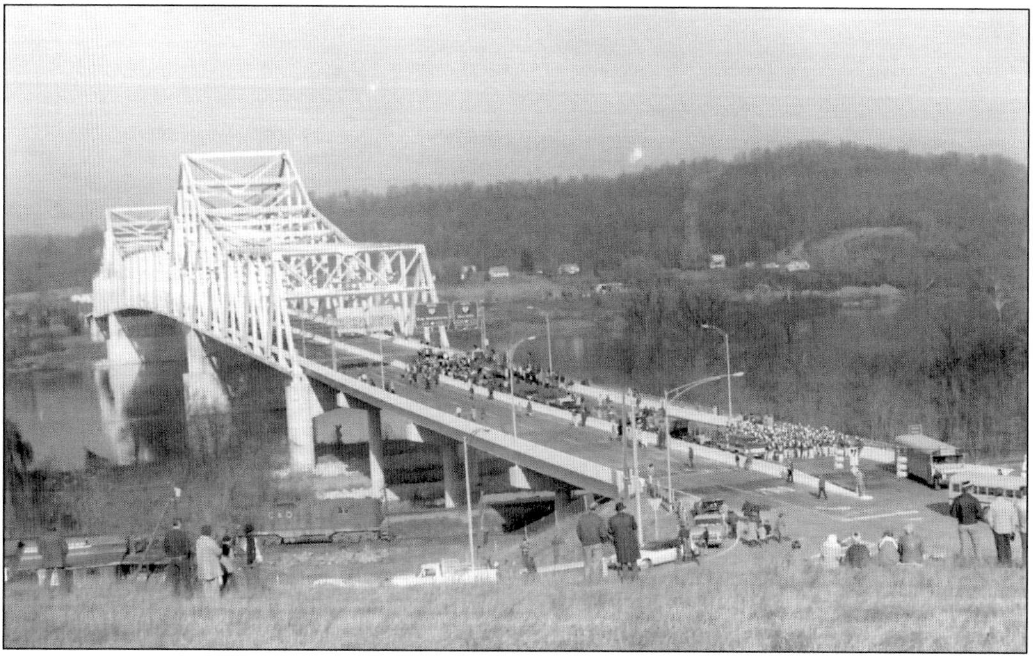

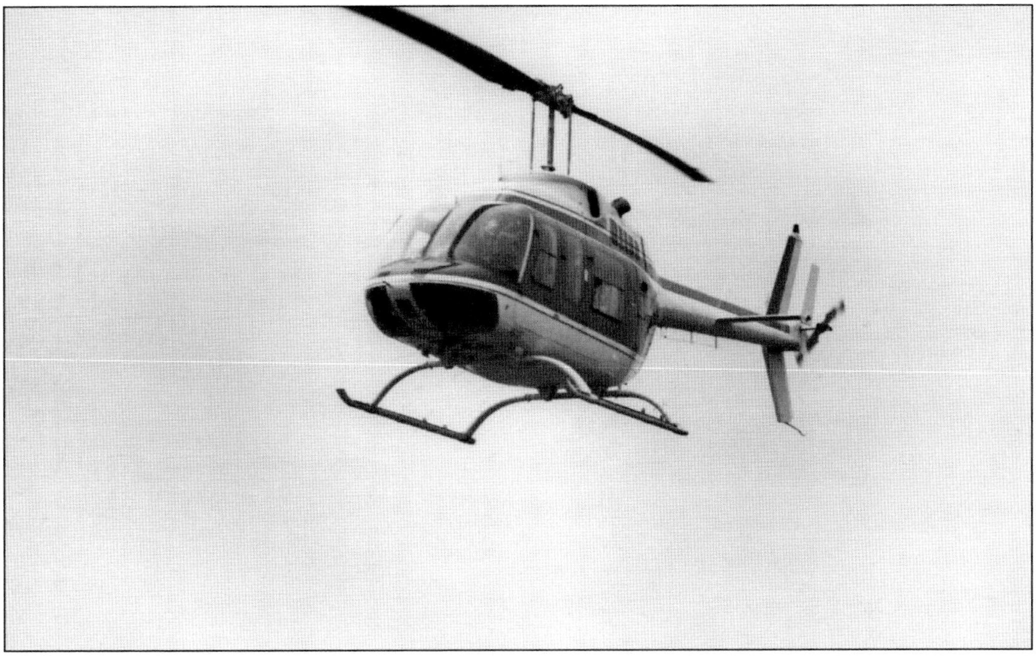

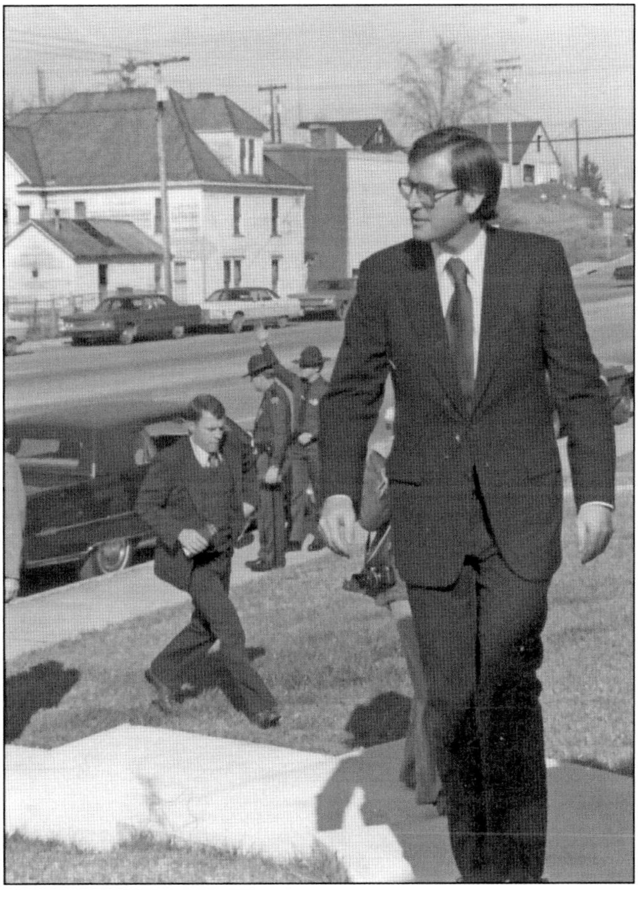

The helicopter brings Gov. Jay Rockefeller and Sen. Jennings Randolph to speak at the dedication of the Hi Carpenter Bridge. Also scheduled to take part were Rep. Robert Mollohan of West Virginia and Rep. Clarence Miller from Ohio. Rockefeller and the other dignitaries were honored guests at the St. Marys Presbyterian church for a luncheon in the fellowship hall. Gov. Jay Rockefeller walks to the luncheon at the church. The author's mother, Mary Ellen Dittman, helped serve the dinner. Notice the large house behind the governor. It was torn down and replaced by the building now known as the Shake Shack. (Both courtesy of Rev. Daniel Simmons.)

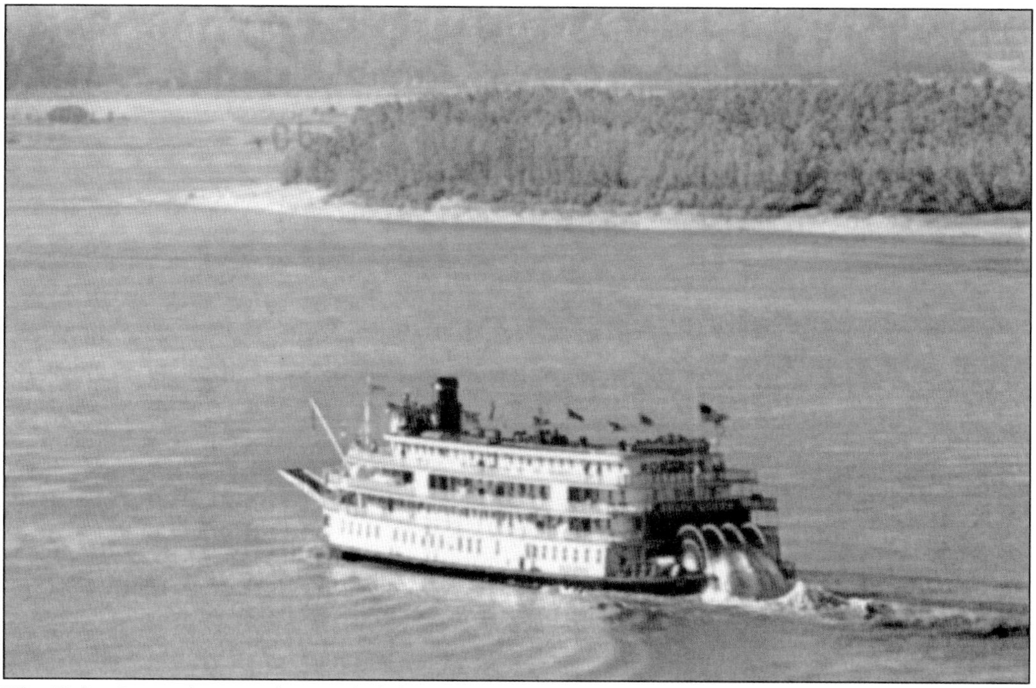

The *Delta Queen* frequently traveled the Ohio River as well as many other boats. The *Delta Queen* originally had a twin called the *Delta King*, which was built at the same time. The *American Queen* also traveled up and down the Ohio River. (PMC, courtesy of Daniel Pitts.)

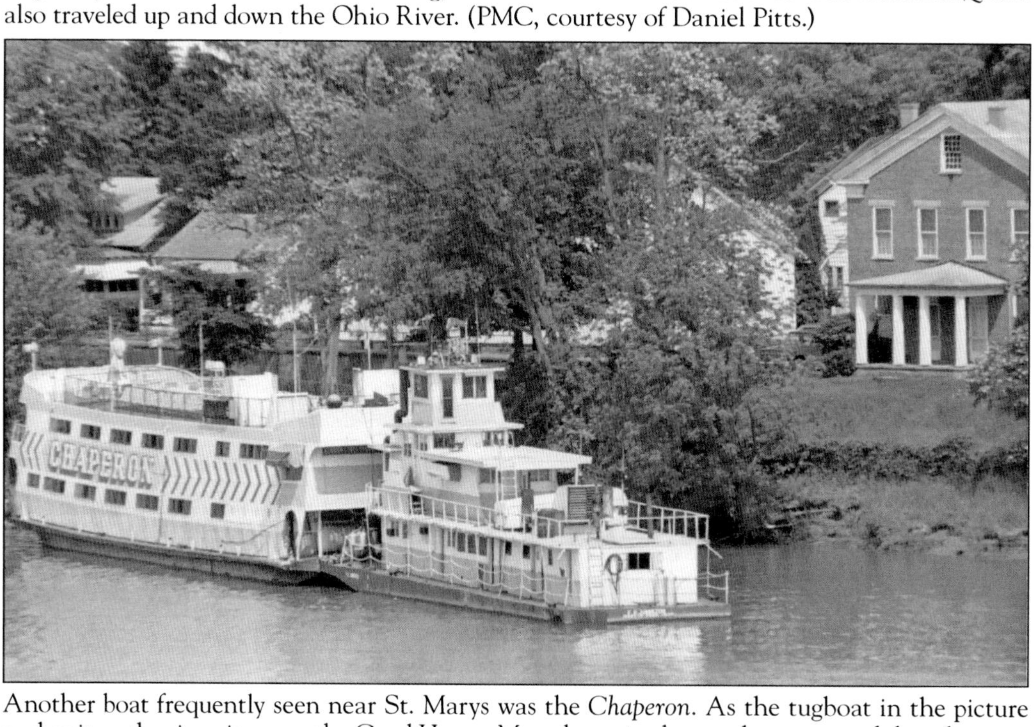

Another boat frequently seen near St. Marys was the *Chaperon*. As the tugboat in the picture pushes it up the river, it passes the Creel House. Many boats in the past have stopped there because in the early days the Creel House, then called the Cain House, was such a convenient place to find relaxation, food, and a place to sleep. (Courtesy of Rev. Daniel Simmons.)

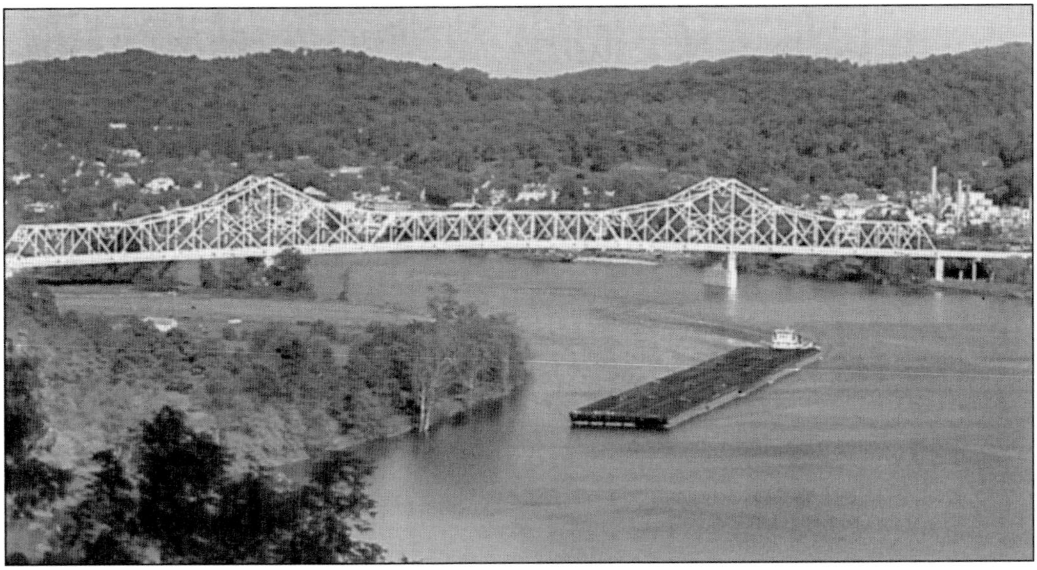

This majestic view of the Hi Carpenter Bridge includes the town of St. Marys and a very typical barge that has just passed under the bridge. Taken from the Ohio side as one goes north past Newport, the view to the right is magnanimous. This wider bridge has four lanes, making travel much nicer than the older two-lane version. This new bridge is also located farther down the river than the original bridge, and it enters directly onto Route 2. The bottom scene is of a tug docked at the base of the Creel House. This shows the northern side of the bridge from West Virginia. (Above courtesy of Rev. Daniel Simmons; below courtesy of Ruth Dayhoff.)

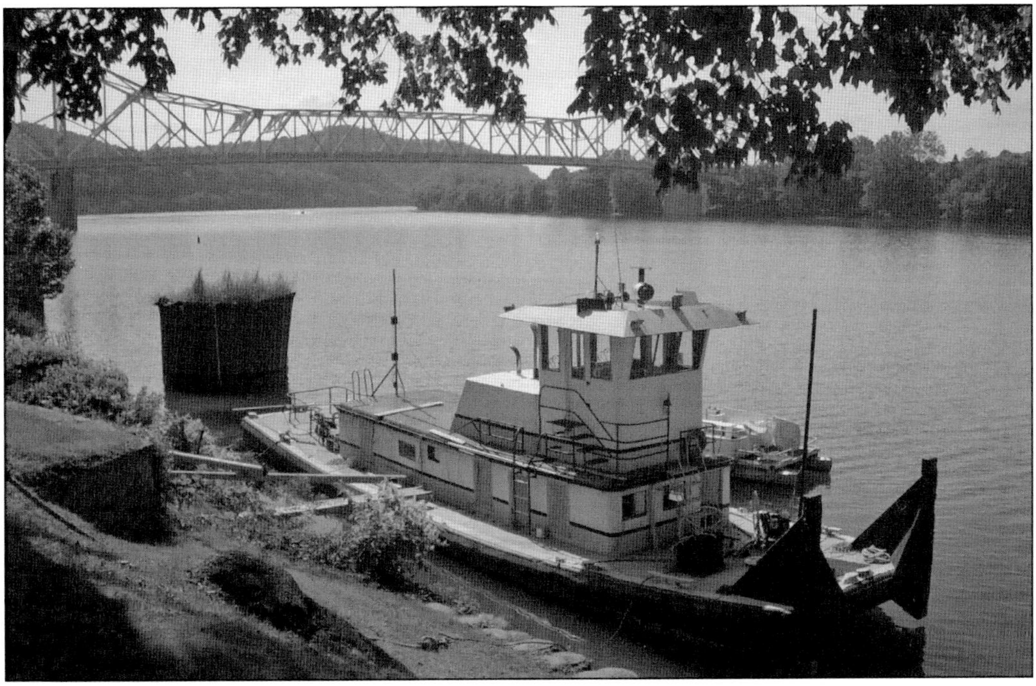

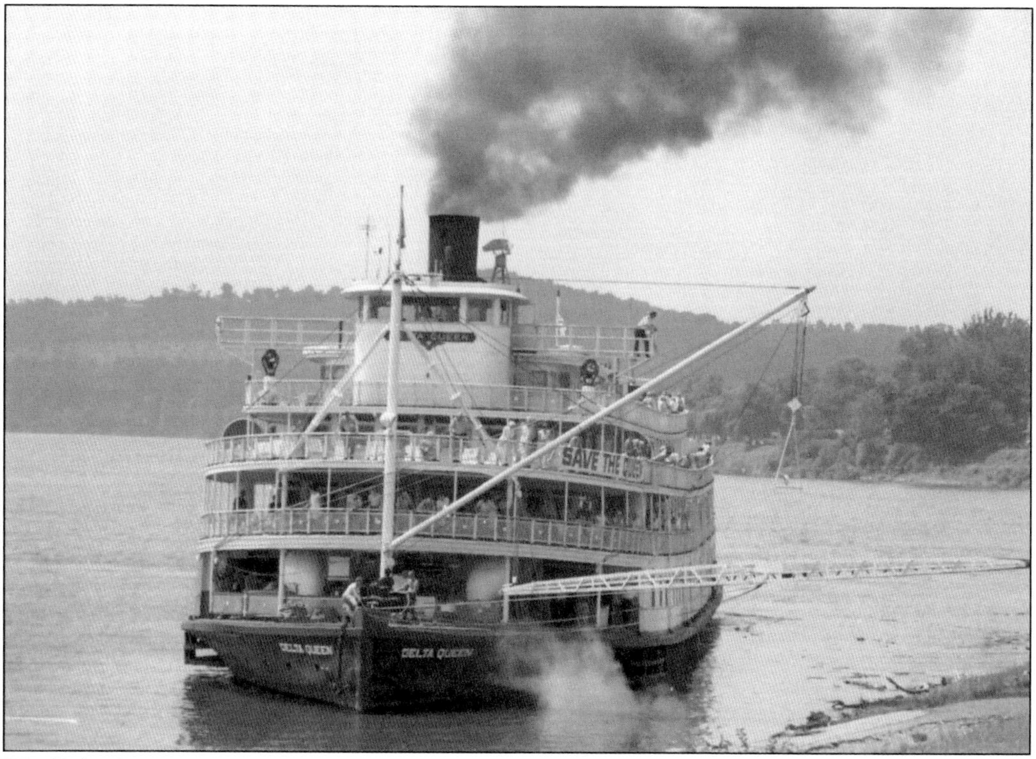

The *Delta Queen* is an American stern-wheeler steamboat. It is a National Historic Landmark. The *Queen* is 285 feet long and 58 feet wide with a capacity for 200 passengers. Its cross-compounded steam engines generate 2,000 indicated horsepower and power the stern-mounted paddle wheel. The decks and steam engines were ordered from the shipyard in Dumbarton, Scotland, in 1924. The photograph above shows the *Queen* coming close to shore, and the photograph below shows the *Queen* passing a barge at the end of Middle Island. These sights have been seen by local residents for many years. (Both courtesy of Rev. Daniel Simmons.)

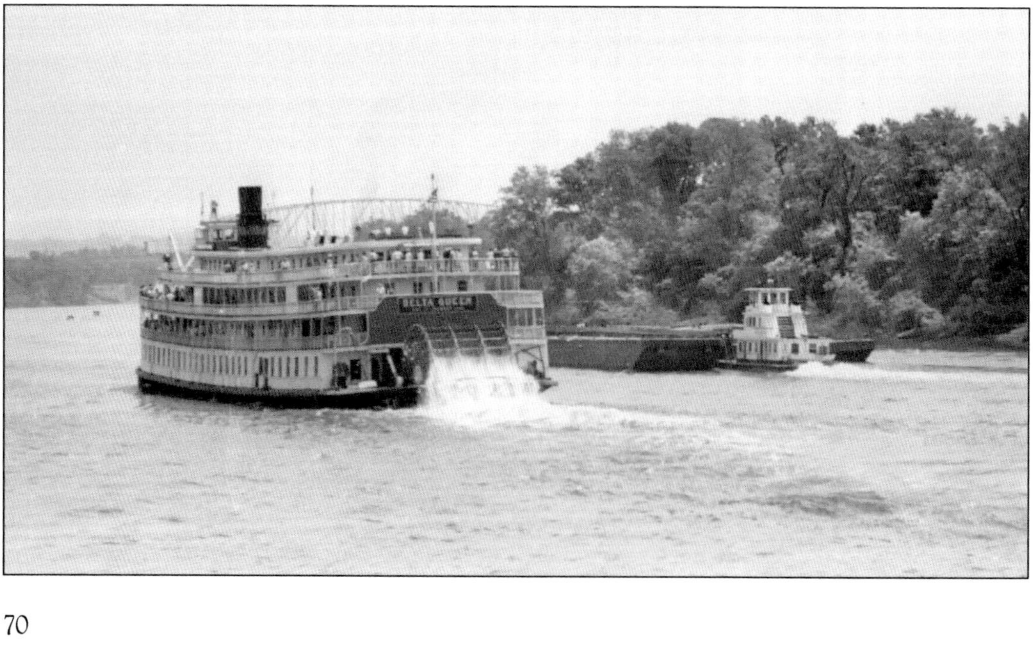

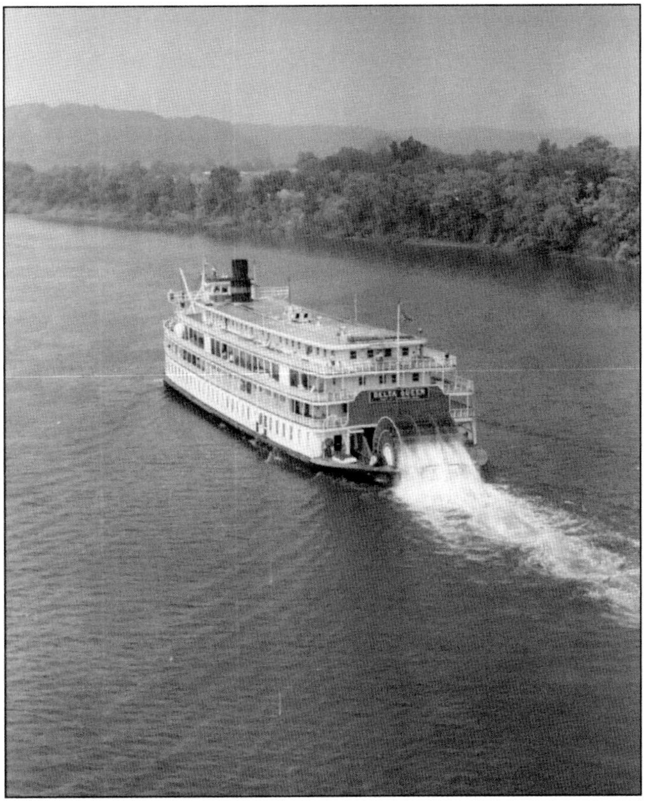

The *Delta Queen* was considered the most elegantly decorated and expensive sternwheeler passenger ship ever. During World War II, it was requisitioned by the U.S. Navy for duty. On August 1, 2007, the owners of the *Delta Queen* announced it would cease operations at the end of the 2008 season. Devotees of the boat launched a "Save the Delta Queen" campaign similar to the one they had in 1970. But sadly, this campaign did not succeed, as the Majestic American Line announced that the *Delta Queen* would not operate in 2009. This will be an unhappy ending to a beautiful and majestic boat that has brought people joy as they watched her glide through the waterways. (Both courtesy of Rev. Daniel Simmons.)

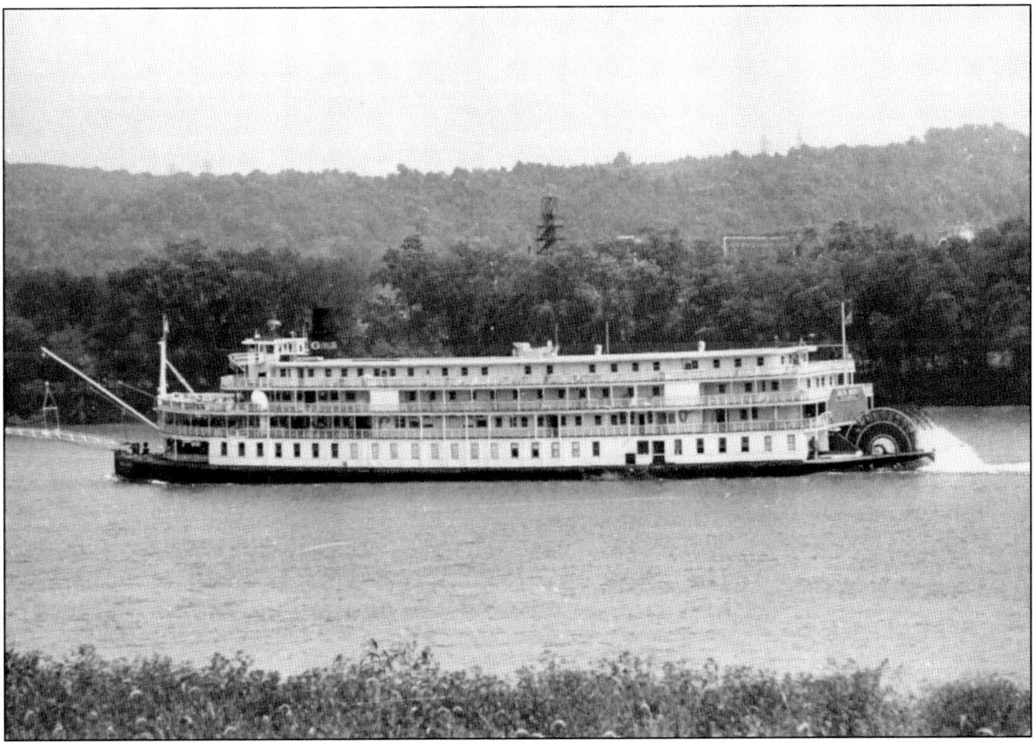

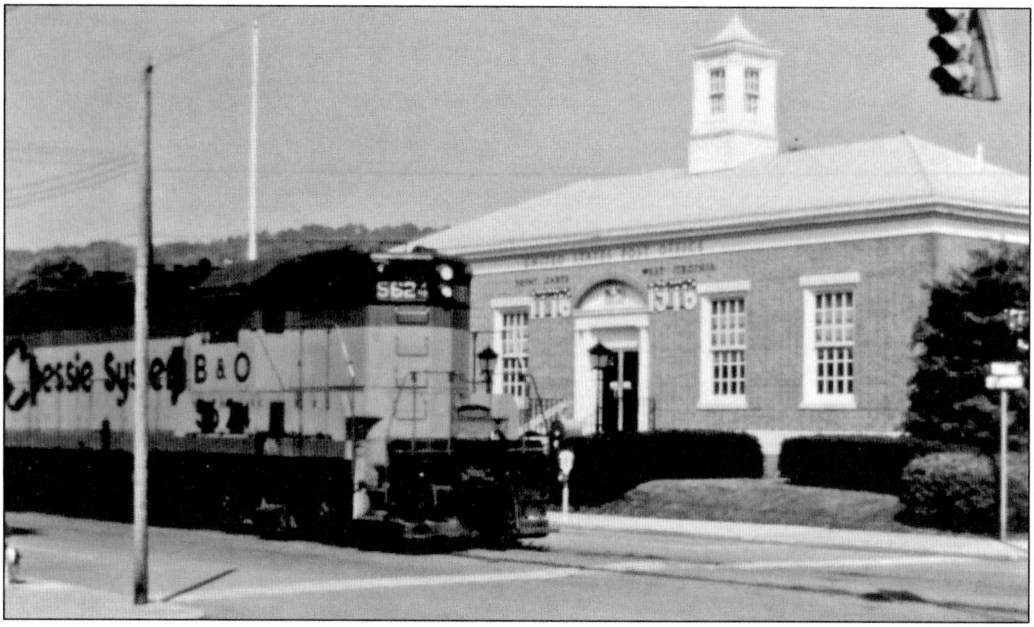

These two pictures were taken of a B&O Railroad train in the late 1970s. Passenger trains no longer come through town. They have been replaced by freight trains, which travel straight through town at varying times. The pictures appear to have been taken just a few yards apart on the corner of Main and Washington Streets and near the Phillips Drug Store. In the background, the present-day post office is a fine example of classical American architecture. Steam locomotives have been replaced by new, modern diesel engines. Below, the train has traveled a little bit farther down Main Street and shows a white house in the background. This house was torn down, and the original Pizza Station replaced it. (Above courtesy of Rev. Daniel Simmons and Barbara Johnson; below courtesy of Rev. Daniel Simmons.)

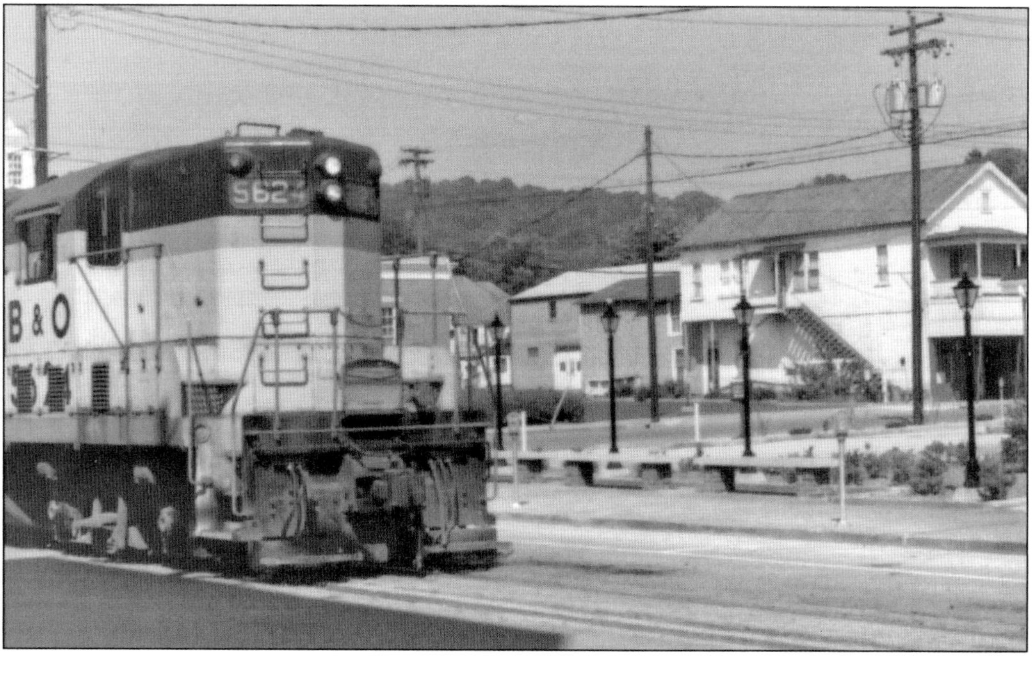

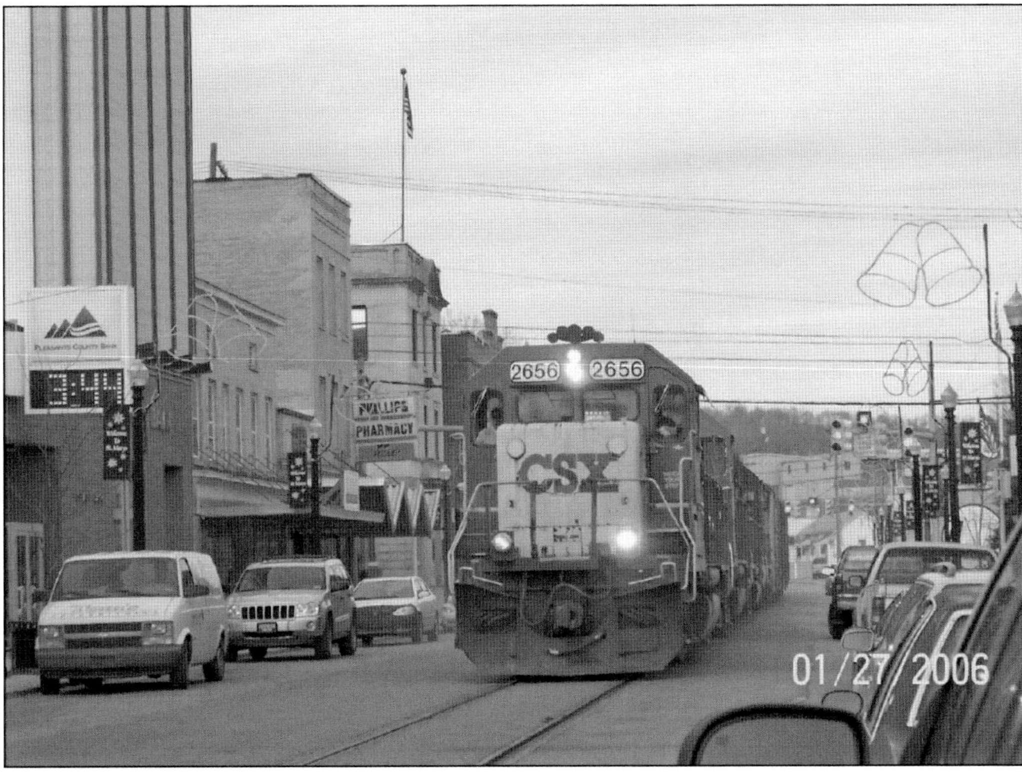

This photographic view shows Pleasants County Bank, Phillips Pharmacy, and the First National Bank, a typical scene that can be quite ominous to a new driver or to an unsuspecting tourist, as there are very few towns with trains chugging their way directly down the middle of town. This train represents the CSX Transportation Company, which traces its beginnings to the B&O Railroad started in 1828. The company transports rail freight around the country with diesel engines instead of steam. Below, the author Ruth Dayhoff took this picture as the train was typically stopped in front of the local Farm Fresh Market for employee refreshments. (Above courtesy of Priscilla Fleming; below courtesy of Ruth Ann Dayhoff.)

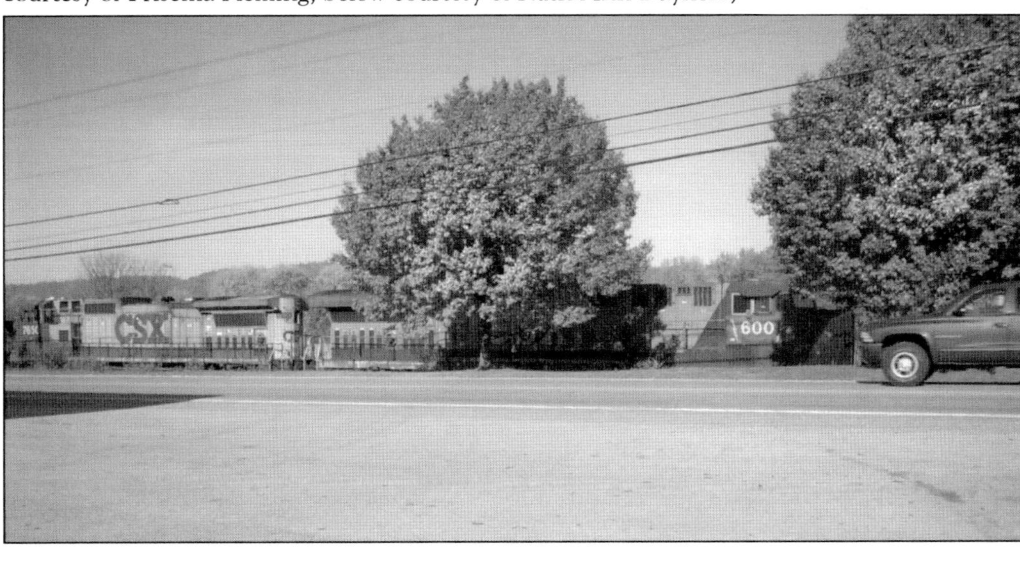

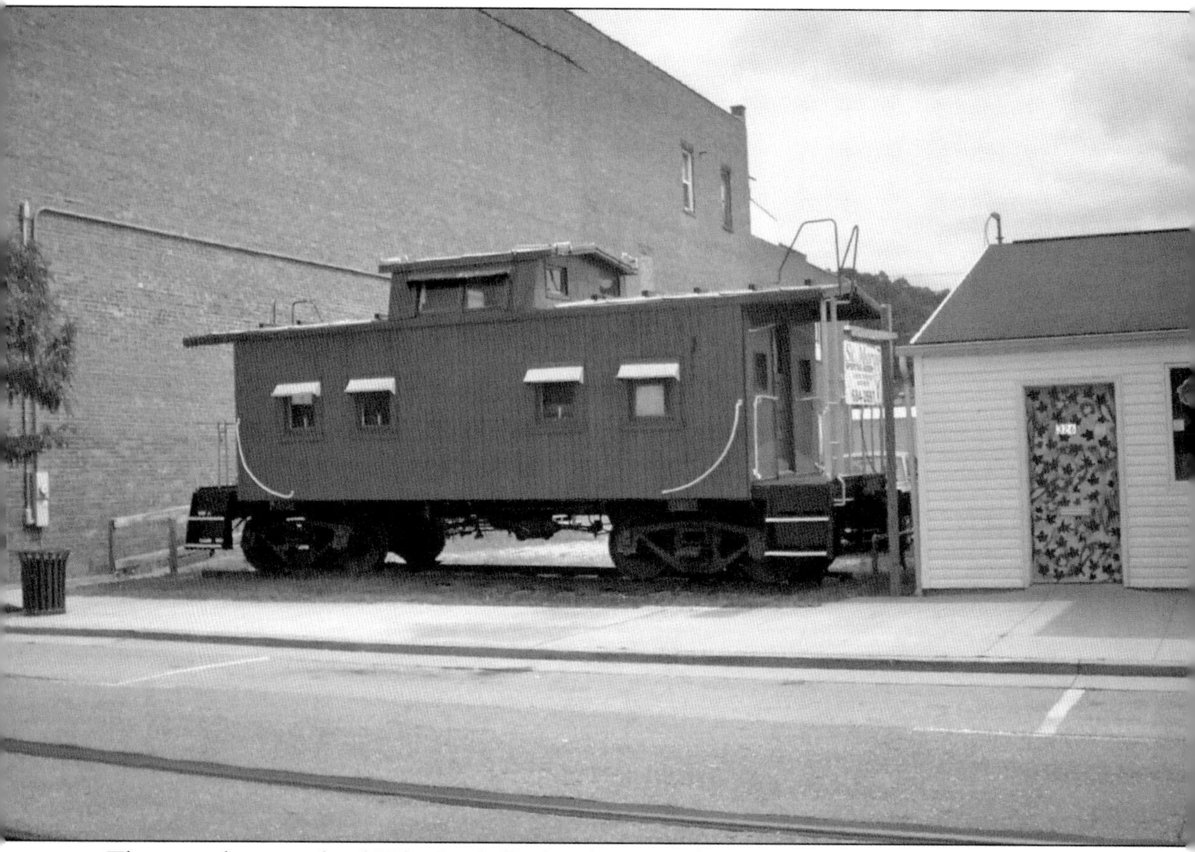

This is a photograph of "The Little Red Caboose," which residents remember came through town at the end of the steam engine train. In 1976, during the national centennial celebration, Orvil Binegar wanted to make a contribution to the celebration. He and Jim McFarland went to Chillicothe, Ohio, to see if they could find a caboose. The caboose pictured above was sitting on a side track looking very lonely. Orvil was able to purchase it for $1. Orvil named the caboose "Old Betsy," and it was placed in the Pleasants County Park for several years, then moved to Belmont beside the Lion's Club building. Now it is on display downtown where everybody can appreciate it. Becky Ingram initiated a contest for the local schoolchildren to name the caboose. Their name for it was "Clickety-Clack." To Orvil Binegar, it will always be "Old Betsy." Whatever the name might be, we are very grateful for this little red caboose that still makes the residents of St. Marys smile. (Courtesy of Ruth Ann Dayhoff.)

Six

Parades, Entertainment, and Activities

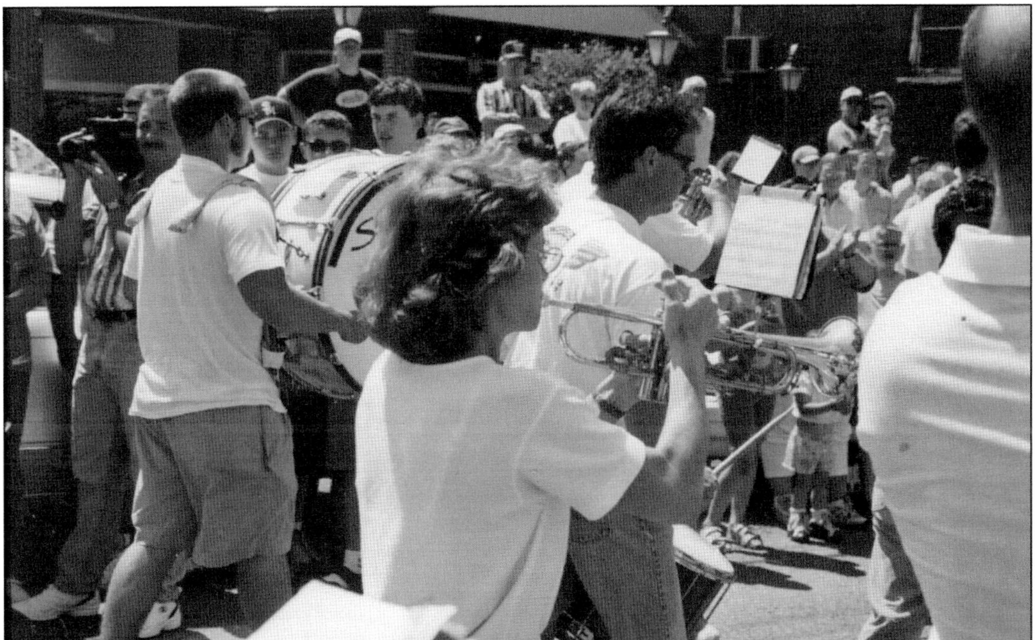

The Alumni Parade is a yearly event in St. Marys. Alumni return each year to celebrate their graduation from St. Marys High School. Special recognition is given to an alumnus of the year. Picnics, boat rides, musical events, special dinners, honorary celebrations, and events of all kinds make this a very special time for Pleasants County. In the foreground, Tammy Hammett Smith marches in the Alumni Band. (Courtesy of Lyle Dayhoff.)

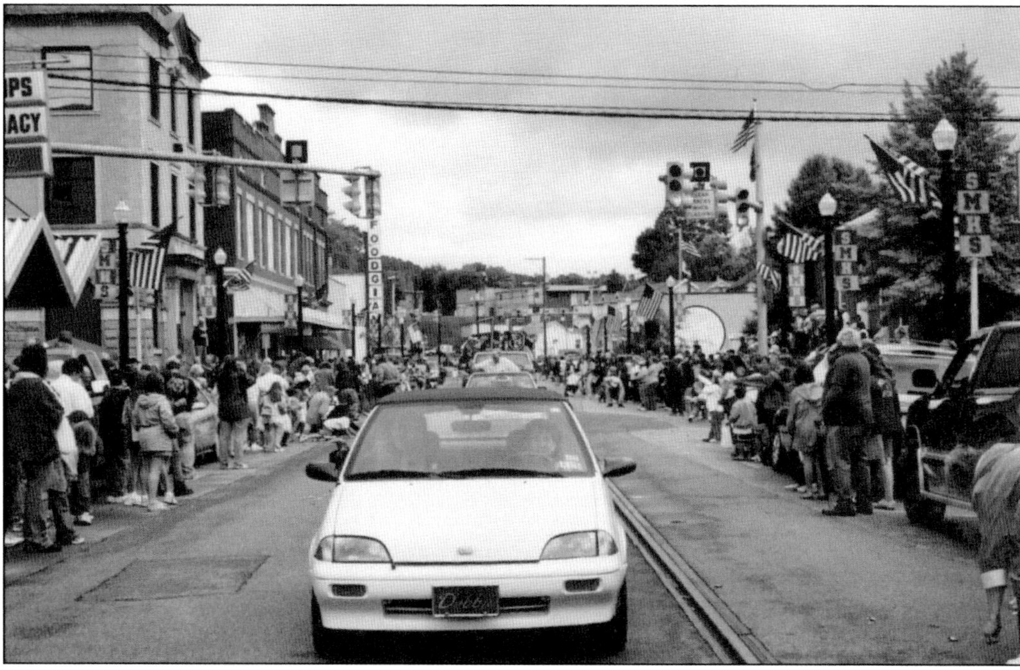

People line the streets of St. Marys to watch the Alumni Parade held every year at the end of May. After the parade, classes meet at the marina for lunch and fellowship with classmates. Below, men from the class of 1945 gather at a marina shelter. They are, from left to right, (front row) Don Irey, Lyle Dayhoff, and Robert Kiester; (second row) Bill Northrop, Bill Bullman, Bill Snider, Bill Fitzpatrick, Wilfred Rogers, Robert Davis, and Hal Smith. (Both courtesy of Lyle Dayhoff.)

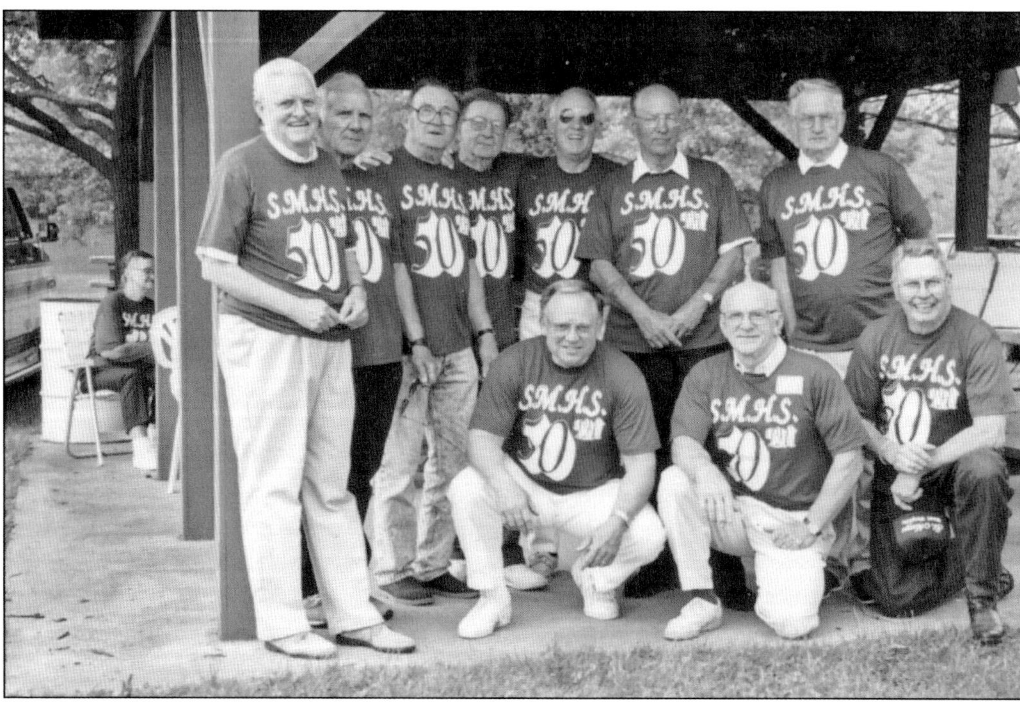

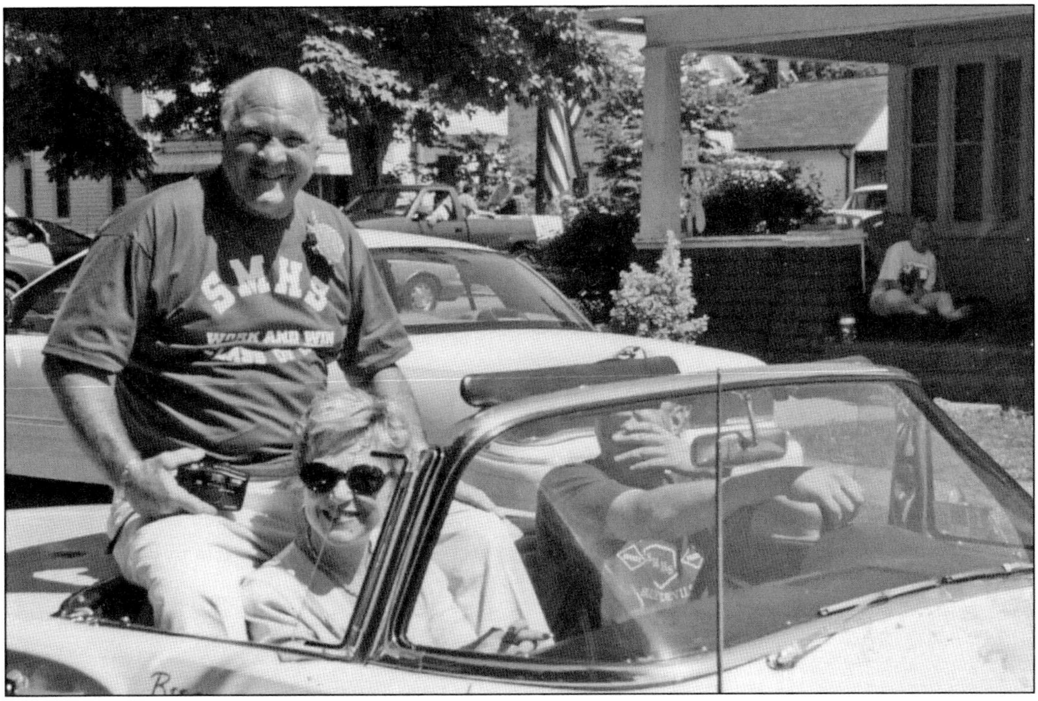

Bill Reynolds, class of 1948, is honored because he made St. Marys very proud as a professional football player for the Cleveland Browns. Another alumnus, Jim Procopio, was a baseball minor league catcher for the Braves. Below, the county is celebrating the nation's 200th birthday (1776–1976). In the background, you can see Davis Motor Company and the Food Giant. A float covered with flags and a covered wagon make their way through town. (Above courtesy of Lyle Dayhoff; below courtesy of Rev. Daniel Simmons.)

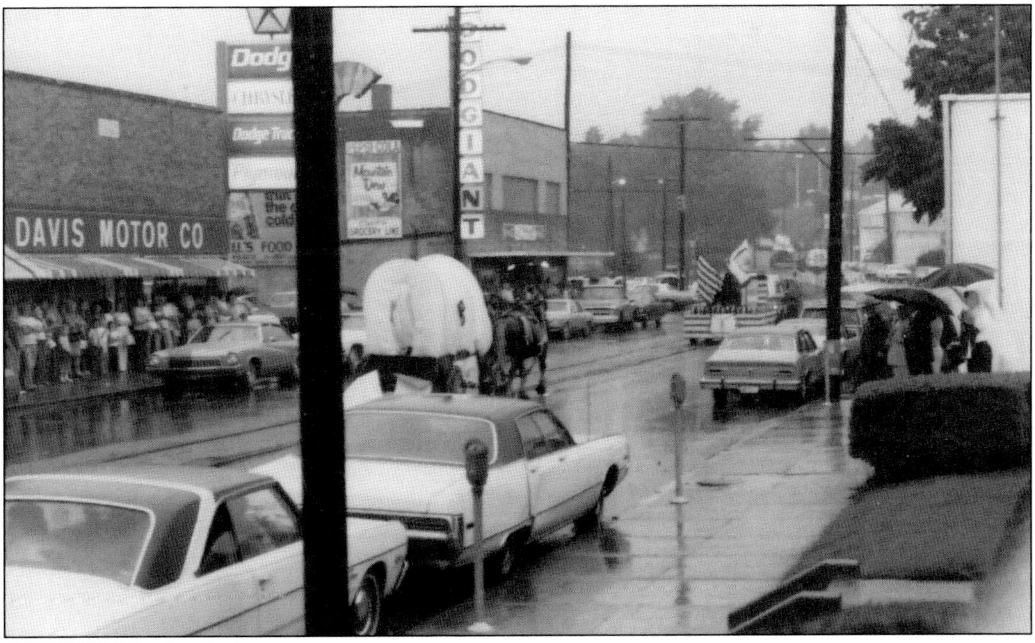

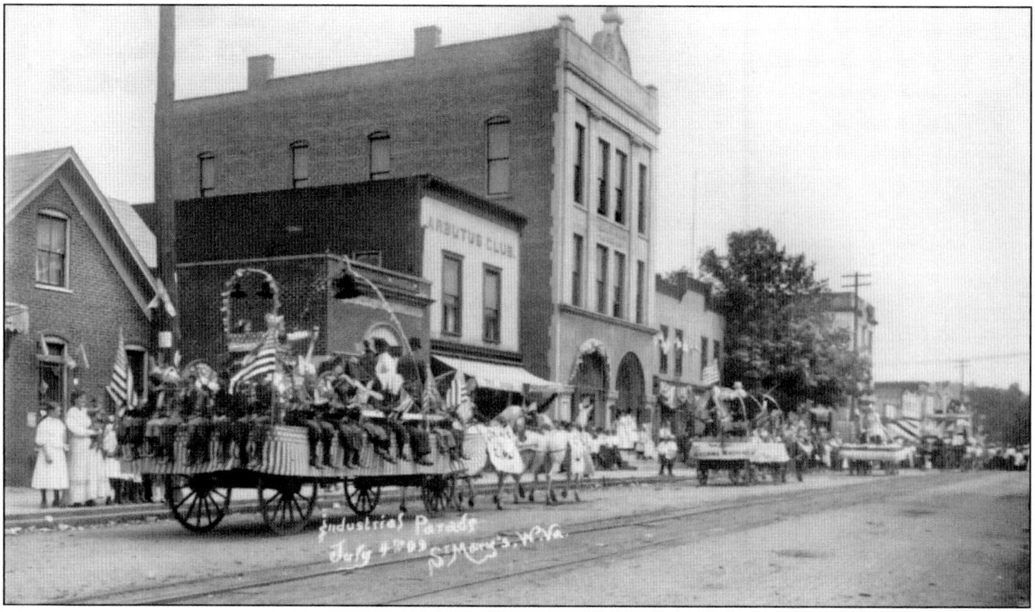

The industrial parades were usually held on July 4 by the various industries around the county. Each industry created a float to advertise their goods and services. High competition for prizes and placement between the floats brought out the creativity of each industry. These photographs were taken on July 4, 1909, with flags flying on the float above. The Arbutus Club, the labeled building, was the first social club for men in Pleasants County. This club brought high-class plays and operas to the auditorium, then located where the present library now stands. Below, the military band provided music as it marched down Main Street. People are hanging out of the window to get a closer look. (Both JEGC, courtesy of Dale Brown.)

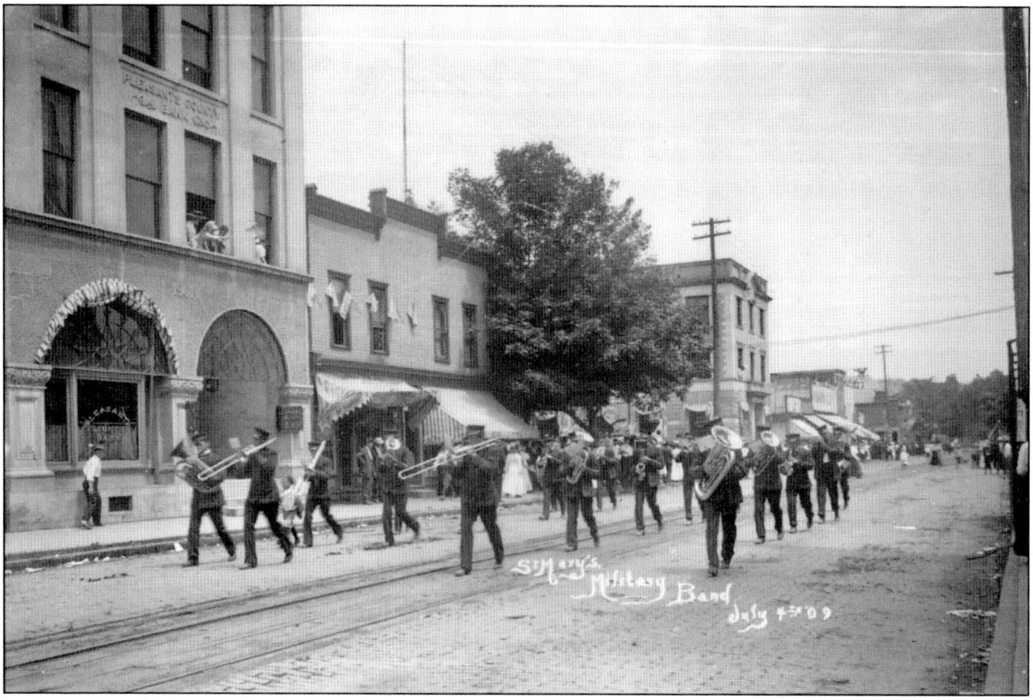

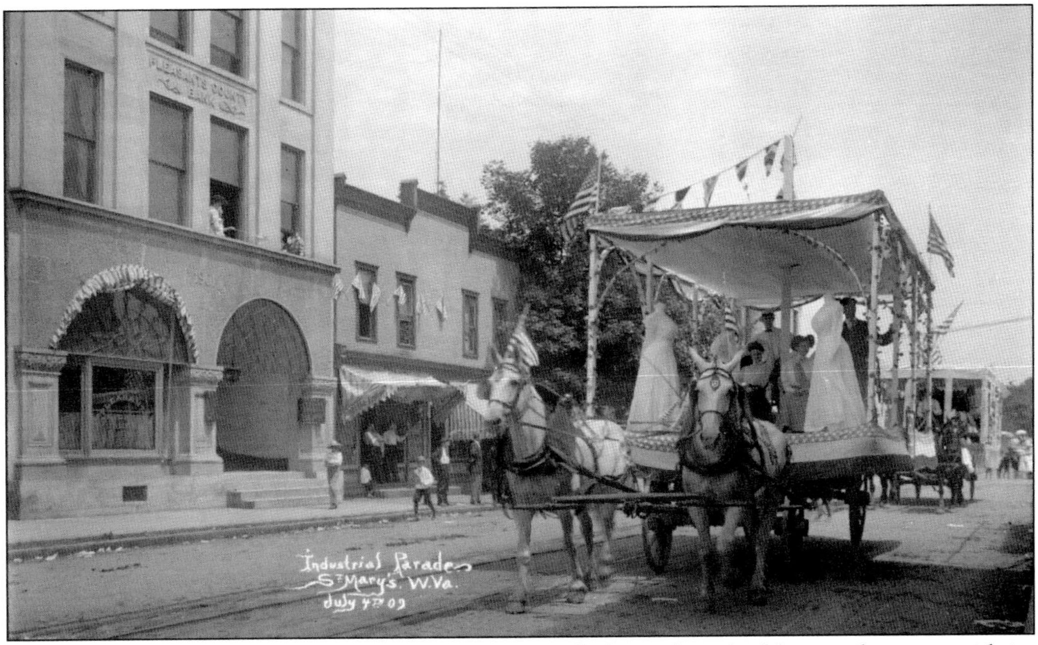

The float in the photograph evidently represents a clothing shop, building up business with its grand exhibit. Notice the beautiful long dresses on the mannequins in the parade. Much effort was made to make this float an eye-catching one by advertising the wonderful garments available to citizens of the town. Below, McMahon's Balloon Ascension has advertised its wares by flying a large balloon above the store, which was located three awnings up from the First National Bank. Many coupons were dropped from the balloon, which could be collected for free merchandise from McMahon's Store. This added some real excitement to the parade. (Both JEGC, courtesy of Dale Brown.)

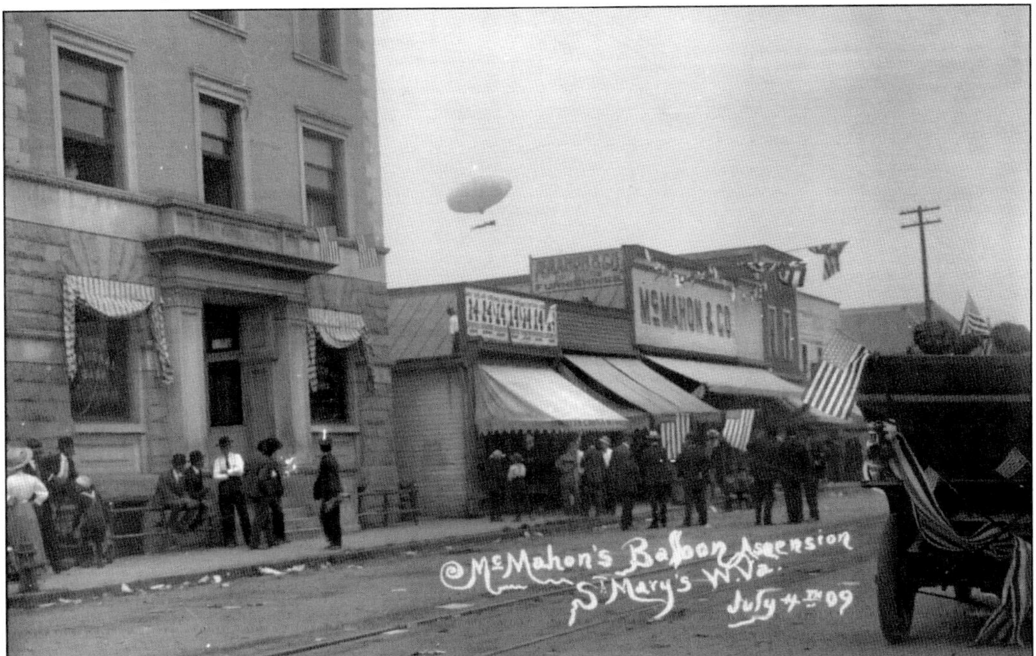

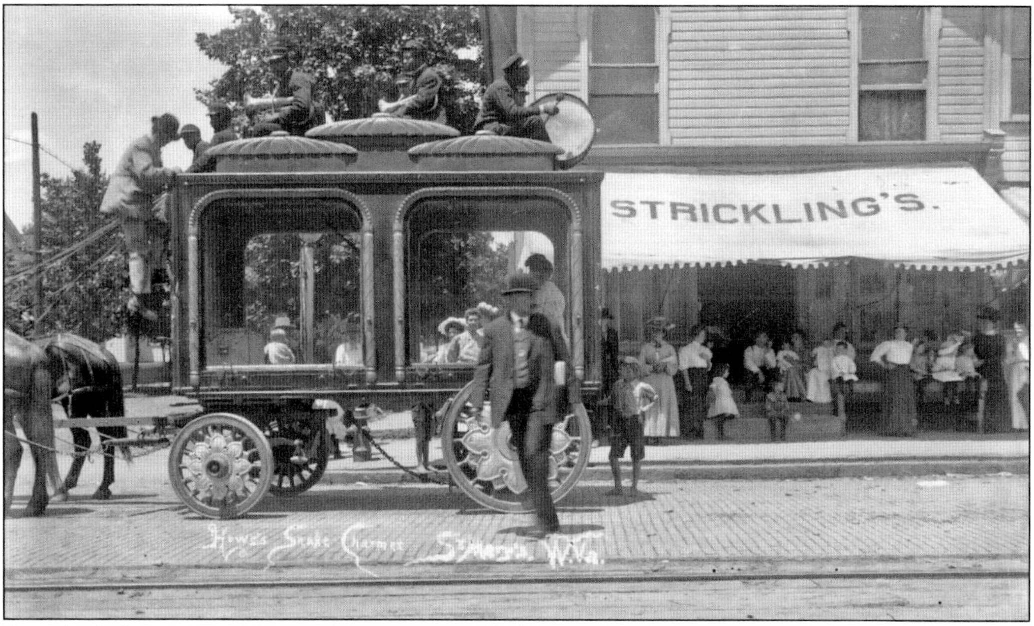

Everybody loves a parade, and the citizens of Pleasants County are no exception. In the days of the early 20th century, parades drew large crowds. According to the 1909 *Pleasants County Leader*, "They came early and remained late and the city had the largest crowds they had ever had in ten years." Parked in front of Stricklings business, in a horse-drawn wagon, is the Snake Charmer Wagon from Howe's Circus. Below are beautiful horses and horse-drawn carriages with spectators enjoying the show. Women in long dresses of the time like those in the picture were expected to ride horses sidesaddle. (Both JEGC, courtesy of Dale Brown.)

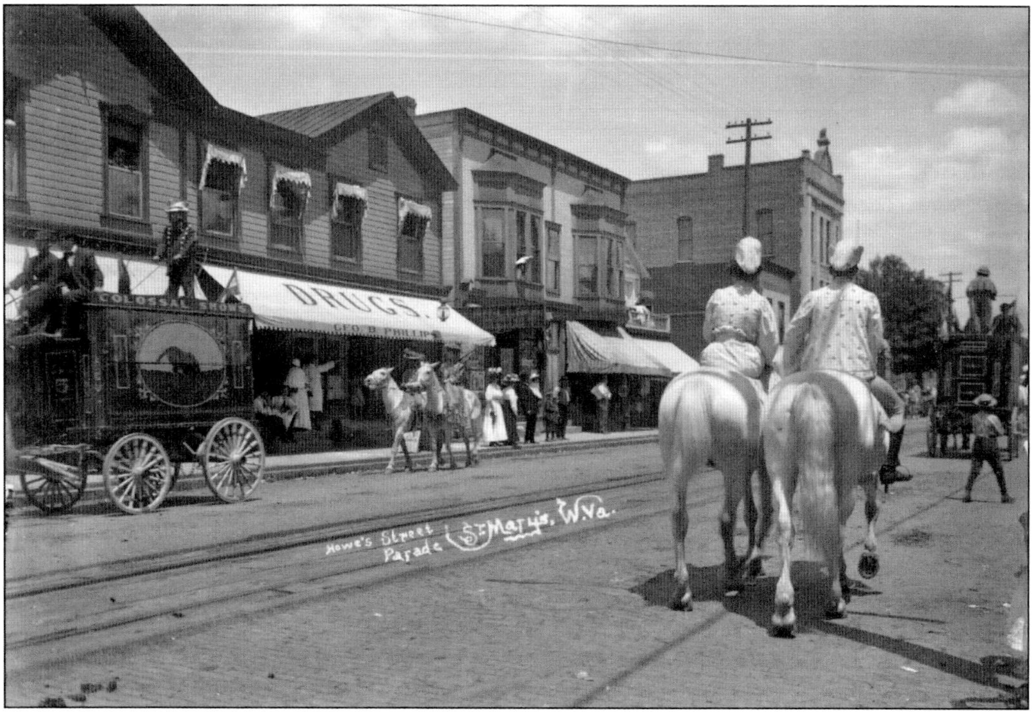

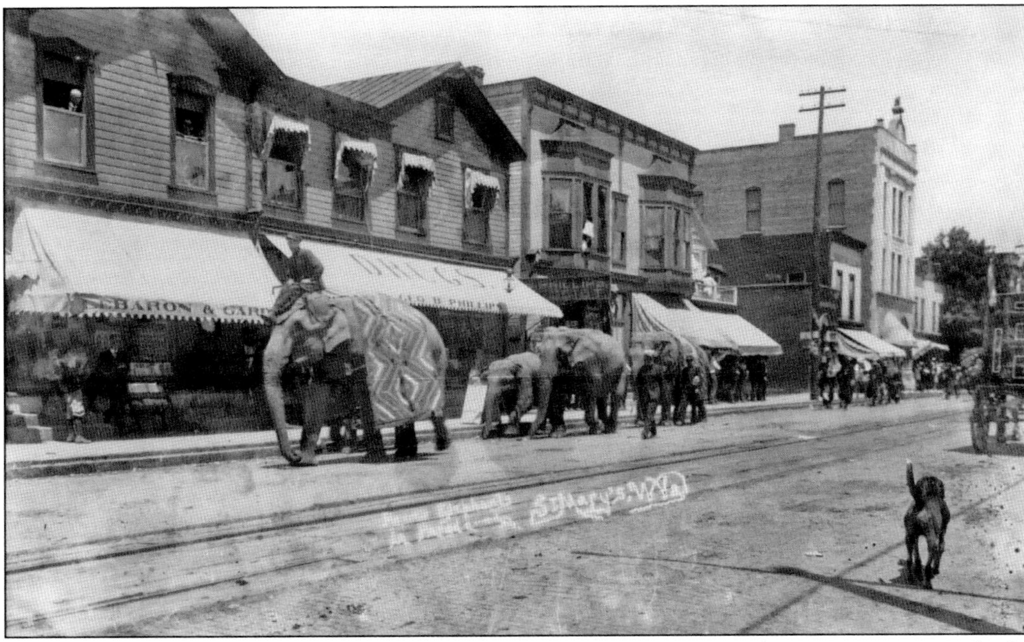

Not very often does one see elephants marching down Main Street. This is an exciting sight for both young and old. The Howe Circus had wonderful parades to whet the appetite of spectators and encourage everyone to come to the Howe Circus in Pleasants County Park and see the spectacular sights. Below is the calliope, a wonderful contraption that makes music with air bellows. Children would come running whenever they heard it. Calliopes were also used on the showboats to let people know they were in town. This one is traveling down the dusty unpaved streets of St. Marys. (Both JEGC, courtesy of Dale Brown.)

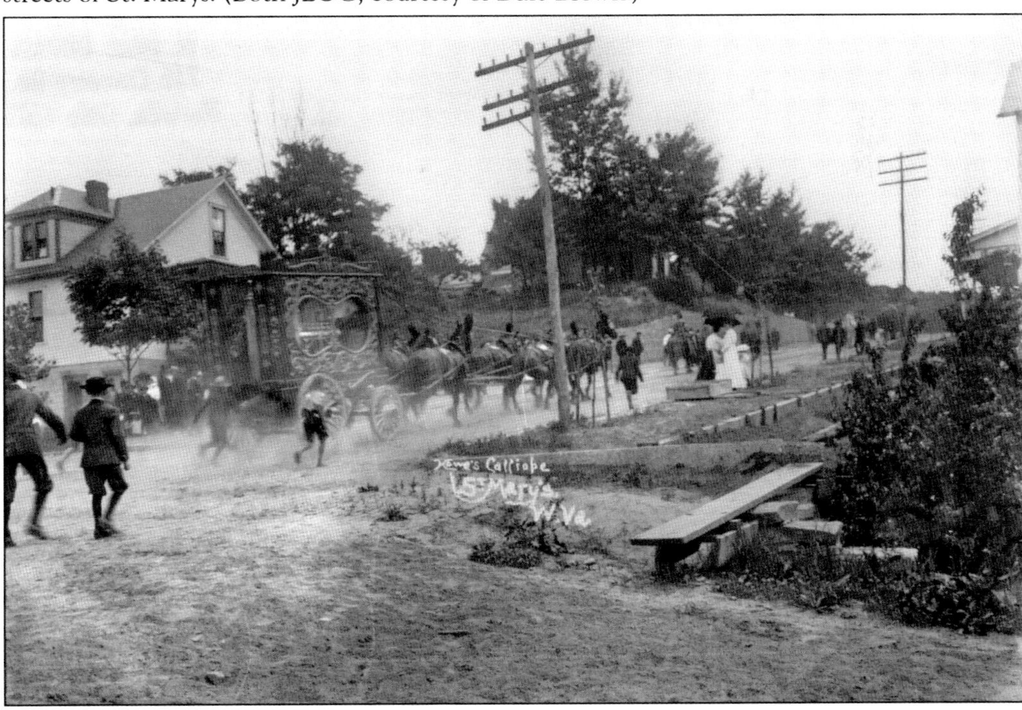

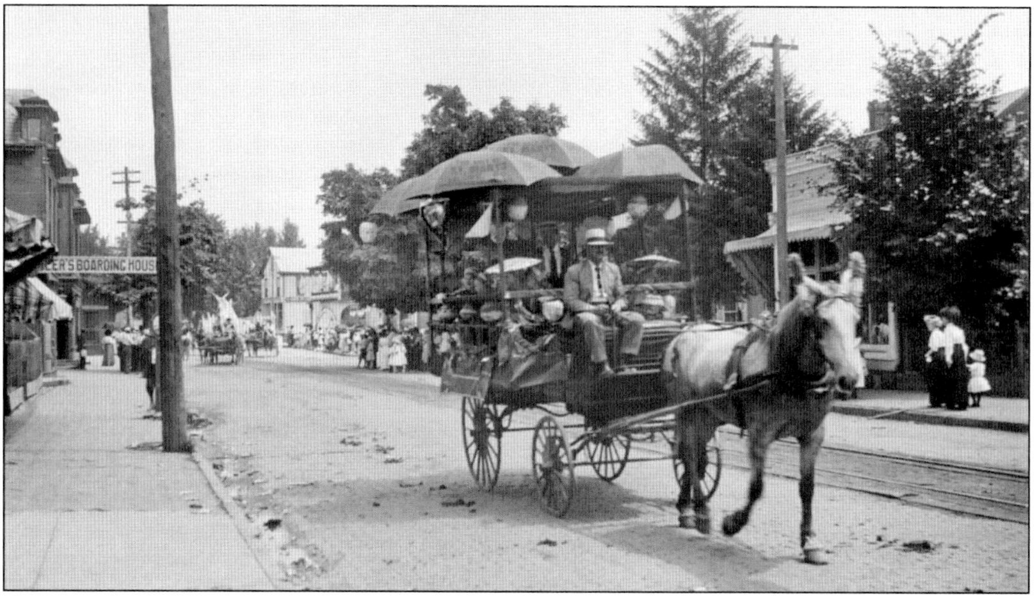

A horse-drawn carriage is traveling down a bricked St. Marys street. Umbrellas shade the driver as he uses them as "For Sale" signs. Notice the woman and little girl enjoying the parade as it travels down Main Street, which is easy to recognize because of its obvious railroad track. Below, Winers Clothing Store advertises in this industrial parade. The Industrial Parade of 1909 was more than one and a half miles in length and traveled throughout the town. Smart businessmen made sure that they used this great opportunity to make their business and products known to all the people. (Both HCWC/Mark Williams, courtesy of WVDCHSA.)

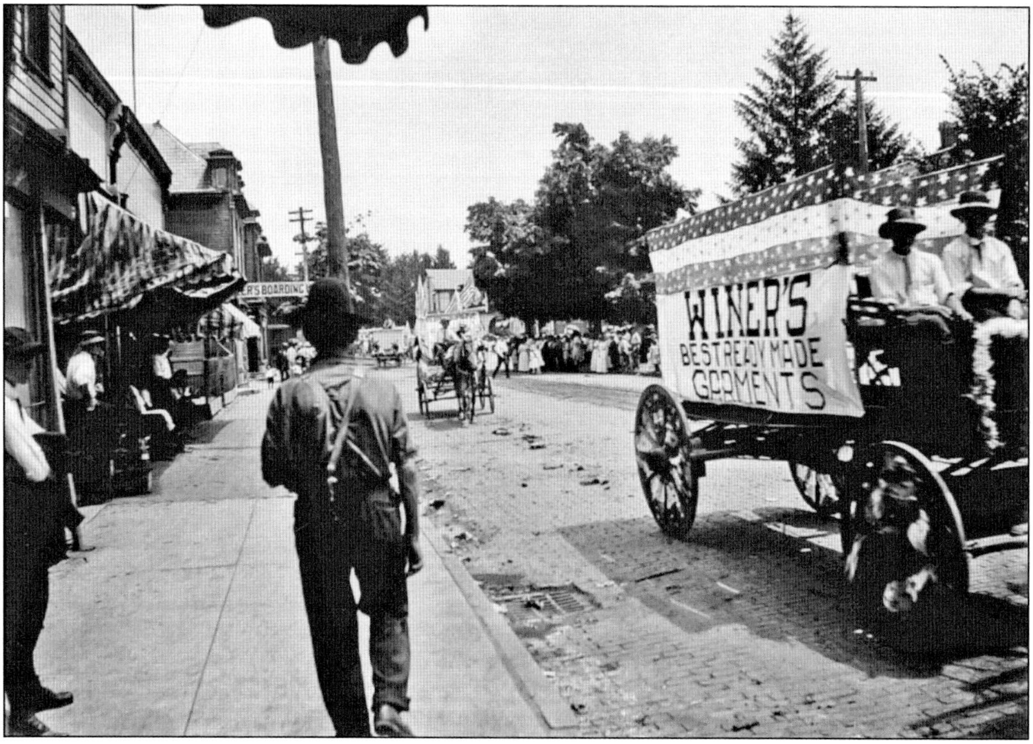

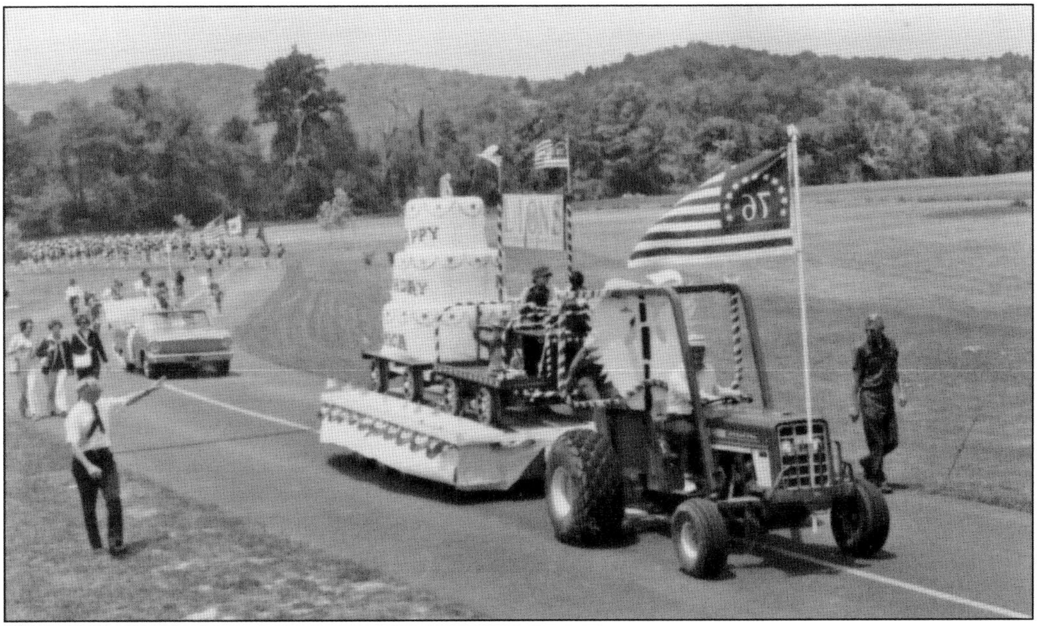

Above, the 1976 Centennial Parade starts at the marina by Middle Island and travels through town. A giant birthday cake commemorates the event of our nation's 200th birthday, one of many events held in St. Marys. Below is the typical Christmas parade with Santa welcoming in the holiday. Children will soon line up to tell Santa all the things they want for Christmas. Author Ellen Dittman Pope's father, Charlie Dittman, was Santa Claus in the parade one year. Ellen sat on his lap in one of the parades and did not know he was her father. She asked for 100 dolls. (Both courtesy of Rev. Daniel Simmons.)

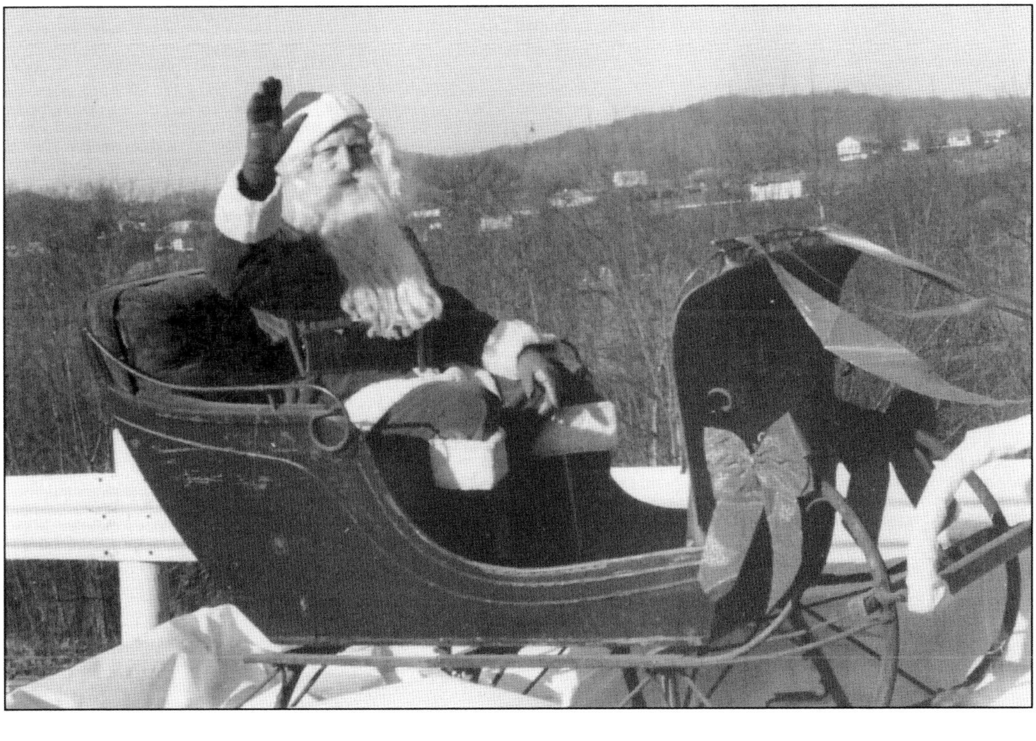

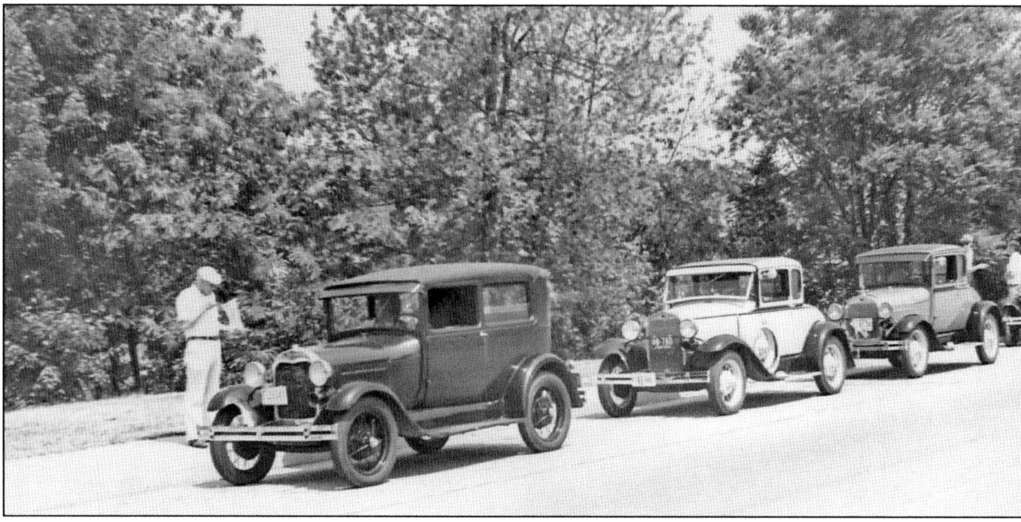

Pleasants County exceeded nearly every rural county in the Union with the largest number of cars, according to the 1914 census. There were 35 cars in the county at that time. Before long, garages came into existence. In 1921, there were so many cars that an automobile association was formed, with James D. Dinsmoor as president. Residents still enjoy cars from that era, as seen in the car show above. (Courtesy of Rev. Daniel Simmons.)

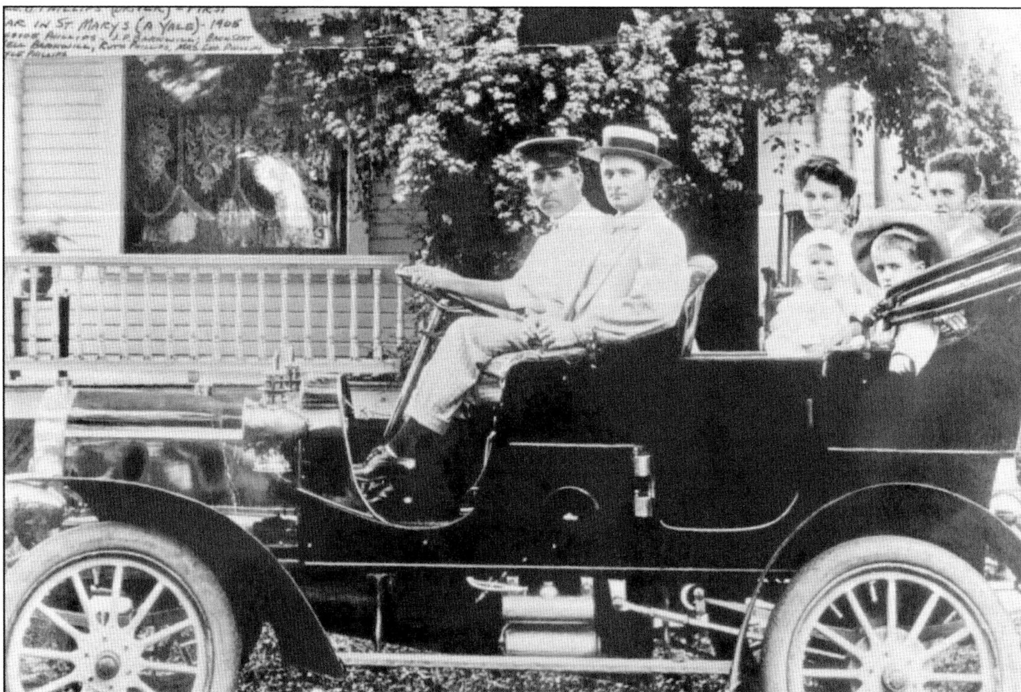

The first car in St. Marys was a Yale model, a manufacturer that has never been heard of since. This car from 1905 had no top, doors, windshield, or headlights. George B. Phillips was driver and owner, while J. P. Barkwell, Nell Barkwell, Ruth Phillips, and Lyle Phillips rode. In 1906, John C. Dinsmoor brought the second car. By 1909, there were seven cars in St. Marys. (PCHSC, courtesy of WVDCHSA.)

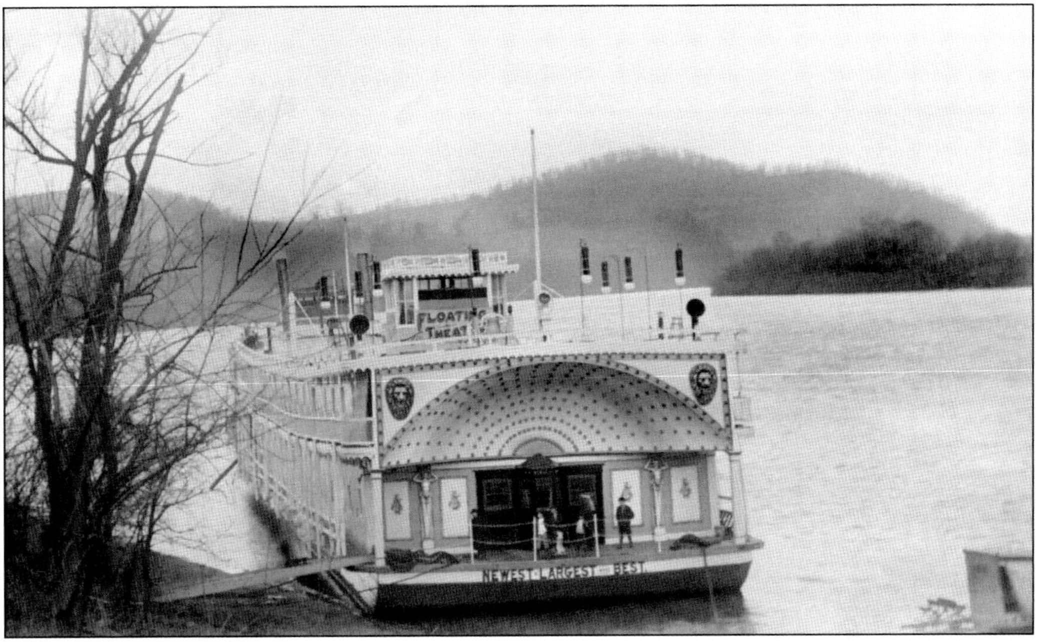

This floating theater (above) would anchor along the levee in front of St. Marys. It could comfortably seat 150 but could squeeze in 200 people. The company included an orchestra of three pieces, consisting of 10 members, only one of whom was a woman, who performed the acts. The performances included sleight-of-hand tricks, songs and dances, African American minstrels, and acrobatic feats in one act. All of this consumed three and a half hours of a show that was as good as any performed in city variety theaters and all for 35¢. The boat would navigate from side to side, touching little towns as it floated downward with the tide. The showboat below represents even larger boats that continued the tradition of entertainment on the river. (Above HCWC/Mark Williams, courtesy of WVDCHSA; below courtesy of Sandra Cronin.)

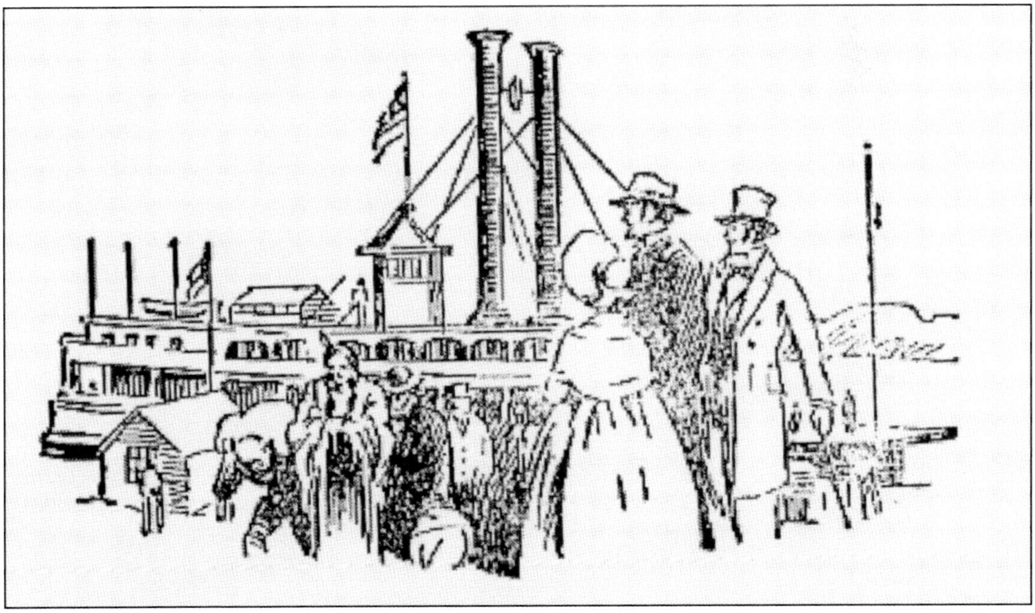

MINSTREL CAST

Musical Director .... John D. Brisbane
In Charge of End Men .... C. T. Strickling
Interlocutor ....John White
Accompanist .... Patricia Morgan
Premier End Men .... C. T. Strickling, Joffre George
Speciality .... C. A. Ruttencutter

END MEN

C. T. Strickling	Joffre George
Paul Johnson	Bill Spence
Delno Webb	Harry Bradfield
Don Wright	Bill Clovis
Harold Spencer	John Walton
Leroy Darling	Tom Watson
Fred Riggs	Lewis Dutton

MEN'S CHORUS — — John Israel, Arthur Miller, Joe Roby, Charles Dittman, Lane Ogdin, Warren Hall, Richard McCullough, Douglas Gorrell, John Fitzpatrick, Bill Lauhon, Jim McKnight, Jim Vogel, Bill Reed, Robert Keister, Dick Hupp, Bruce Knight, John Kyle, Larry Morris, William Wolfe, John Lowther, Sanford Satterfield, Jim Riggs, Mike Duffy, Jack Boley, Jim Webb, Kramer Sellers, Jim Smith, Heman Dillon, Franklin Riggs, Tim Robinson, Ken Williams, C. S. Himmiger, Darrell Harding, David Snodgrass, Gene Lowther, Richard Pickens, Charles Chapman, Larkin Spence, Cecil Jones, Gary Snively.

GIRLS' CHORUS — — Pat Gilpin, Jeanette Wilson, Margaret Ingram, Sue Strickling, Mary Ellen Gibbs, Karen Armentrout, Shirley Riggs, Faith Darling, Peggy Underwood, Judy Grimes, Marjorie Parsons, Paula Foley.

ORCHESTRA — — James Taylor, Jack Carpenter, Delmar Williamson, John Hammett, Cecil Boyd, Harold Davis.

MAJORETTES — — Roberta Ingram, Barbara Farren, Patty Gilpin, Gloria Abicht, Susie Strickling, Shirley Auberle.

COLOR GUARD — — Frances Mercer, Nancy Morris, Sharon Hammett, Claudia Fleming, Janet Stanley.

This is a copy of the program of one of the minstrel shows given in the Main Theater in the late 1950s. Readers from Pleasants County will recognize many of the names. The performances consisted of music, comedy, acting, and just general fun. Practically the whole community became involved. Sometimes one organization would sponsor it, sometimes another. But the whole community benefited and worked together to make this a grand success. (Courtesy of Sandra Cronin.)

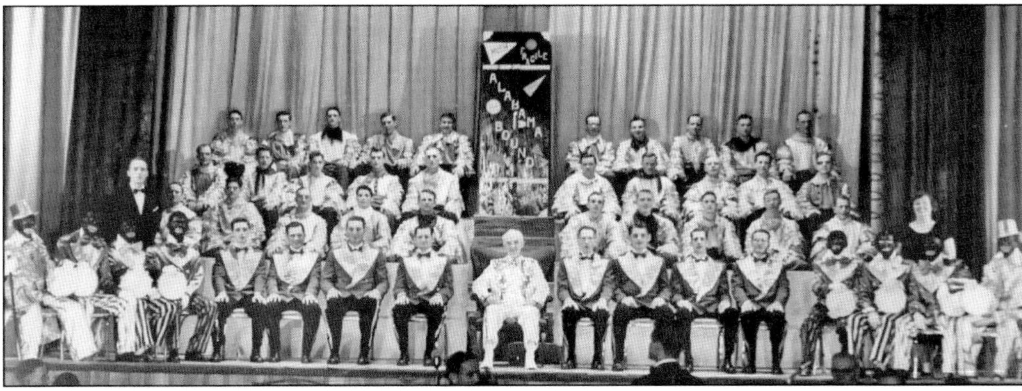

The complete cast of one of the annual minstrel shows is depicted above. The community anxiously looked forward to this event every year. Different organizations put this on, such as the St. Marys Jaycees and the American Legion. Enthusiasm reigned toward this county event. The productions duplicated the showboat entertainment that traveled the rivers of our nation during that time period. These local productions were discontinued in the late 1950s. (PCPLC, courtesy of Eleanor Poling.)

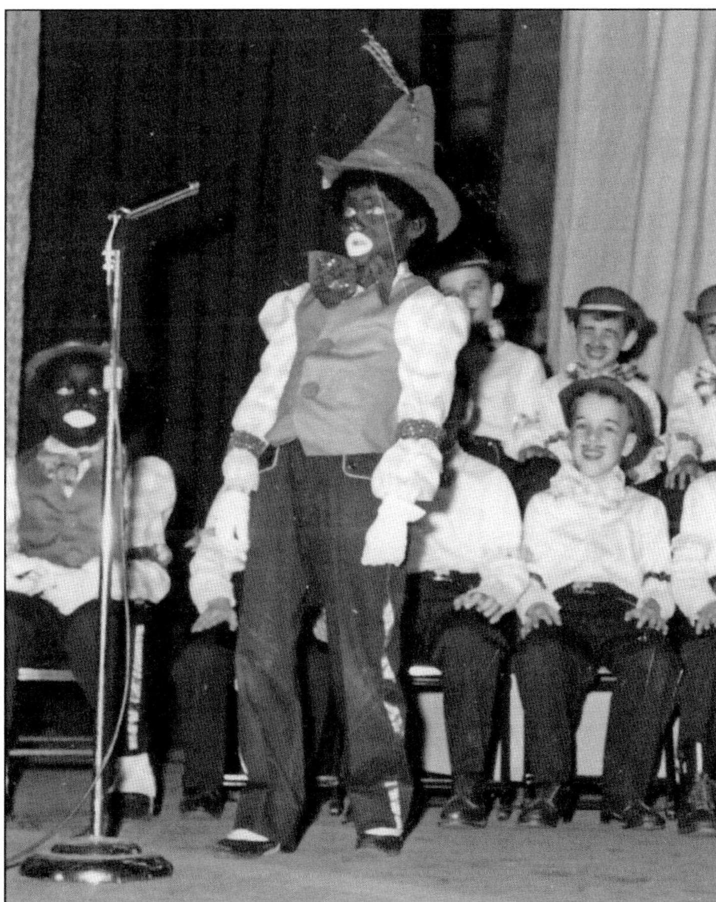

One can see young Charles Morgan Dittman performing the song, "This Old House." He was called back for six encores. This performance was held in the Main Theater about the year 1955. This was a Cub Scout minstrel that duplicated the minstrels presented in the county for many years. (Courtesy of Mary Ellen Dittman.)

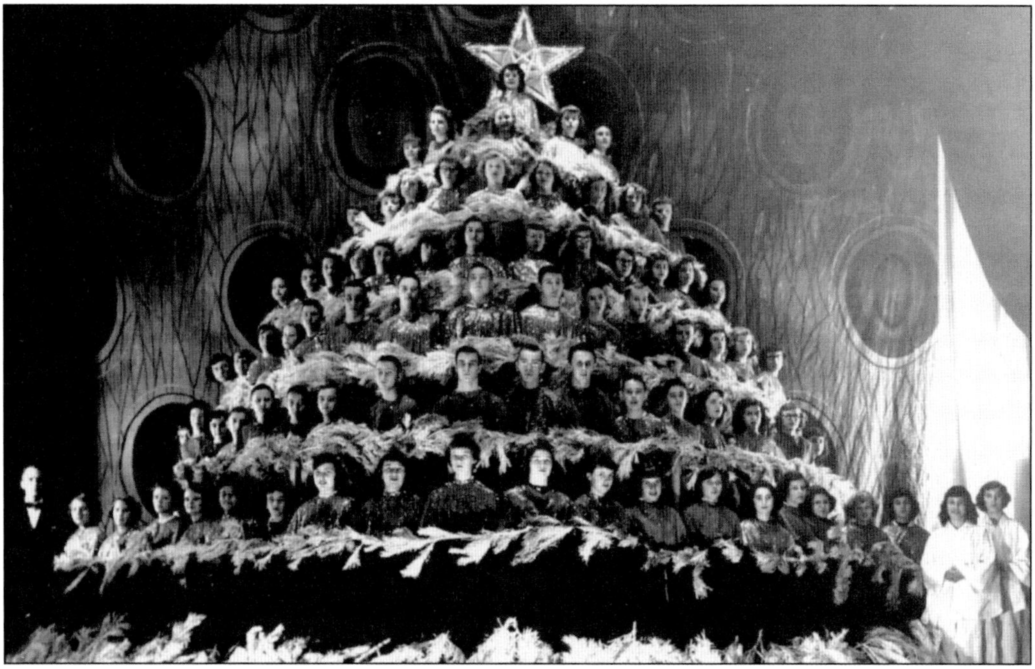

To fully appreciate the singing Christmas tree, it needed to be seen as well as heard. This annual holiday presentation by the Glee Club of St. Marys High School was given in the old Main Theater and featured a program made up of sacred Christmas numbers led by John D. Brisbane. The smiling face in the star at the top is that of Penny Young. (PCPLC from John D. Brisbane's scrapbook, courtesy of Eleanor Poling.)

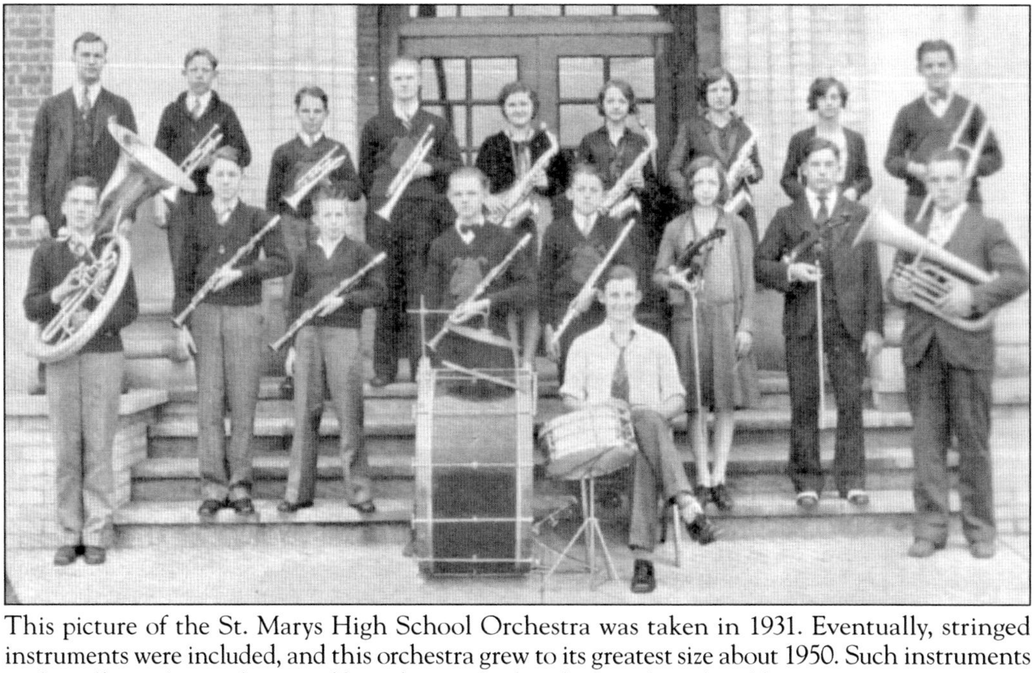

This picture of the St. Marys High School Orchestra was taken in 1931. Eventually, stringed instruments were included, and this orchestra grew to its greatest size about 1950. Such instruments as the cello, violin, and stringed bass disappeared as the marching band became more prominent. (PCPLC, courtesy of Eleanor Poling.)

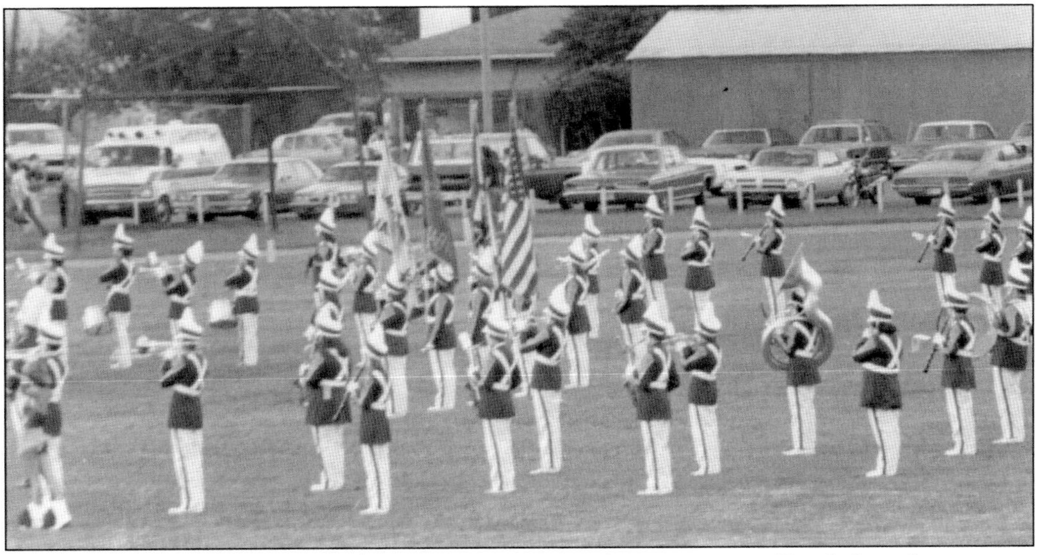

Pleasants County has always had an interest in musical organizations. Bands have been a part of the community since 1890. Here the St. Marys High School Marching Band prepares for the coming season. One of the many highlights of the band's experience was when they were chosen to march in the Rose Bowl Parade in California. (Courtesy of Rev. Daniel Simmons.)

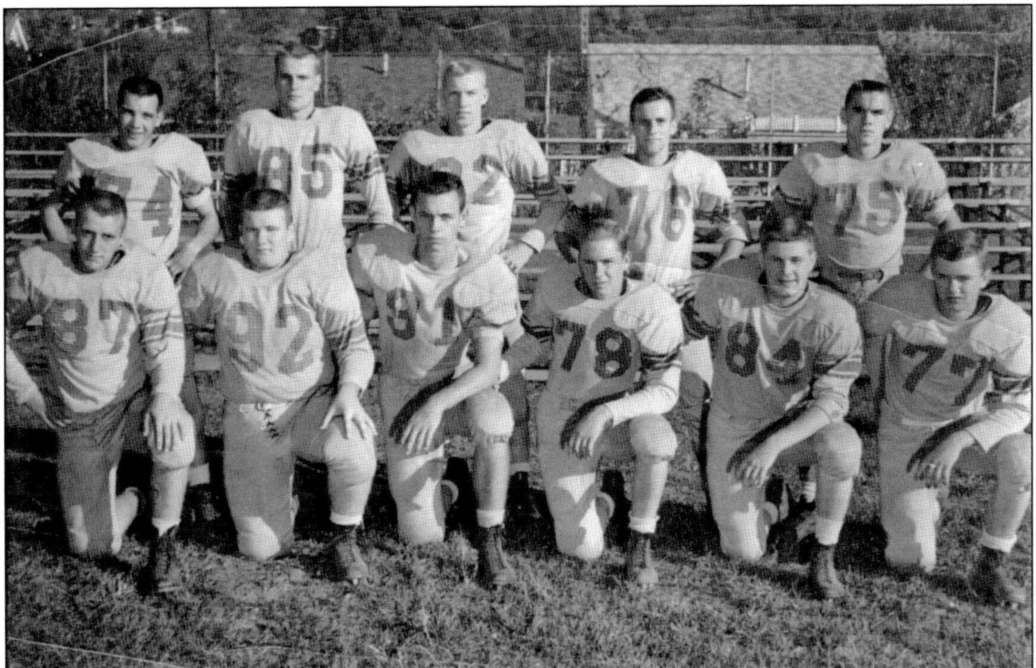

This is the Little Kanawha Senior football team of 1956. Sheldon Hays, known as Mr. Touchdown, ran 600 yards, made four touchdowns, and four extra points in one game. Shown are (first row) Beryl Bills, John Bogard, Roger Gerke, Charles McKnight, Gary Ingram, and Jim McKnight; (second row) Bob Faucett, Tom Weber, John Renner, Junior Reynolds, and Sheldon Hays. (Courtesy of Pat Hays.)

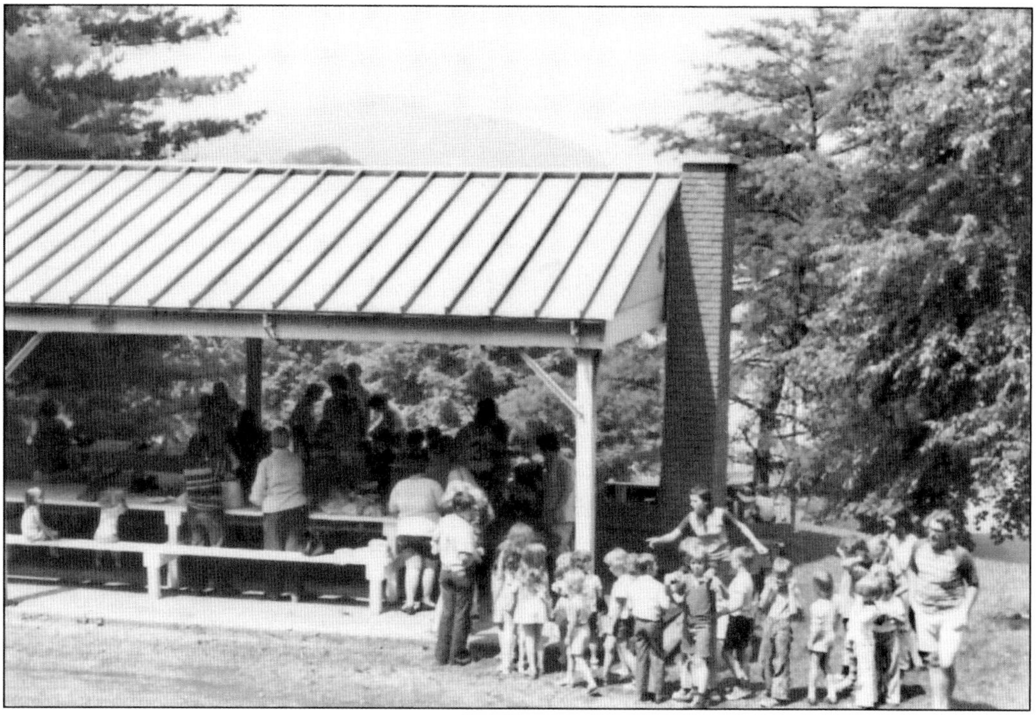

The Pleasants County Park, originally called Williams Park and later Kiwanis Park, is a site for many fun activities. Above, the children are having a picnic under one of the newer shelters that have been added. Constant upkeep makes the park beautiful for the enjoyment of all. Ball games, carnivals, hiking, nature walks, swimming, and picnics are all a part of life at the park. Look closely below, and see if you can identify the activity. The Cunningham Carnival is in full session. In times past, circuses were very prominent and exciting. Horse shows, fairs, and Scouting activities all have made this place a delightful playground. (Both courtesy of Rev. Daniel Simmons.)

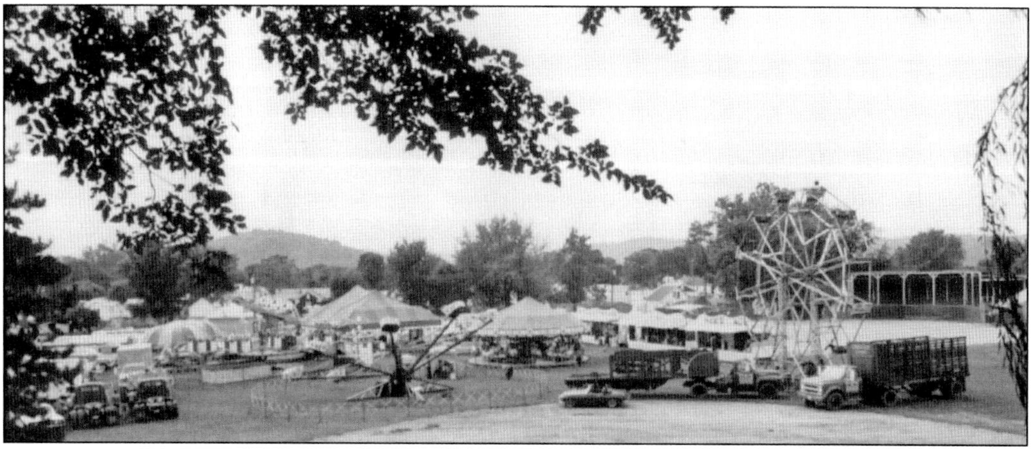

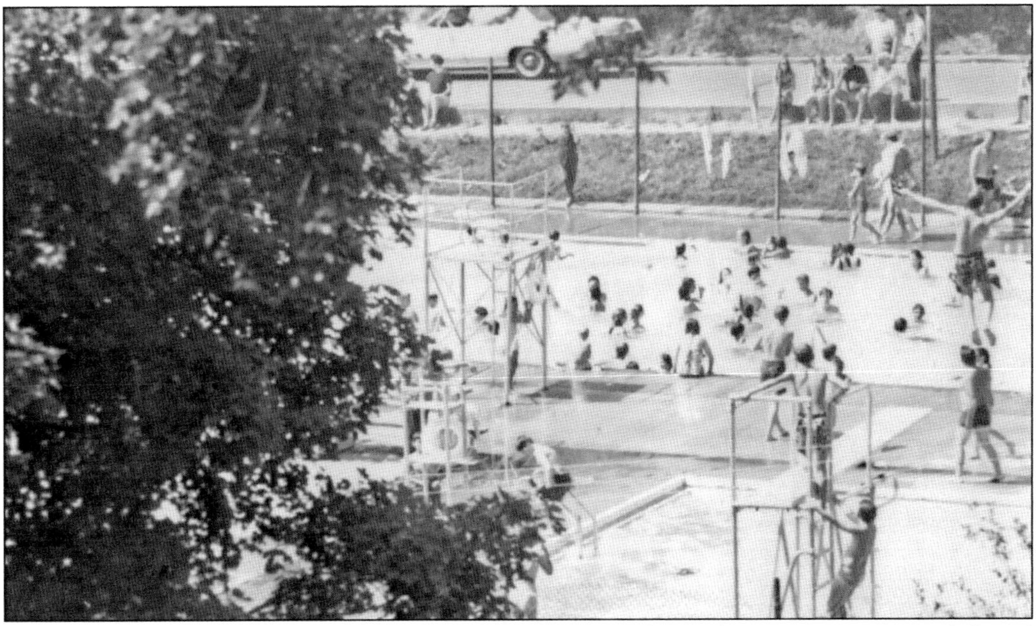

Probably the most popular park activity was swimming in the pool. Lessons were provided, and lifeguards cleared the pool when weather threatened. Mamie Clovis was a noted ticket-taker. Lifeguards the authors remember well were Sam White (later a lawyer and judge) and Richard Hamilton Jr., son of beloved Dr. Hamilton, Sr. Richard saved author Ellen Dittman Pope's life from drowning as a child. (Courtesy of Rev. Daniel Simmons.)

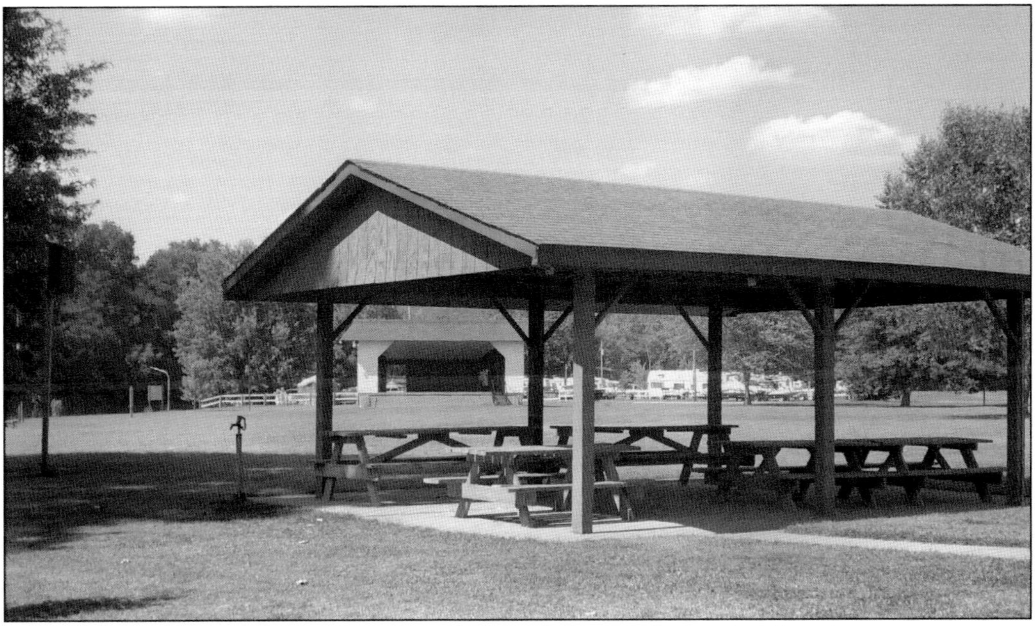

The Pleasants County Marina is a second area of pleasure. It was developed in recent years to accommodate the many river activities. The annual Bass Festival brings people from all over the United States to compete with their fishing skills. It is located at the mouth of Middle Island Creek as it flows into the Ohio. Parades, reunions, and performances make this a valuable asset to the community. (Courtesy of Ruth Ann Dayhoff.)

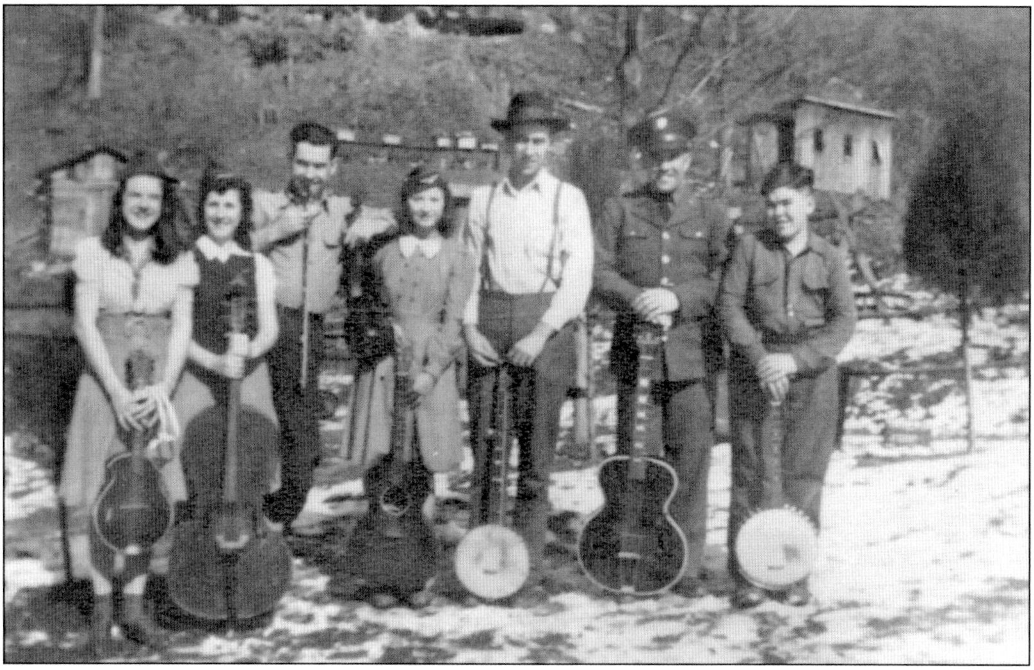

Music plays a big part in the lives of the Cronin family. This is a photograph of the musicians in earlier days; their music is made from a wide variety of musical instruments as each member of the family has his or her own specialty. The family plays for local festivities, senior citizens. homecomings, and more. From left to right in the picture above are Elaine Cronin Fox, Grace Cronin Cunningham, Michael J. Cronin, Margie Lamp Dodd, Lewis Cronin, Harl Cronin, and Blaine Cronin. Below is a photograph of the Cronin family cemetery. It is quite unique because the family members build beautiful images of their instruments to decorate the graves of those of their family who have passed away. This cemetery is located along the countryside between Pleasants and Wood Counties. (Above courtesy of Barbara Dean; below courtesy of Ruth Ann Dayhoff.)

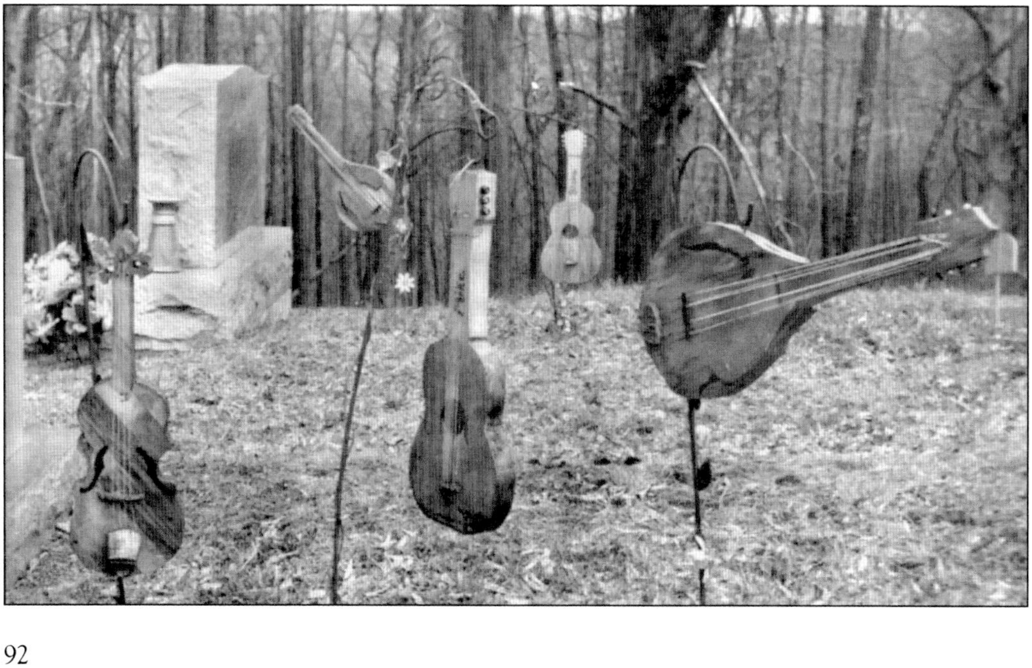

Seven

SERVING THE COUNTY

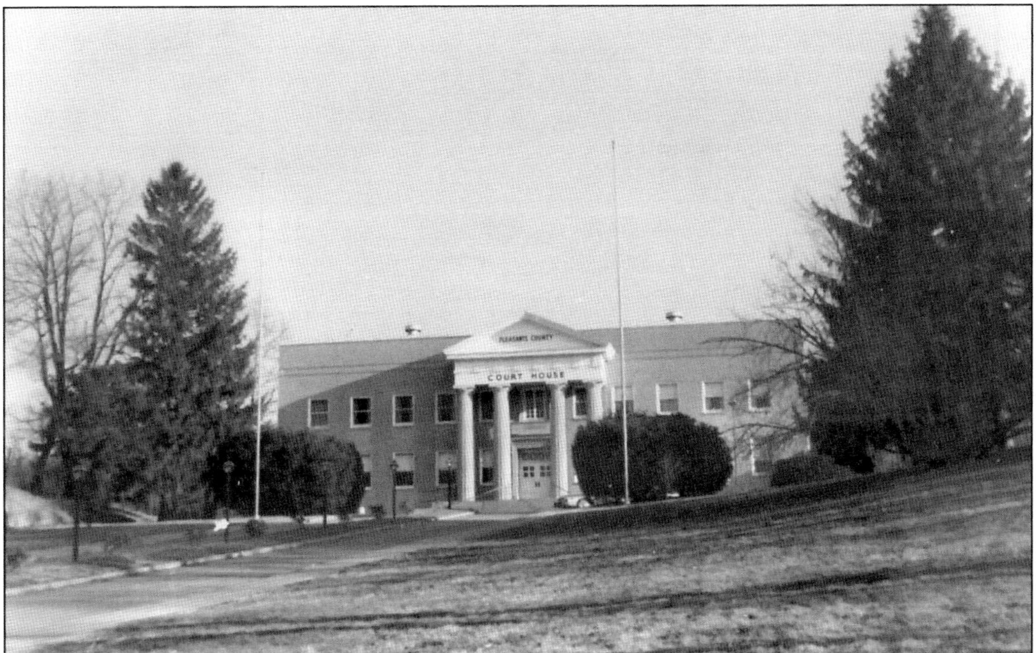

The current Pleasants County Courthouse was built in 1926. Lightning struck the old one, making it unsafe. Grading and landscaping had to be done to the hill because of the difficulty of getting to the courthouse. The approach from George Street when it rained was almost impossible to ascend. This courthouse is listed in the National Register of Historic Places and is a very commanding sight as one enters town. (Courtesy of Rev. Daniel Simmons.)

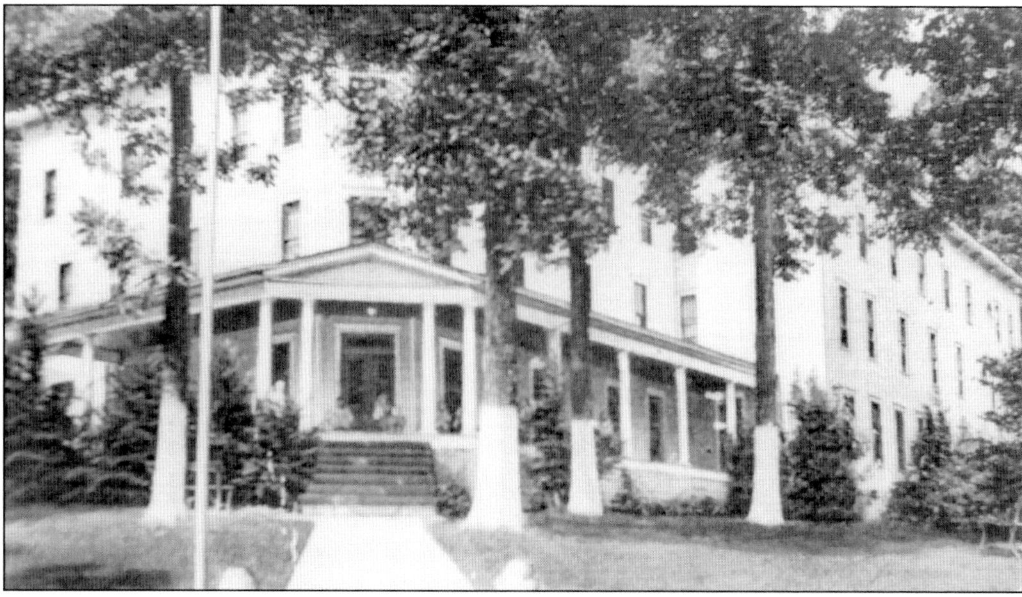

J. W. Grimm built the Borland Springs Hotel in 1908 along Bull Creek. It had 65 rooms, a dining room that seated 90, swimming, canoeing, tennis, horseback riding, and the mineral springs. People thought the springs could cure anything; they traveled many miles to "take the cure." The hotel started having financial problems in the 1940s. In the late 1950s, it served as a chicken coop for 12,500 chickens. (Courtesy of Rev. Daniel Simmons.)

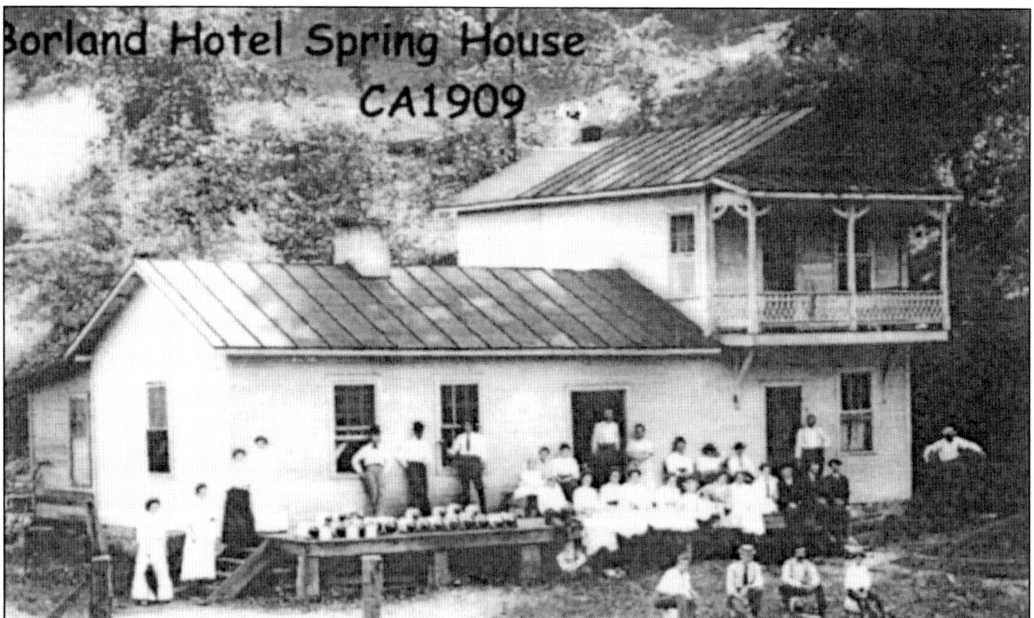

The Borland Springs Spring House was a popular spot for dances, picnics, and public gatherings. It was a peaceful, serene place to visit with purple Japanese irises growing near the springs. Charles Grimm, son of J. W. Grimm, shot and killed John Maidens at the spring house. For many years, people have said this area is haunted. Elsie and Clarence Maxwell were the caretakers in later years. (Courtesy of Mike Naylor.)

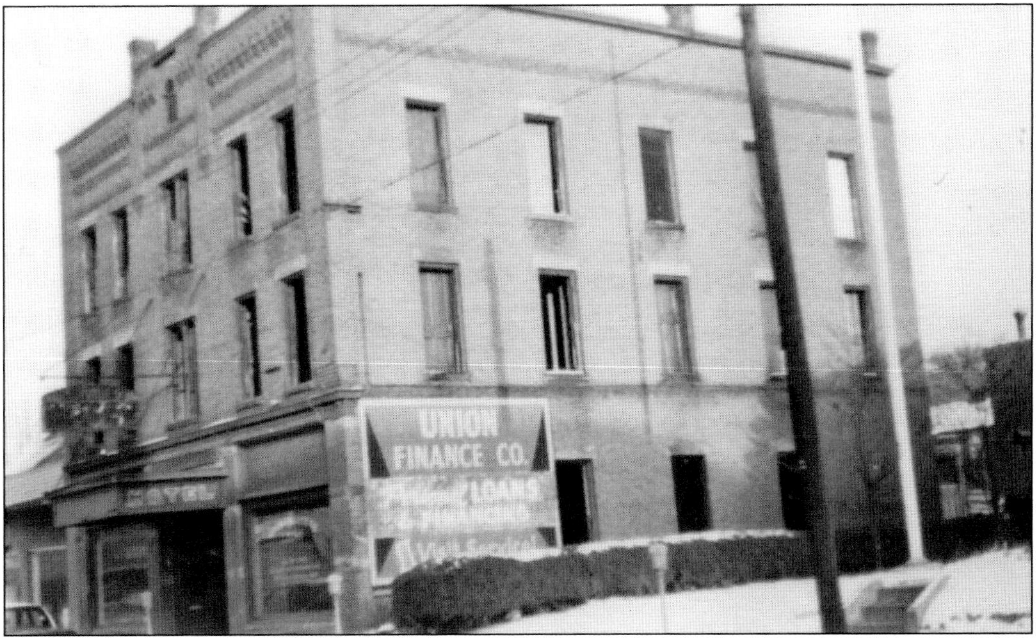

The Haddox Hotel was located where the City Building is today. It was a local hotel in the center of town. At times, it was used as a boardinghouse, assisting new families as they moved into town to take up residence. Sweeney's Sterling Oil and Gas Station was located on the corner of George Street and Riverside Drive. It started as the St. Marys Mill and ground grains with large millstones. Over the years, it housed different businesses and is best remembered for selling Sterling oil products. Charles Sweeney, the owner, recently tore it down and replaced it with Sweeney's Storage Units. (Above courtesy of Rev. Daniel Simmons; below PCPLC, courtesy of Eleanor Poling.)

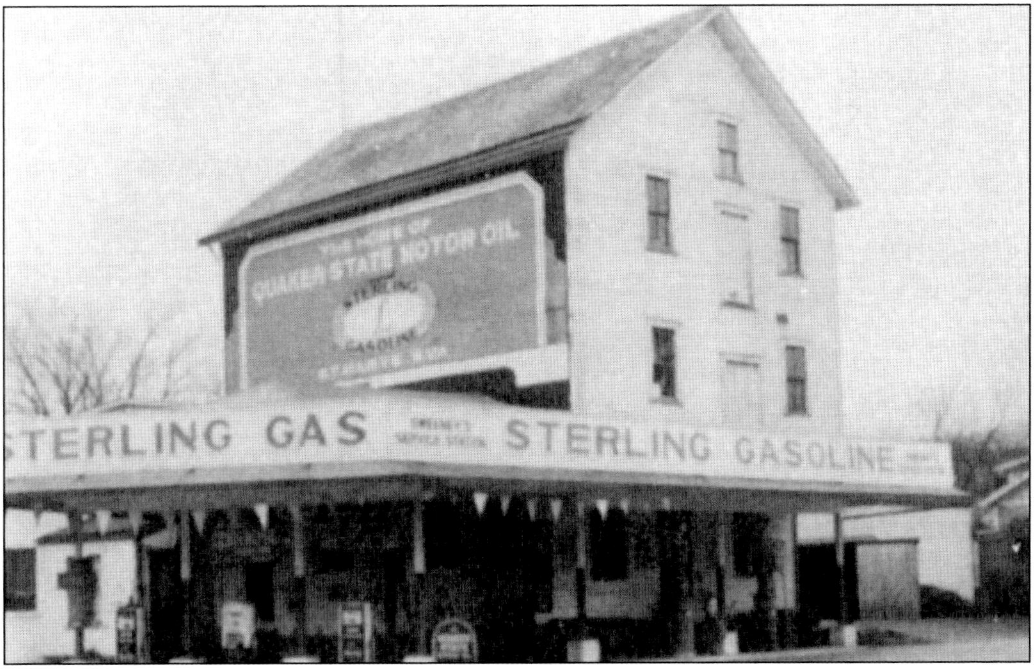

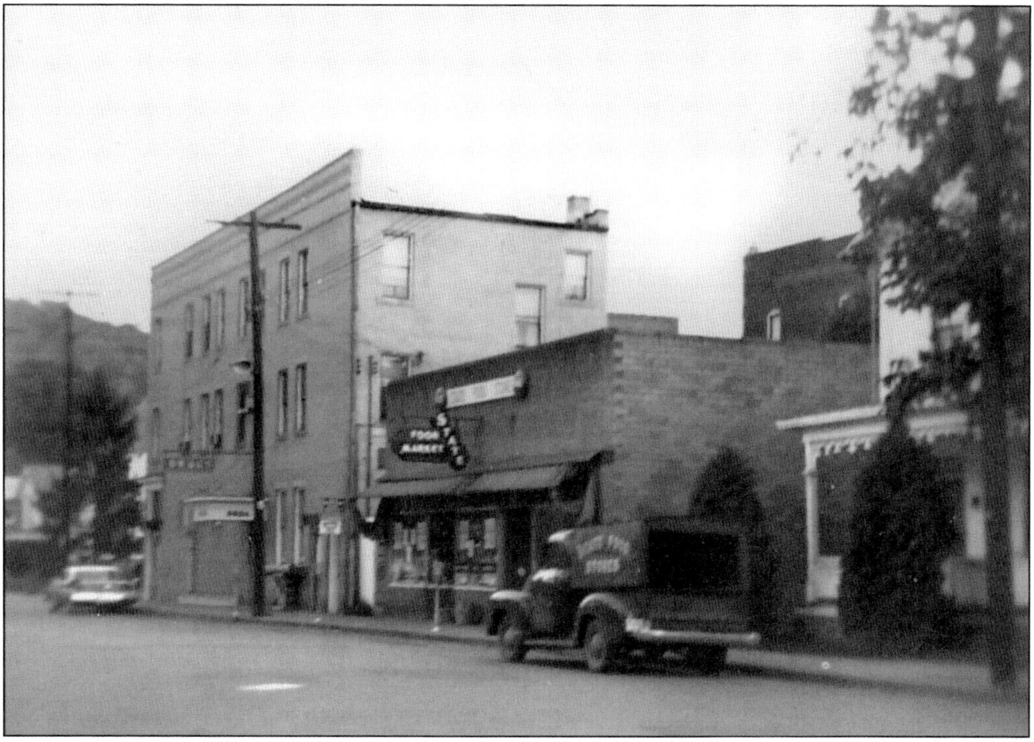

On the corner is Phillips Drug Store, first owned by George Phillips. It has been in business for at least 100 years. The State Store, behind Phillips Drug Store, was owned by Frank Gilbert. It is directly across from the First National Bank. The delivery truck in front was used for home deliveries. Gary Gilbert, son of Frank, made deliveries on foot as a youngster. (PMC, courtesy of Daniel Pitts.)

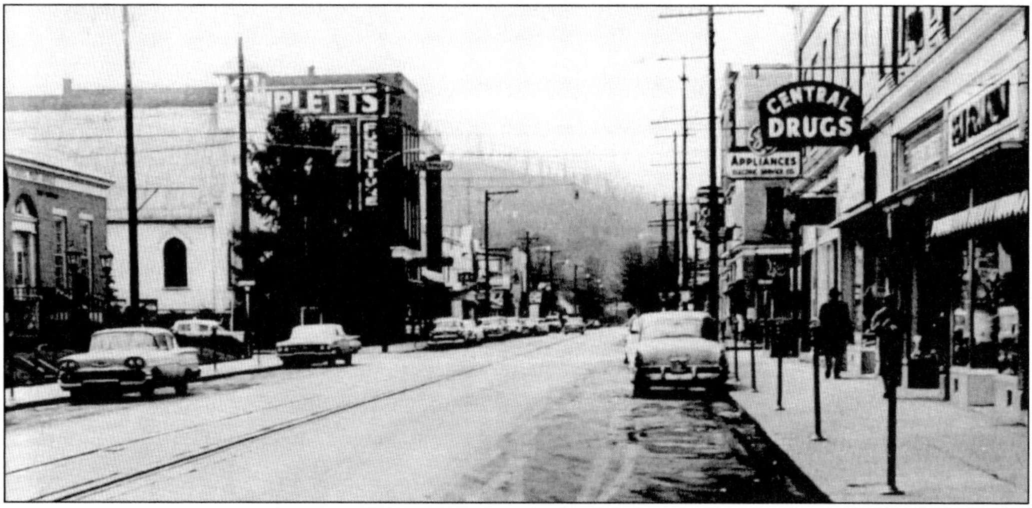

Looking down Main Street, one can see many of the businesses no longer in existence. Beside the post office is the Methodist Protestant church, which burned down in the 1960s. Next comes Tripletts Hardware, and looking across the street is the Central Drug Store and Shouldis's Department Store. In the distance on the corner is Phillips Drug Store. This photograph brings back many fond memories. (PCPLC, courtesy of Eleanor Poling.)

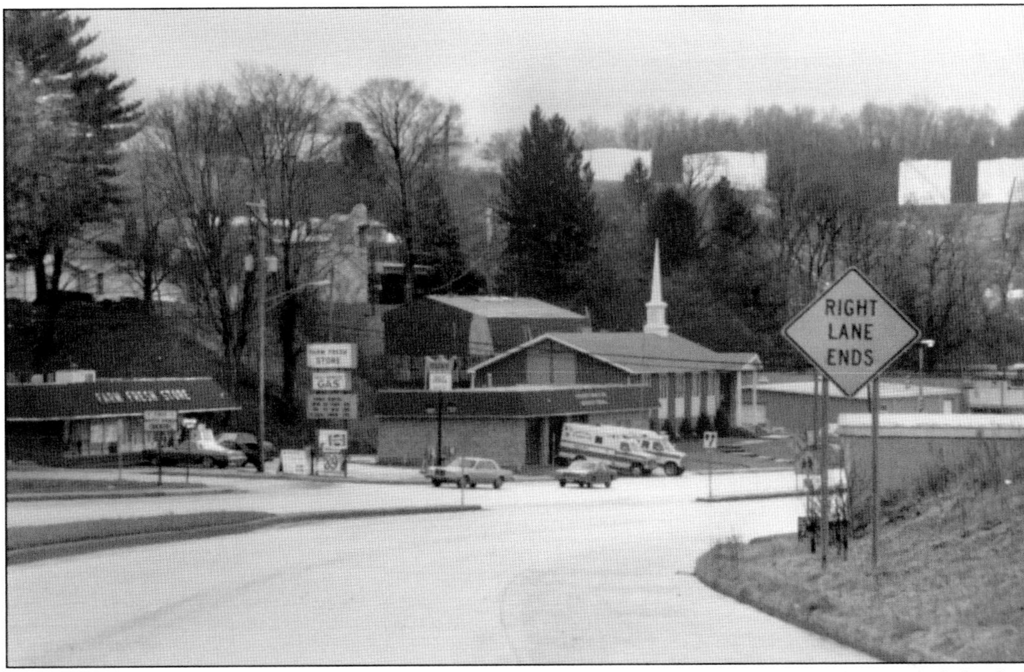

As one travels into town on Route 2, a significant view can be seen. At the top of the hill overlooking the city are six large oil storage tanks of the Quaker State Oil Refinery. You can see the St. Marys Presbyterian church and the emergency squad with trucks exiting to assist someone in need. The four-lane highway of Route 2 travels through town, leading to Belmont and Parkersburg. (Courtesy of Rev. Daniel Simmons.)

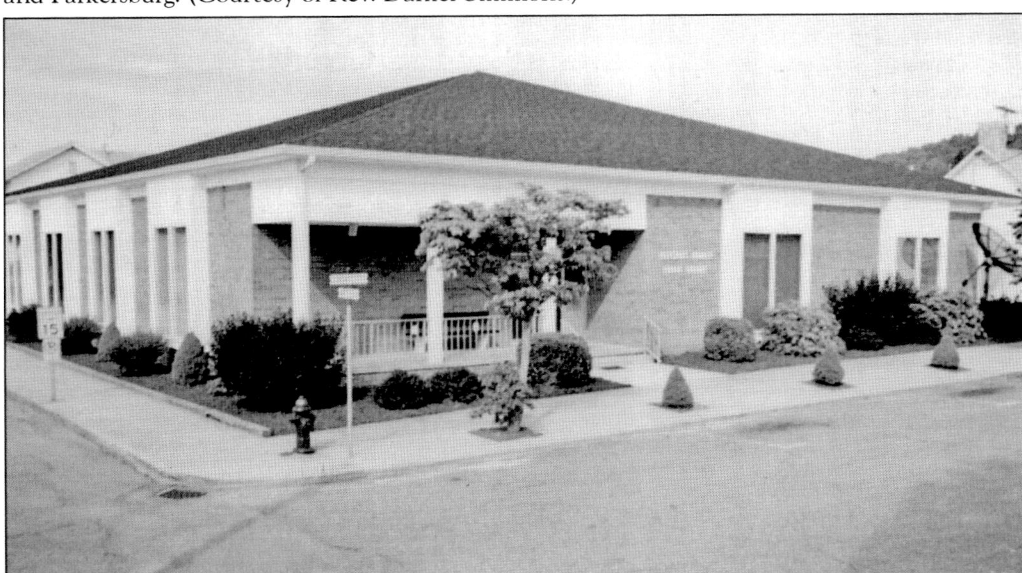

Pleasants County Public Library is located on Lafayette Street and was built in 1974–1975. Many residents have fond memories of checking out books in the old library, which was upstairs in the old Robey Theater, formerly known as the auditorium. This new library recently had an addition built on to it in 1998–1999, named after Dr. Richard Hamilton, one of the town's most beloved physicians. (PCPLC, courtesy of Eleanor Poling.)

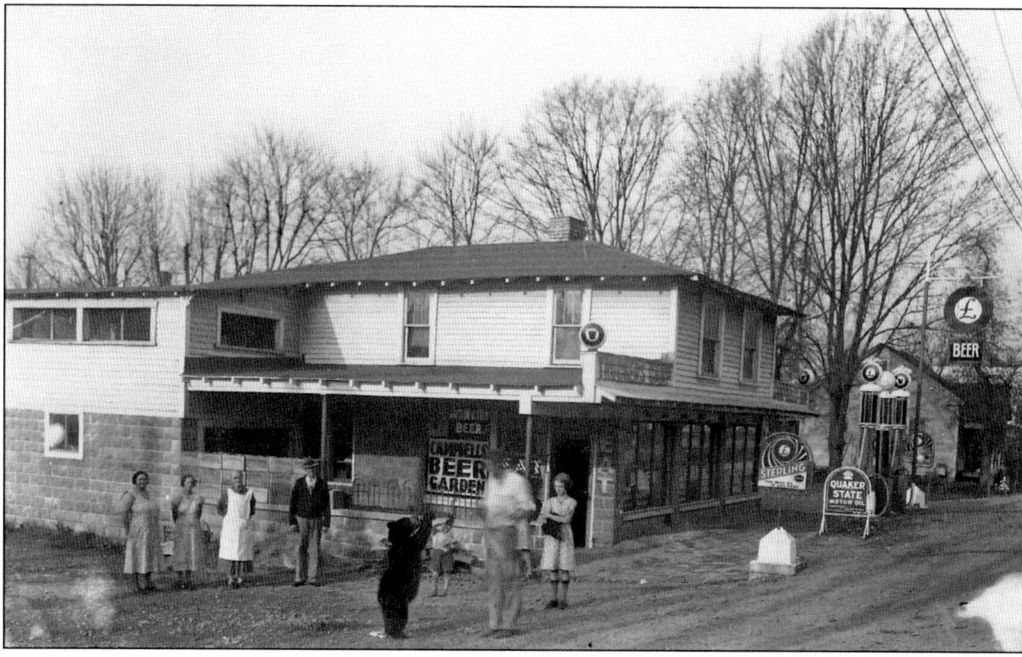

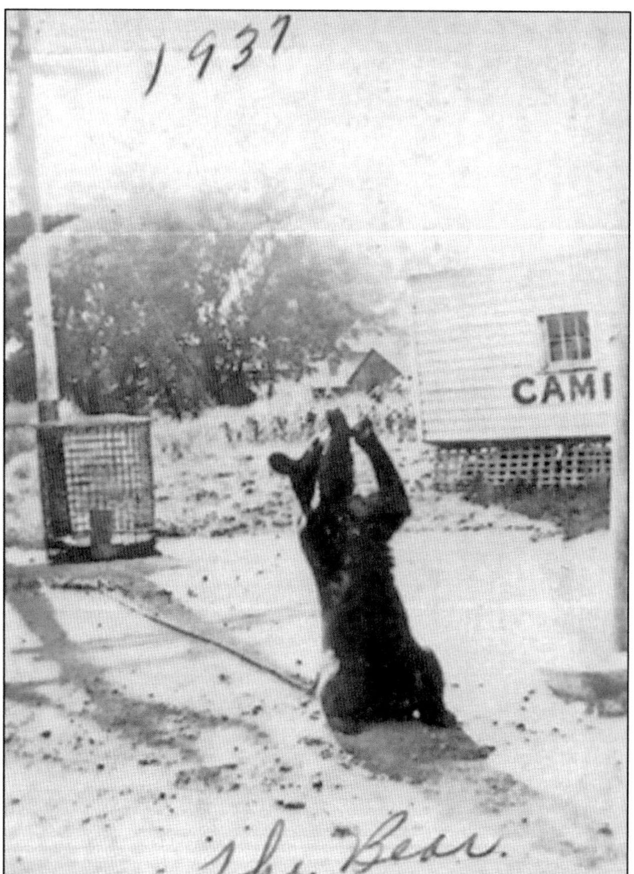

Bob's Place, owned by Robert H. Campbell, was located where the Go Mart now stands coming into St. Marys from Route 2. It was a grocery store, restaurant, and service station in St. Marys for more than 50 years. In 1934, Bob got a real black bear for the entertainment of his customers. The bear would wrestle, box, and dance to the enjoyment of everyone who saw it. The bear cage was an old oil drum with holes cut in it so the bear could breathe fresh air. The bear's cage was used in 1949 as the jail during the city's 100th birthday celebration. The picture below shows the bear drinking something delicious. His cage can be seen behind him. (Above courtesy of Jeff Little; left courtesy of Cynthia Hicks.)

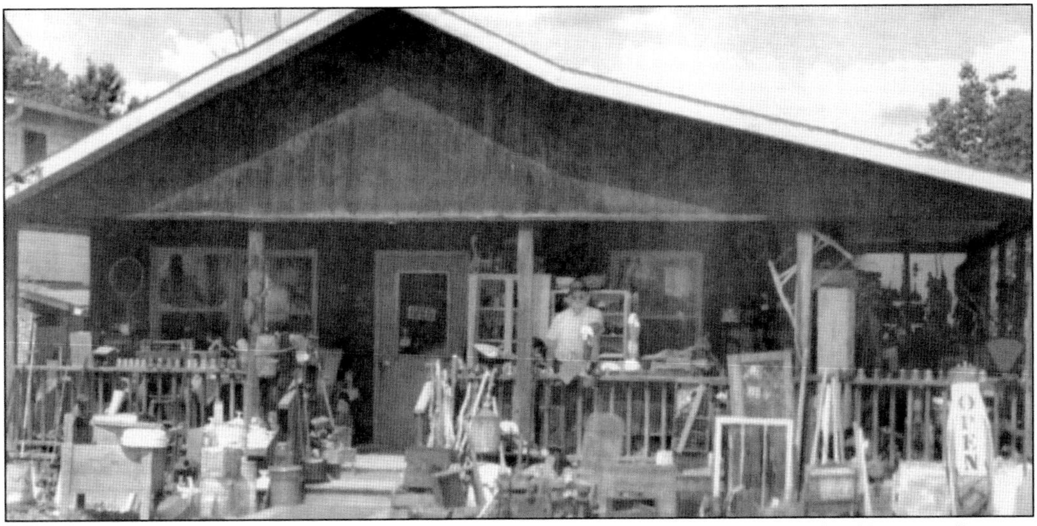

Chester and Betty Bills started the Antiques and Collectibles in 1988. He had been collecting things for years and finally decided to start a business to sell them. Chester specializes in oil field and petroleum memorabilia. His store is located on Route 2 across from Wendy's. After an airplane crashed and demolished his roof, he was able to build the establishment above. (Courtesy of Mary Sue Ross.)

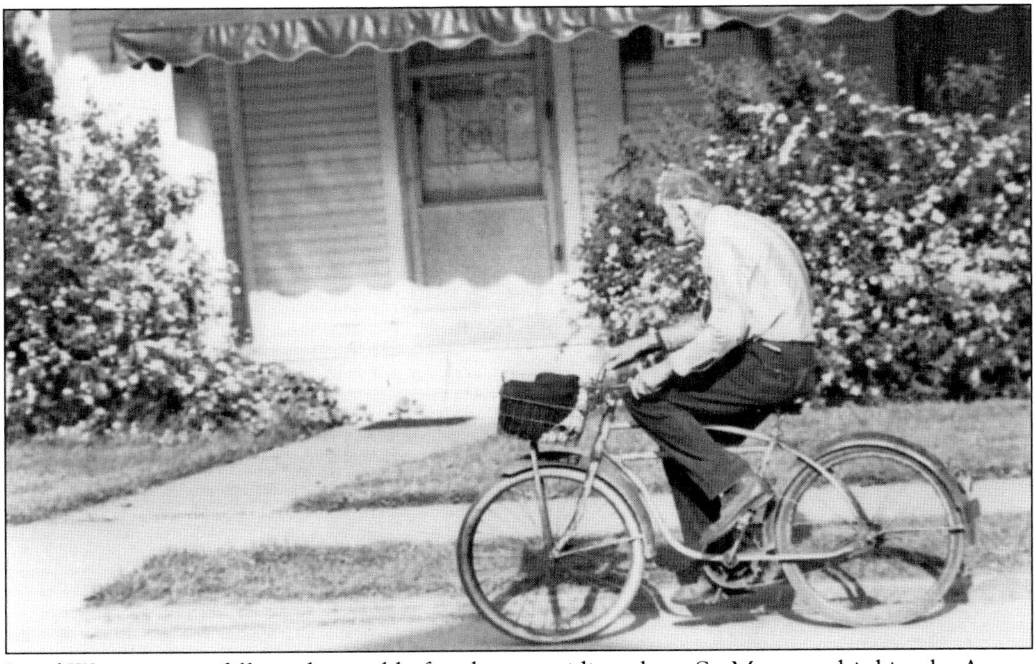

Laird Watson was a fellow who could often be seen riding about St. Marys on his bicycle. A very hard worker, he mowed lawns and did odd jobs for people who could use assistance. Laird was a kind and unique man, a symbol of our community. He had dignity and respect even though he had very few earthly belongings. When he passed away, residents felt a true loss. (Courtesy of Rev. Daniel Simmons.)

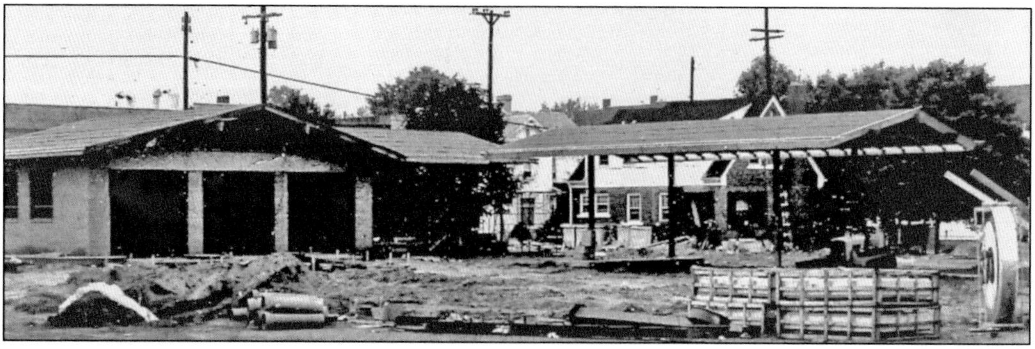

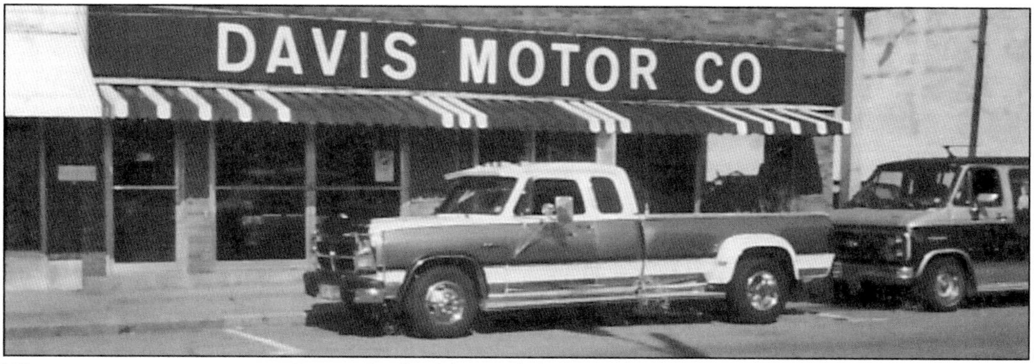

The construction picture shows the building of the Exxon Station, currently owned by Larry and Malcom Webb. The Davis Motor Company, a Dodge and Plymouth Agency, was on Main Street in business from 1932 until the late 1990s. Below is an advertisement for the other garage in St. Marys, the Clovis Motor Company. Since 1913, Clovis had the first Ford franchise in town. In 1950, they purchased the filling station and Firestone Store across the street from their first building, shown below. In 1972–1973, the modernization of Route 2 through St. Marys forced them to tear down this first brick building. Bob Yoak purchased the business in 2007. (Above (top) courtesy of Larry Webb; above (middle) courtesy of Thelma Davis; below PCPLC, courtesy of Eleanor Poling.)

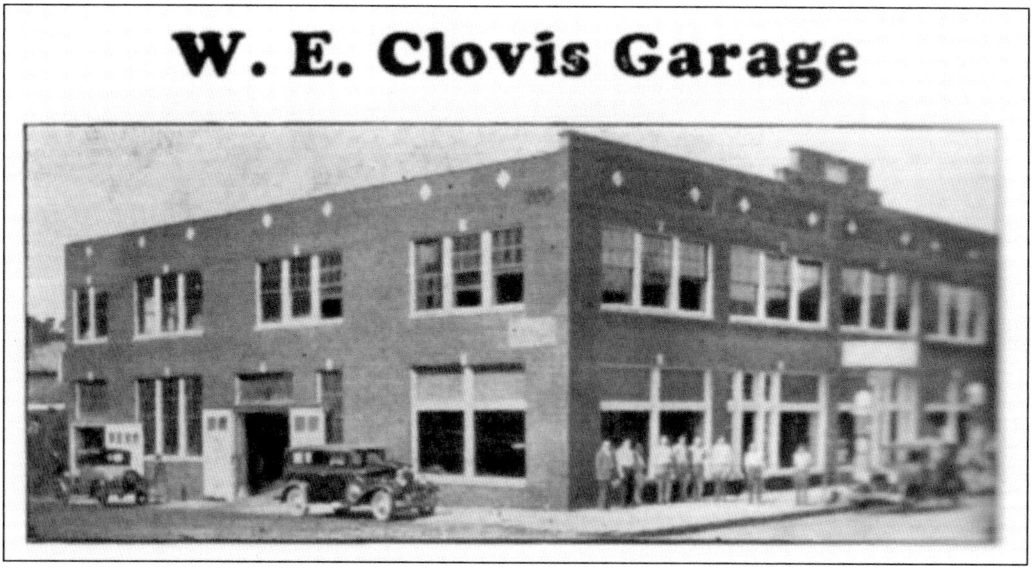

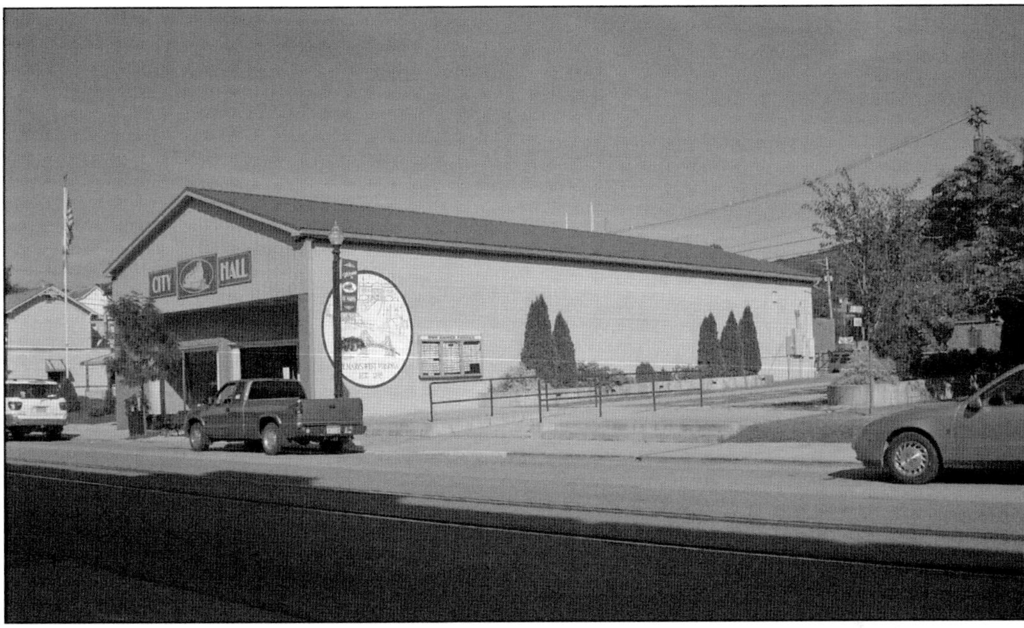

The St. Marys City Building is located on Main Street where the Haddox Hotel once stand. Paul Ingram is the current mayor. On the side is painted the city motif. There have been three different designs: first, on the 1949 centennial "Bells of St. Marys" booklet; second, on the 1980 History of Pleasants County; and third, this motif designed by Carla Wince. (Courtesy of Ruth Ann Dayhoff.)

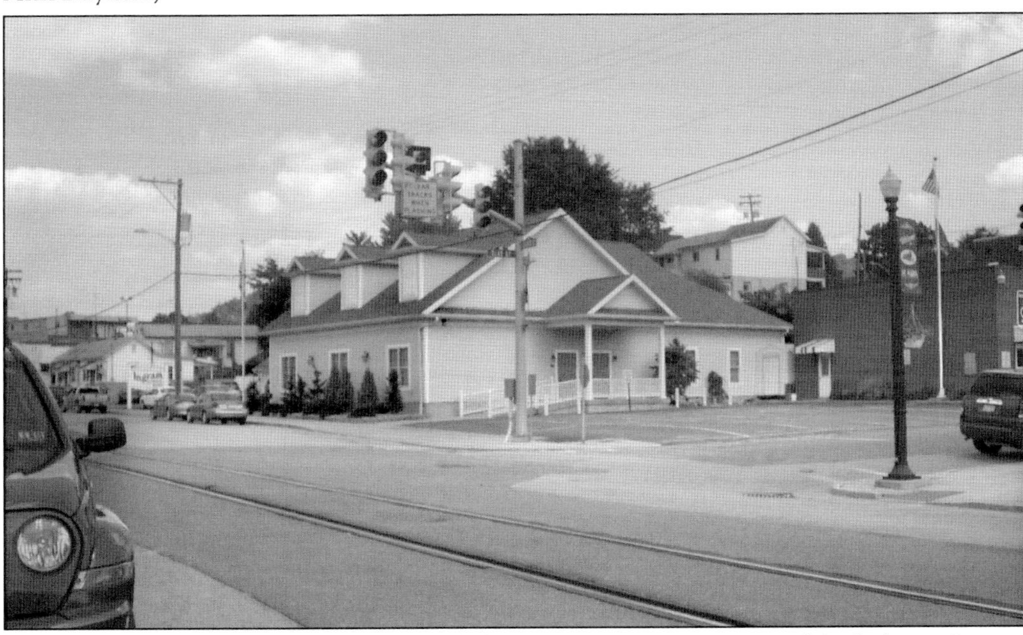

Charles "Charlie" Ruttencutter established the Ruttencutter Mortuary and Ambulance Service. His son, Charles Abram, better known as "Junkie," joined his father with the business. Upon Junkie's death, the business was sold to Harvey Hatfield and is now owned and operated by Paul Ingram and his wife, Becky. The name is now Ingram Funeral Home and is still in the same location but completely renovated. (Courtesy of Ruth Ann Dayhoff.)

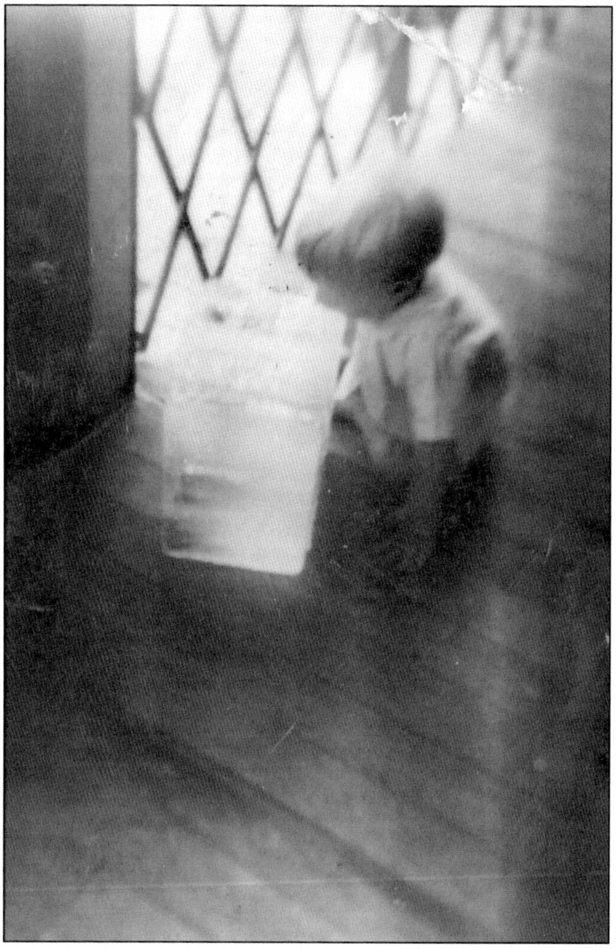

Have you ever licked a large piece of ice and found yourself frozen to it? Young Charles Weekley is in that predicament in the photograph at left. Tom Weekley, his father, worked delivering ice for the Ice House in St. Marys and milk for Joy's Creamery. Other employment included working at the mill, the marble plant, and as caretaker of the IOOF Cemetery to support his wife and eight children. He represents the typical, hardworking residents of the county. The photograph below shows Tom and his six-month-old son, Charles. (Both courtesy of C. F. Weekley.)

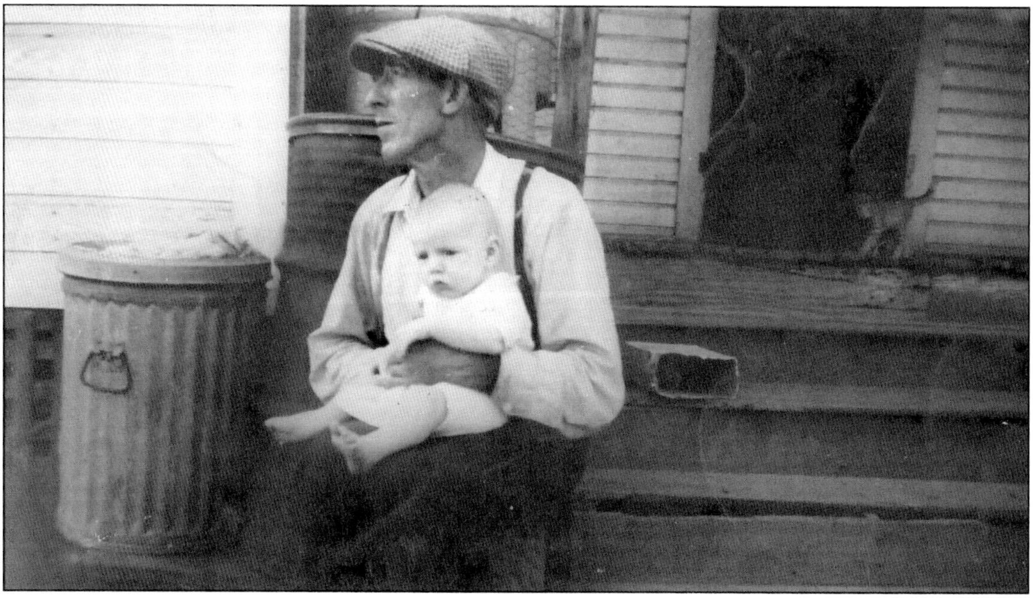

Eight

People, Past and Present

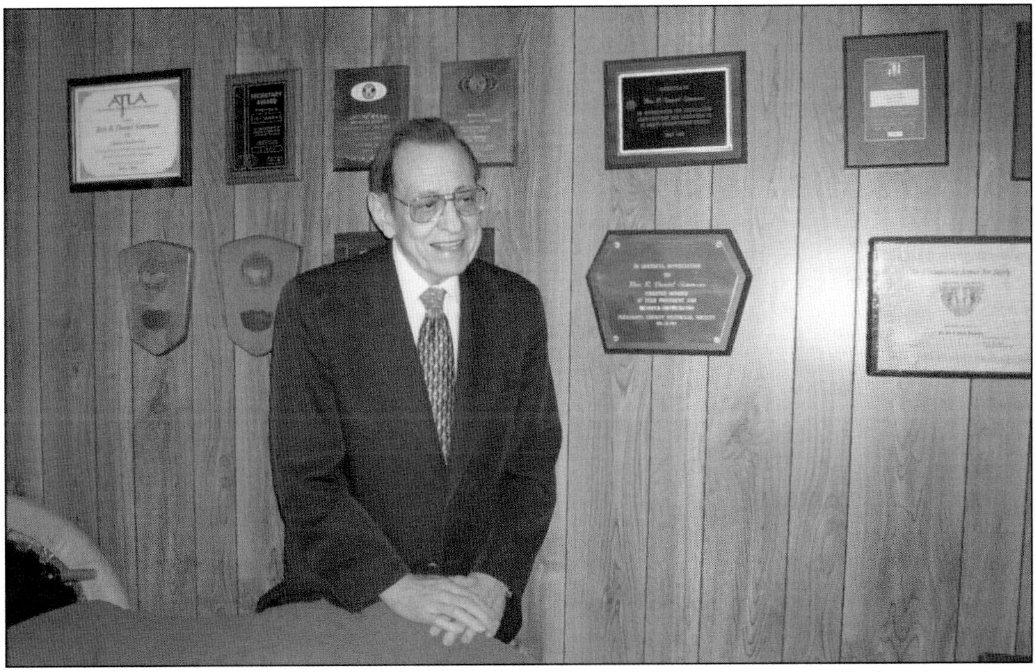

Rev. Daniel Simmons, a freelance photojournalist, contributed many photographs from his private collection for this book. His other accomplishments include serving as president of the Ministerial Association for 21 years, vice president of the Pleasants County Commission on Aging for 17 years, and he was a charter member and president of the Pleasants County Historical Society for 17 years. The plaque to his left commemorates his service. (Courtesy of Ruth Ann Dayhoff.)

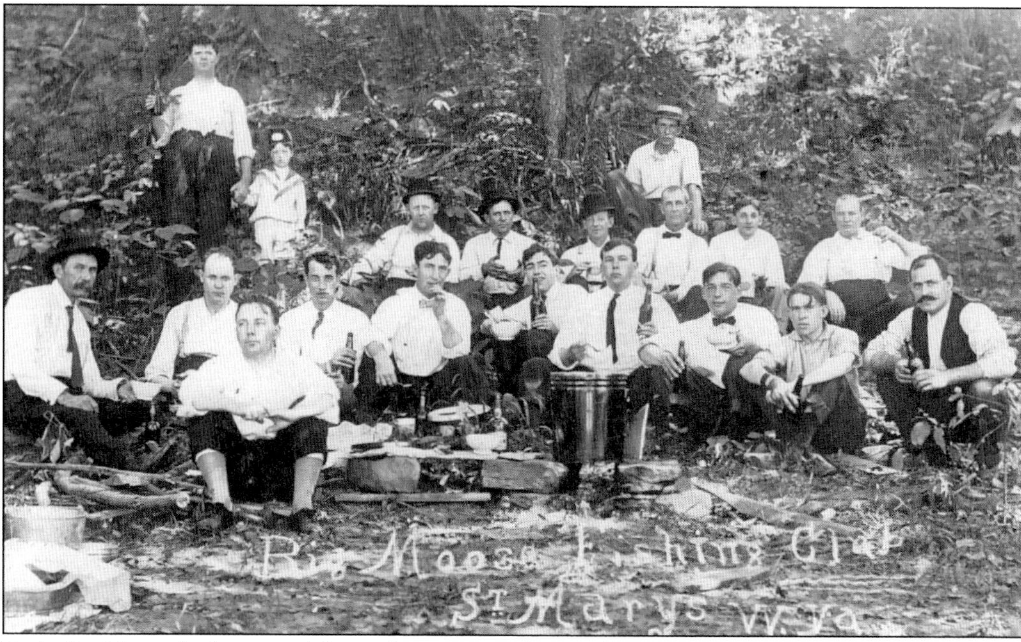

Early St. Marys had many clubs and activities that no longer exist. One of those was the Big Moose Fishing Club. Above are the men involved with this organization. There is still a club called "The Moose" in the area. Names of the members above have been lost in the annals of time. (Courtesy of Andrew Clovis.)

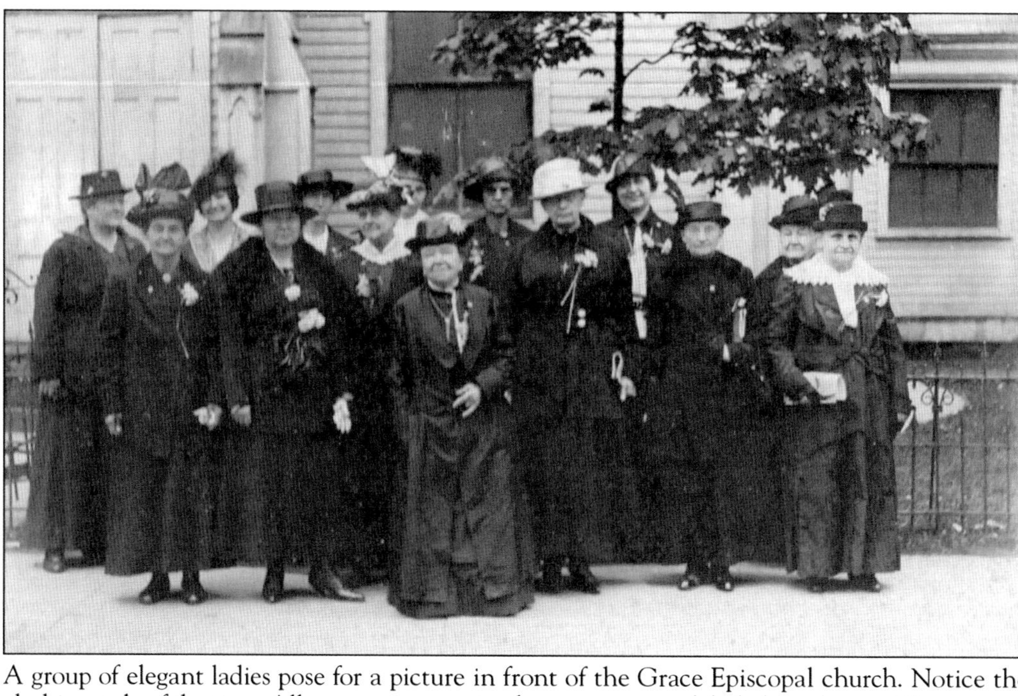

A group of elegant ladies pose for a picture in front of the Grace Episcopal church. Notice the clothing style of the time. All women are wearing hats, scarves, and dark, long dresses. The purpose of the gathering is unknown and leaves a lot to speculation. (Courtesy of Andrew Clovis.)

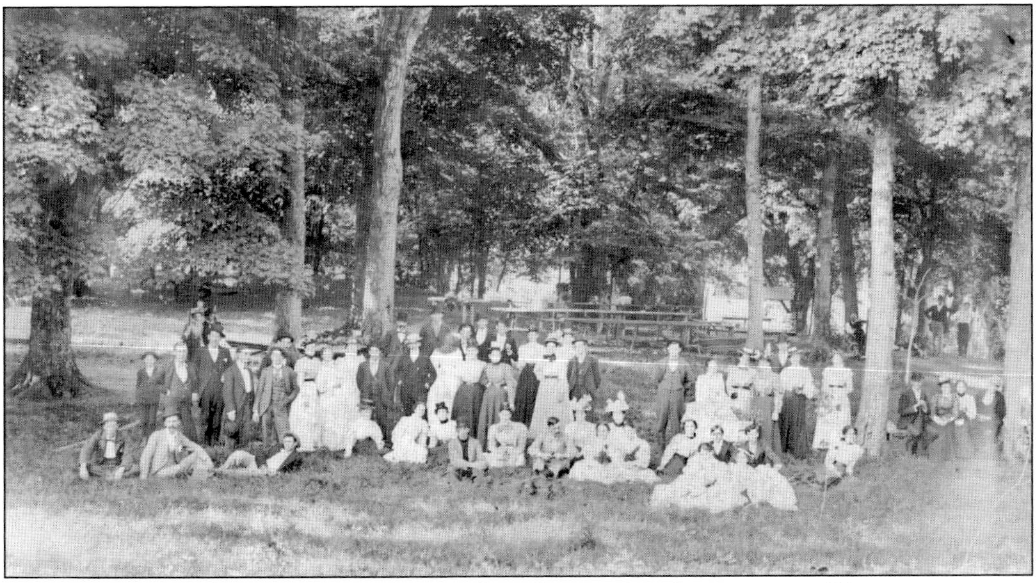

Some youth from Pleasants County have gathered at a park to have a picnic. This picture is very old, and the people shown here are all unidentified. However, the old-fashioned styles on the women are quite captivating. These types of dresses were quite constricting, so most of the ladies were limited to quiet activities. (Courtesy of Jeff Little.)

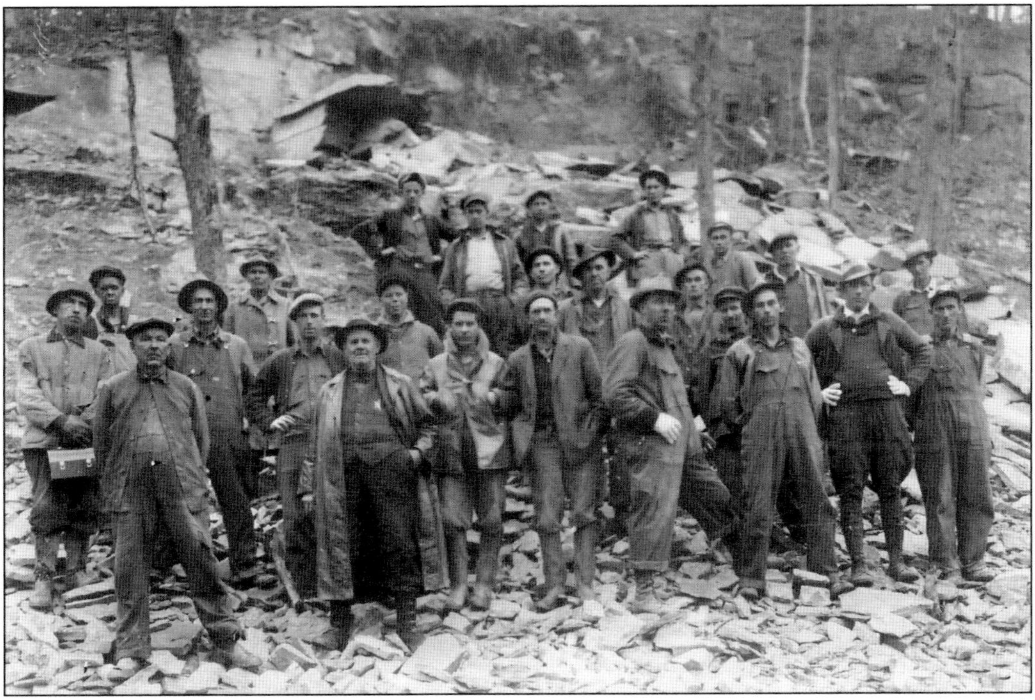

These hardworking men are taking a break for lunch. In 1945, the Calco, or American Cyanamid, plant was being built. These men are preparing the property for plant construction. Their job was to dig the trenches for the pipe. One of the men was Theodore Parsons, and it was his job to lay the pipe in the trench. Charlie Dittman inspected the pipe and later became head of the maintenance department. (Courtesy of Mary Ellen Dittman and Jeff Little.)

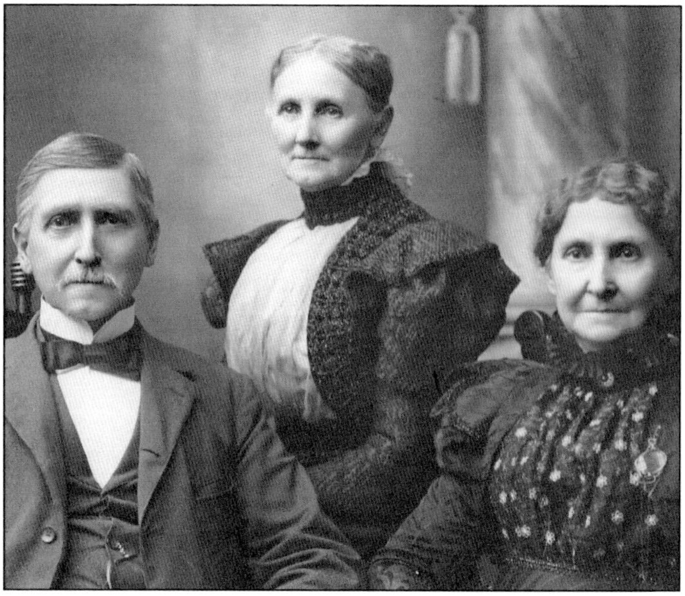

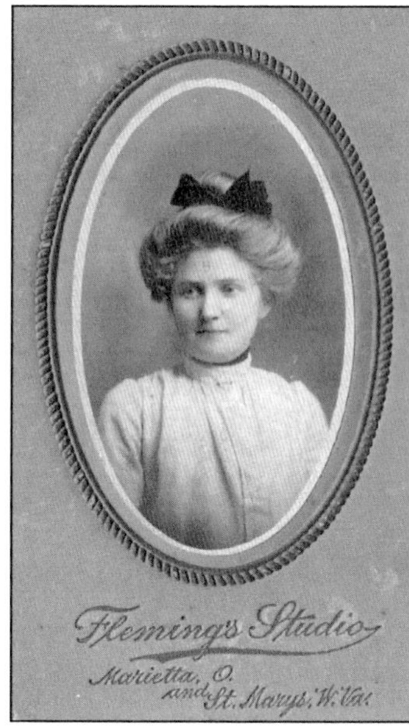

The elegant portrait on the left above is of Harvey and Mrs. Katherine McCollum with aunt Emma McCollum, who taught school in Pleasants County. Their son, Dr. James Riley McCollum, came to St. Marys to work in the hospital with Dr. Grimm. The right photograph above is of Mable McComas McCollum, wife of Dr. James Riley McCollum. Dr. McCollum served as the mayor of St. Marys and in the House of Representatives in Charleston. The photograph was made by Flemings Photo Studio, which had businesses in St. Marys and Marietta, Ohio. Below, James Edwin Green attempts to do his wife Edith's work while she is visiting her sister. Notice the note on the stove that says, "If wife would only come back!" He is trying to thread a needle and sew up the hole in his sock. (Above (both) PMC, courtesy of Daniel Pitts; below JEGC, courtesy of Dale Brown.)

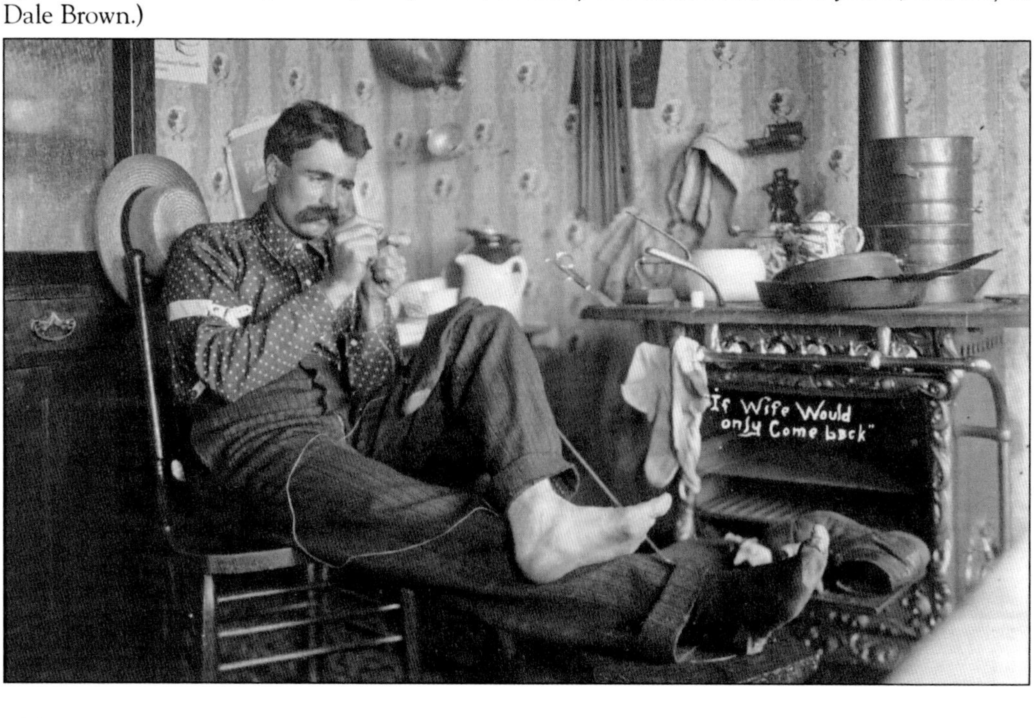

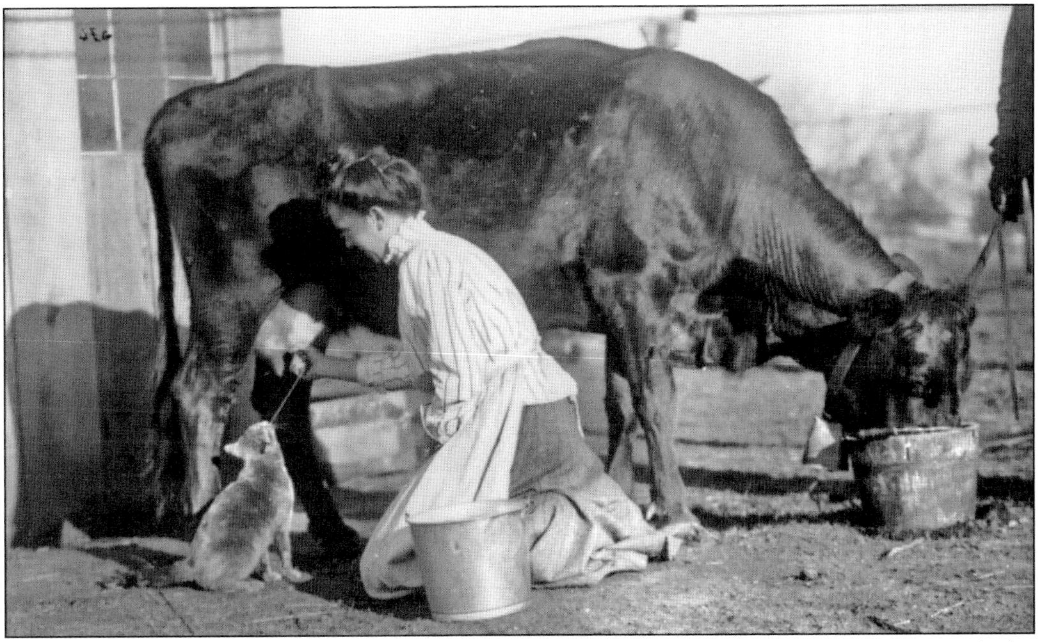

Julia Goetgeluck was the sister of Edith Green. Green's husband, James Edwin Green, took the picture above and many photographs of places and events of Pleasants County. In order to take those pictures, he carried supplies that weighed 50 pounds. Julia has been milking her cow and giving Blue Boy, the cat, a drink now and then while her husband works on farm machinery. Below is Julia's husband, Oscar, who was a native of Belgium. This photograph was taken at their home, Forest City Farm, just below Vaucluse on Route 2. Notice the fine furnishings, the beautiful needlework, and the relaxed atmosphere. (Both JEGC, courtesy of Dale Brown.)

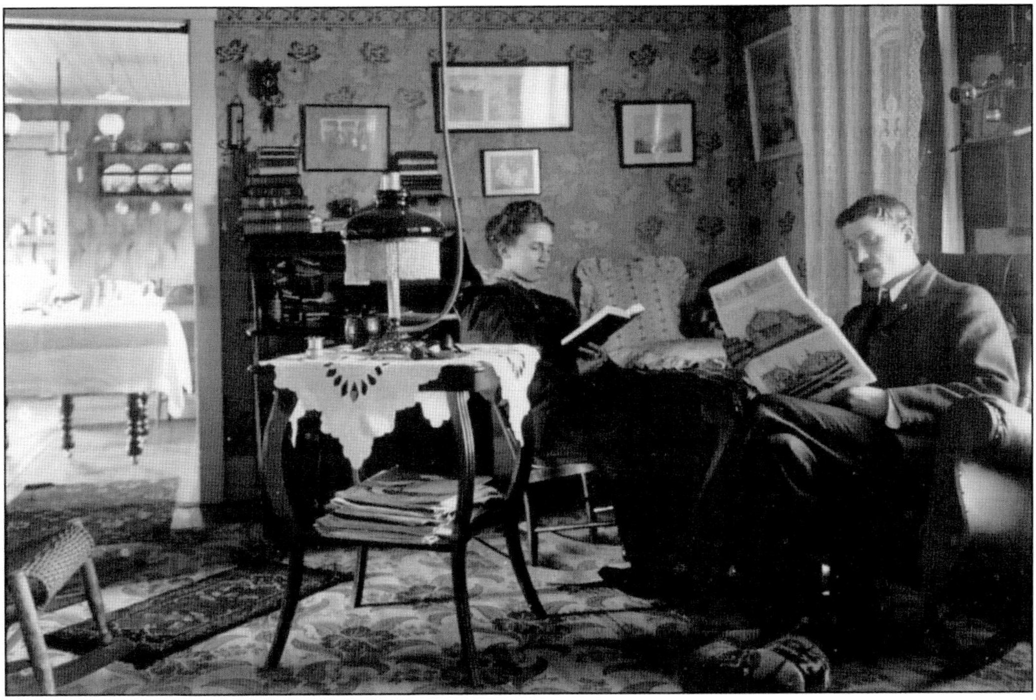

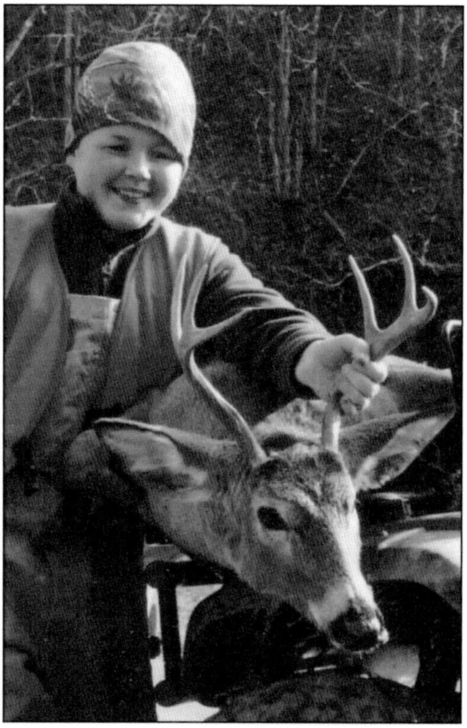

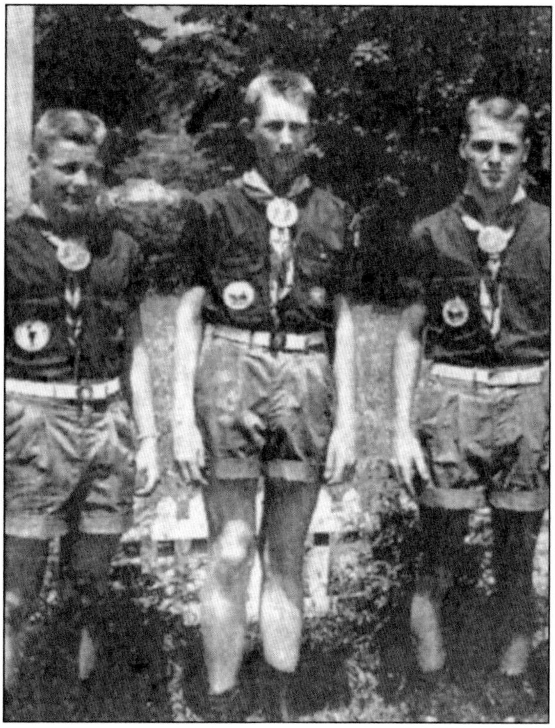

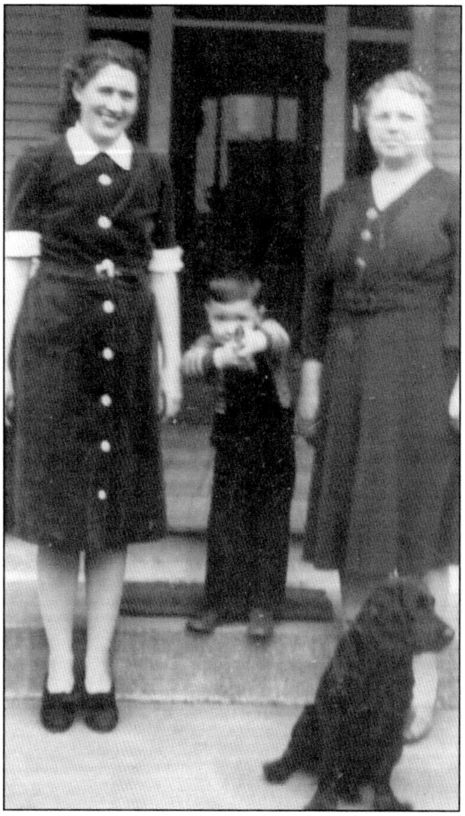

Above left, 13-year-old Benjamin Barnes is showing his trophy six-point white-tail buck. He bagged this first buck on Saturday, November 29, 2008, while hunting with Robbie Adams on the Katherine Smith farm. As seen in the photograph by his wide smile, he is enjoying this newfound sport just like the earliest settlers did in this beautiful county. Above right, three local Boy Scouts are on their way to Camp Philmont in New Mexico. They are, from left to right, Gary Ingram, David Pitts, and Tom Weber. These young men have made the county proud. They were very active in sports and Scouting and were fine examples for the youth of Pleasants County. Left, standing on the front porch are Evelyn Clovis, Theodore Clovis, his grandmother Mamie Clovis, and their dog. Evelyn's memories have been quite helpful in writing this book. Mamie worked with county youth all of her life. Ted's interest in history has inspired many. (Above left courtesy of Sonya Adams; above right courtesy of Mary Ellen Dittman; left courtesy of Andrew Clovis.)

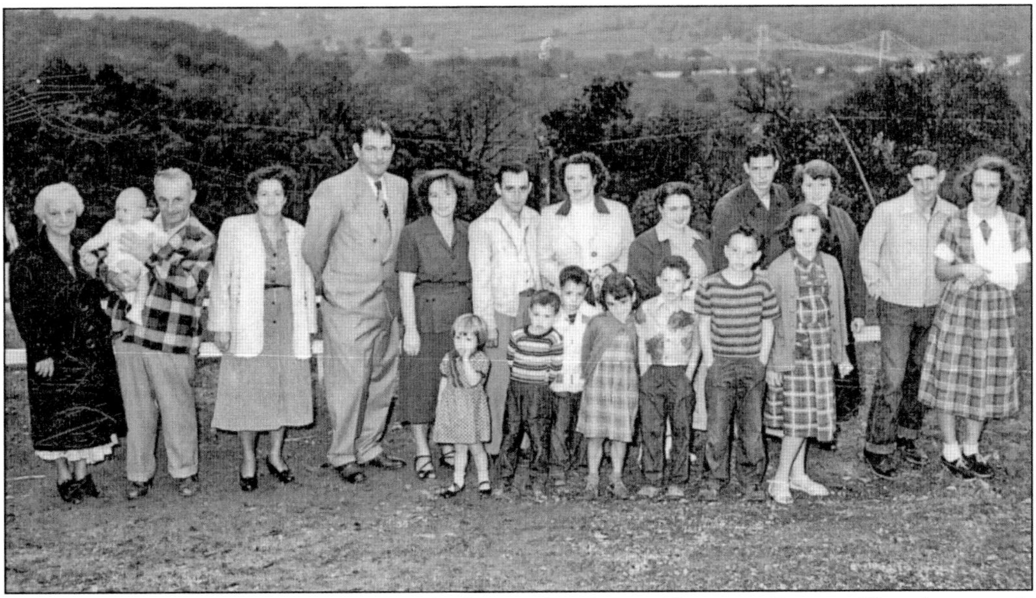

The West and the Wolfe families were the largest families in Pleasants County. The photograph above depicts the West family, which included, from left to right, (first row) Marilyn, Marion, David, Carol, Daniel, William, and Vivian (son Jay is not pictured); (second row) Grandma Lawson, Clint West with baby Joseph and wife, Cassie Bills West, James, Edna, Eugene, Ruth, Betty, Norman, Irma, Delbert, and Nancy. (Courtesy of Mary Sue Ross.)

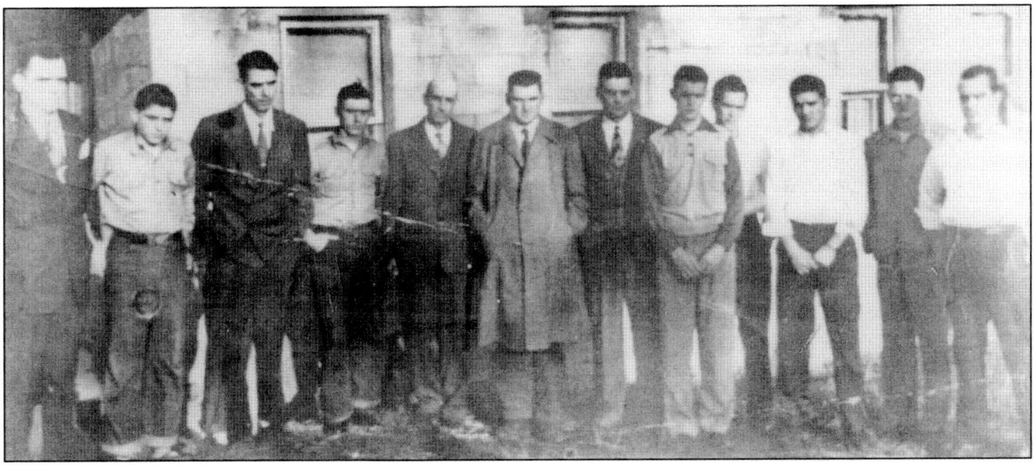

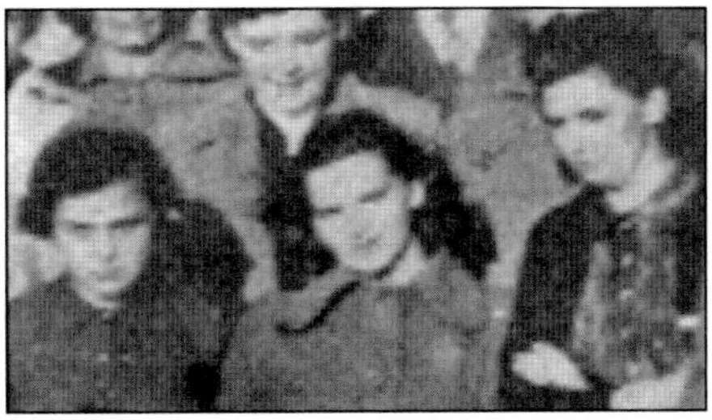

This is the Wolfe family after the funeral of their mother, Amanda, wife of John Harrison "Polar" Wolfe. Above, pictured from left to right are Melvin, Richard, Jim, George, John "Polar," Edward, Howard, Joe, Ernie, William "Jup," John, and Milton. The girls (right) are, from left to right, Sue, Betty, and Garnet. Jennings is not pictured. Gerald, Laura, and Andrew are deceased. (Courtesy of Betty Winland Wolfe and William R. Wolfe.)

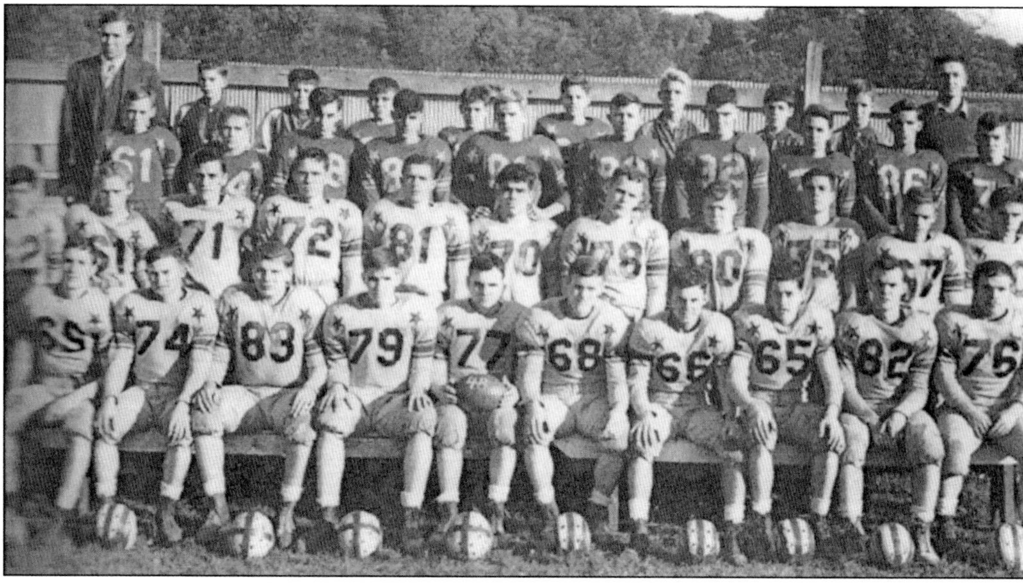

The St. Marys Blue Devil football team of 1948 was the only undefeated team in St. Marys High School's history. In 2008, a few members of the 1948 team unit returned for a reunion. They were welcomed by the 2008 football team. This 1948 undefeated football team reunion included players, managers, and cheerleaders. Below, from left to right, those returning included the following: (first row) Dottie Harper White, Barbara Shouldis Reckard, Dolph Cosper, Brandy Riggs, Grandon Snyder, Jim Snyder, and John Chips; (second row) Jerry Wagner, Frank Bills, Delno Winland, and George Lee. (Above PCPLC, courtesy of Eleanor Poling; below courtesy of Richard Moore.)

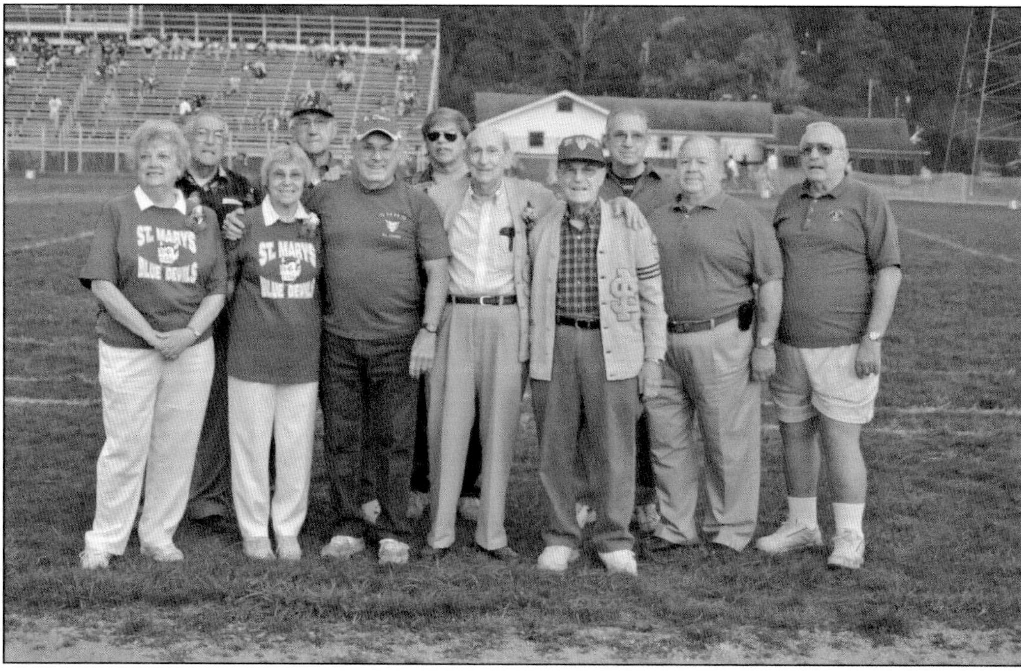

Nine

Schools and Churches

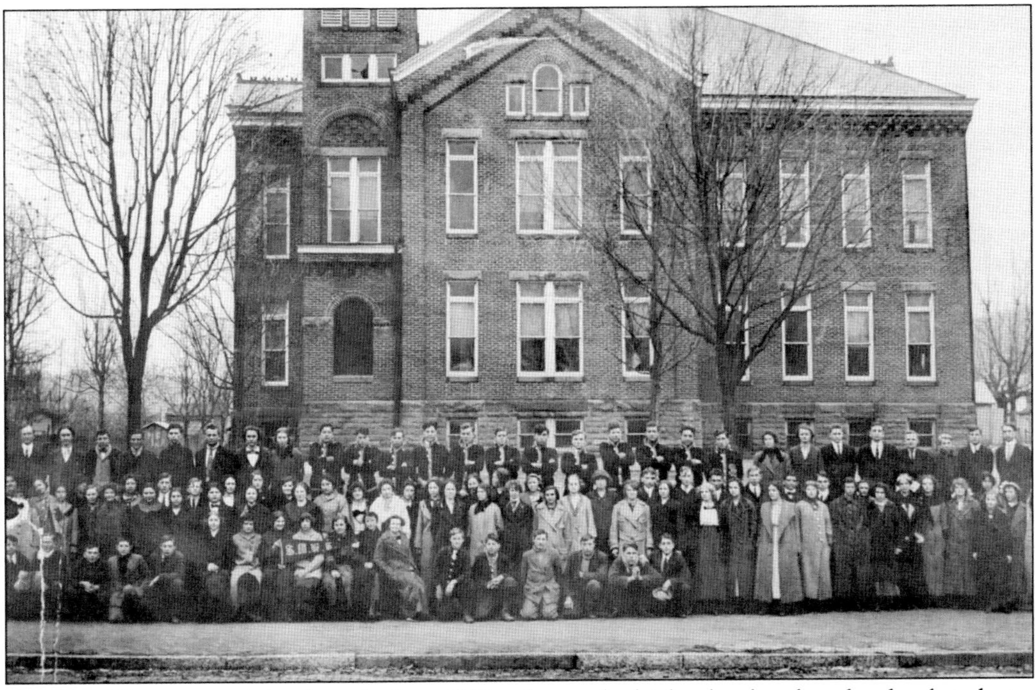

St. Marys Elementary School was built in 1898 to house the high school and grade school students. Teacher training was also held there for about two weeks. This picture was taken in 1913–1914 of the students and faculty. In 1951, the school was closed and remodeled. Students were transported and taught in the high school basement until completion. Because of the recent renovations, this school is still in use. (PCHSC, courtesy of WVDCHSA.)

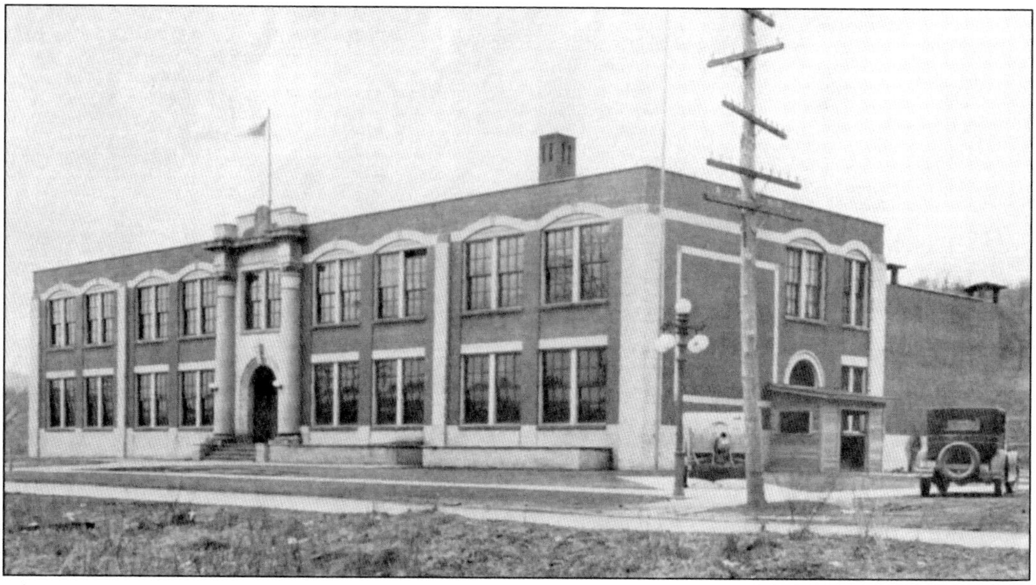

This is a 1928 photograph of St. Marys High School, constructed in 1919. The first high school was combined with the elementary school in 1898. In 1937, more classrooms were added. Many renovations have modernized its present appearance. The citizens of Pleasants County embarked on a program to build a school system second to none. This school is located on the corner of Route 2 and Route 16. (PCPLC, courtesy of Eleanor Poling.)

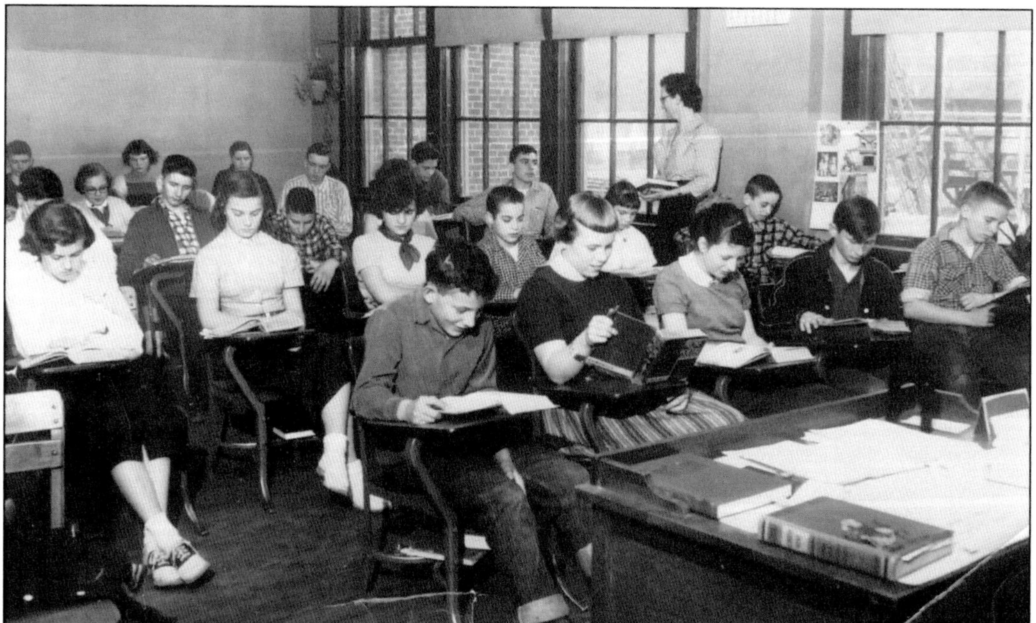

Isabelle Strickling teaches history in 1954. From left to right are (first row) Max Alkire, Mickey Anderson, Wanda Barrett, Gary Bills, and J. D. Dinsmoor; (second row) Judy Crosser, Ellen Dittman Pope (author), Barbara Keener, Wendell Ross, Amy Monroe, and Gary Gilbert; (third row) unidentified, Dale Smith, Larry Brown, unidentified, and Earol Hess; (fourth row) Sally Sunderman, unidentified, Charles Weekley, and Frank Pethel; (fifth row) William Wolfe, Helen Smith, and unidentified. (Courtesy of Charles Weekley.)

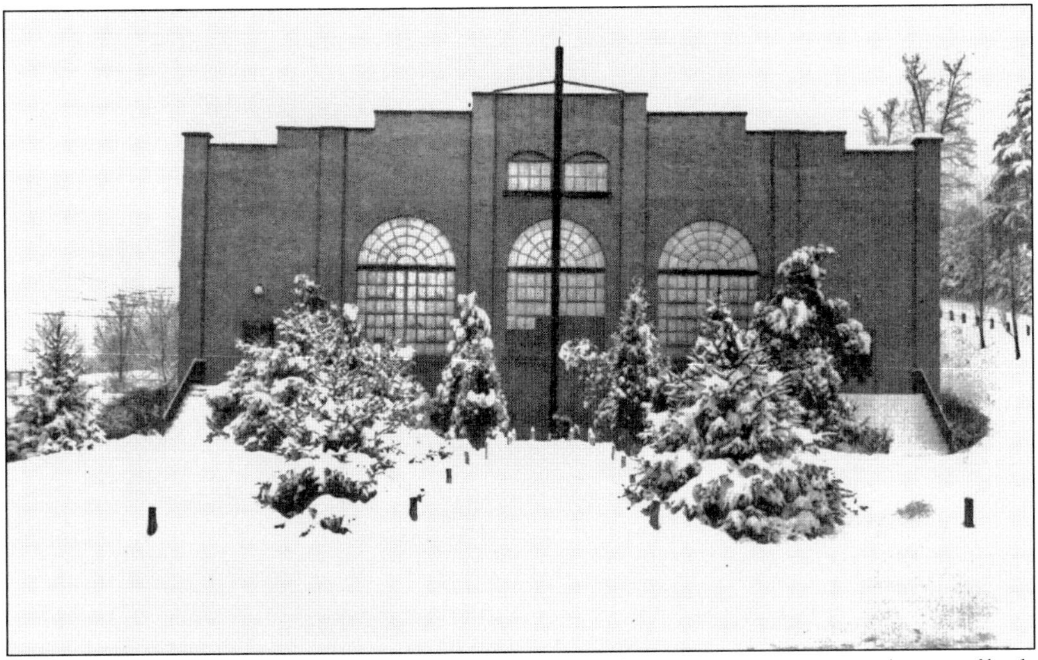

Pictured above is the American Legion Community Building. For 20 years, it was the site of high school physical education and trade and industrial shop programs. It also had the only bowling alley in town until the Illar family built the Center Theater and bowling lanes. In 1960, it was converted to the Park School. In 1974, it became the Pleasants County Community Center, now renamed the Jim Spence Center. (PCPLC, courtesy of Eleanor Poling.)

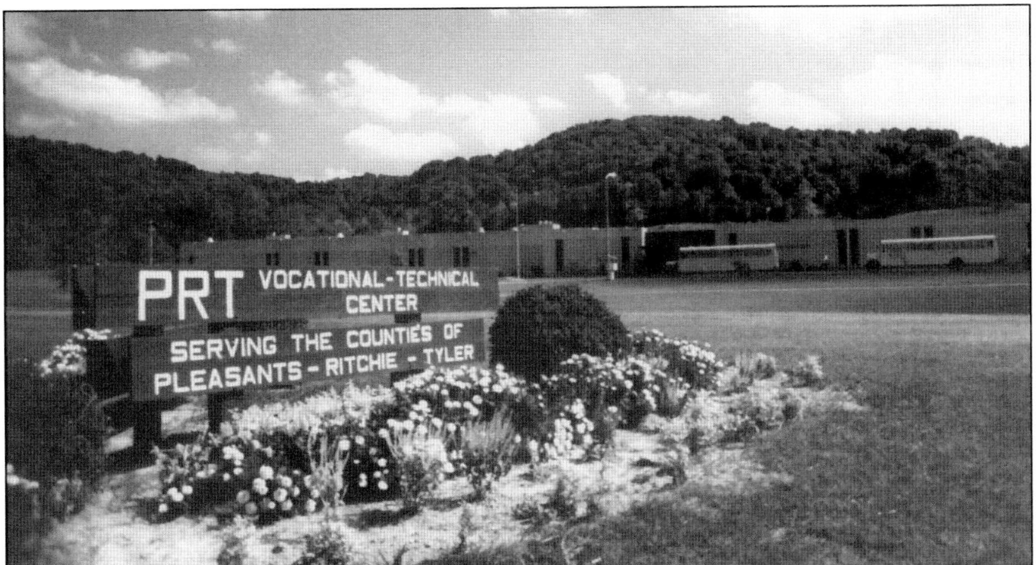

In 1973, the Pleasants Ritchie Tyler Technical Center, better known as PRT, was completed. It is located north of St. Marys on Route 2. In 1942, L. E. Watson initiated the first vocational program in the basement of the community building. It later moved, in 1955, to the high school. The vocational technical vision for the area youth was finally transformed into reality. (Courtesy of Rev. Daniel Simmons.)

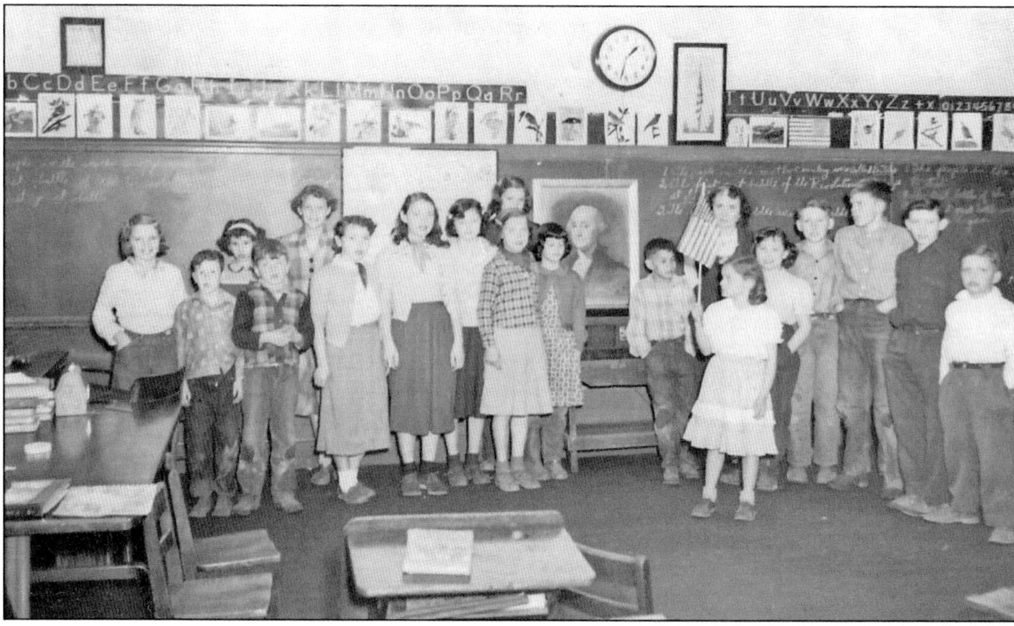

This one-room-school photograph is taken inside the Hebron School in 1953–1954. Pictured from left to right are Frances May, Tommy Smith, Sara Lou Lamp, Carl Colvin, Norma Mosser, Ruth Ann Lamp, Mildred Shultz, Sharon Smith, Martha Colvin, Hazel Colvin, Linda Hadley, Robert Evans, Lucy Houseman (teacher), Carolyn Cross, Becky Evans, Johnny Metz, Phillip Colvin, Eddy Byers, and Joe Cross. (Courtesy of Ruth Ann McPeake and Mildred Harden.)

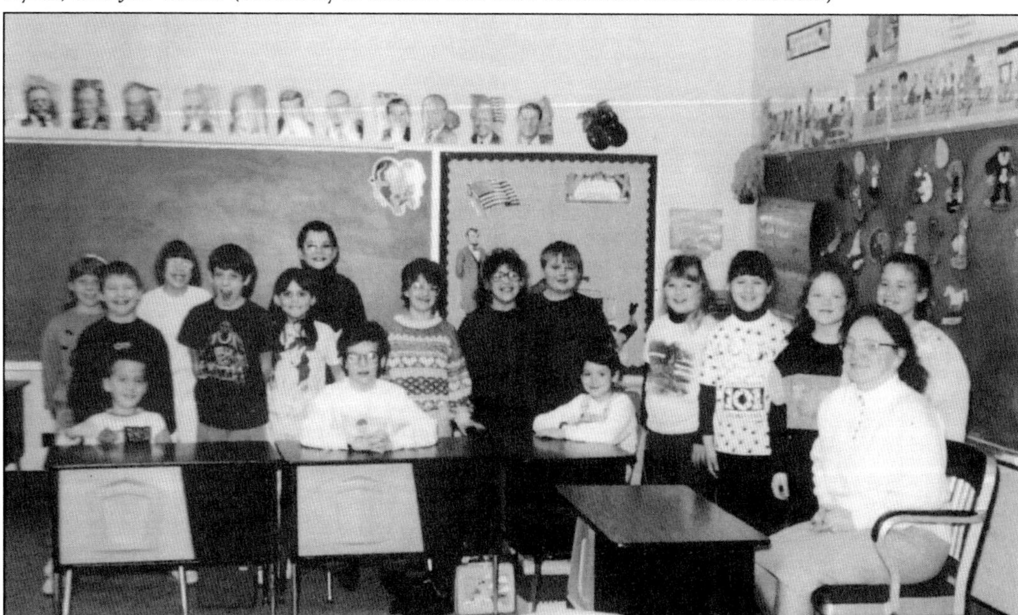

This 1993–1994 Belmont Elementary third-grade class picture shows one of author Ruth Dayhoff's classrooms. It was chosen in memory of two precious children here who died so young. Amanda McBrayer (standing, fifth child from left) died in a car accident the following year. Laura Loar (standing, fourth child from right) died of a sudden illness in the sixth grade. They were best friends. (Courtesy of Ruth Ann Dayhoff.)

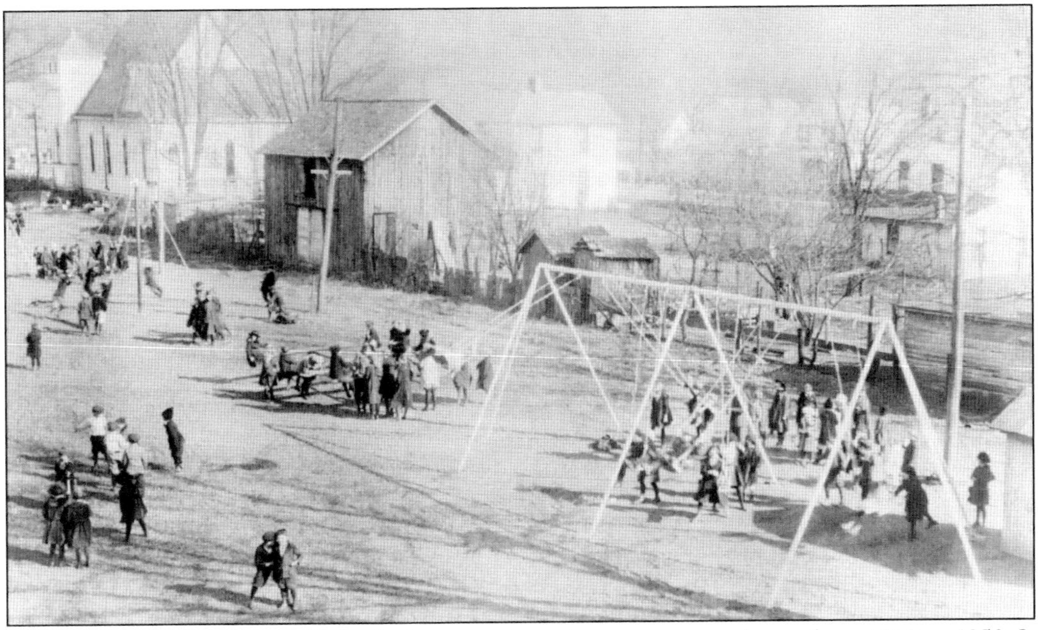

This St. Marys Elementary School Playground was in use, as seen above, from 1920 to 1950. It is still in use today but is somewhat changed. The authors hold fond memories of the recesses they spent playing here. These memories include waiting on a swing to be free, hanging onto the merry-go-round for dear life, jumping rope, playing hopscotch, and playing seven-up with a ball and a wall. (Courtesy of WVDCHSA.)

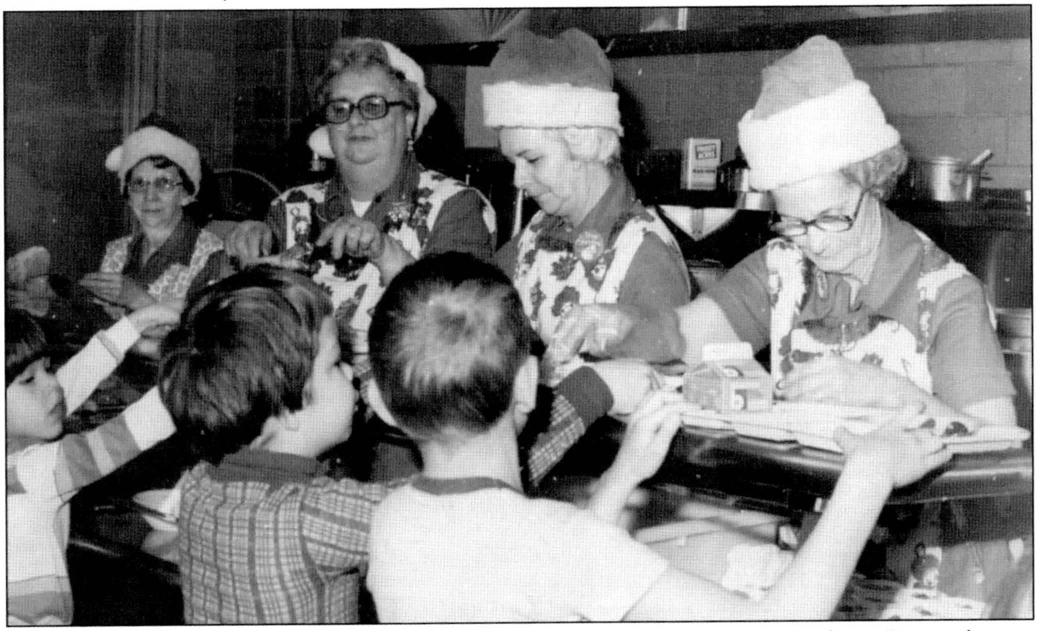

Schools of today cannot function well without cooks. Lunch is a favorite "subject," according to Mary Ellen Dittman, and cookies were the favorite. She specialized in chocolate chip. Dressed as Santa's elves, the St. Marys Elementary School cooking staff pleasantly perform their job. From left to right are Emma Robinson, Lillian Butcher, Phyllis Dent, and Mary Ellen Dittman. (Courtesy of Mary Ellen Dittman.)

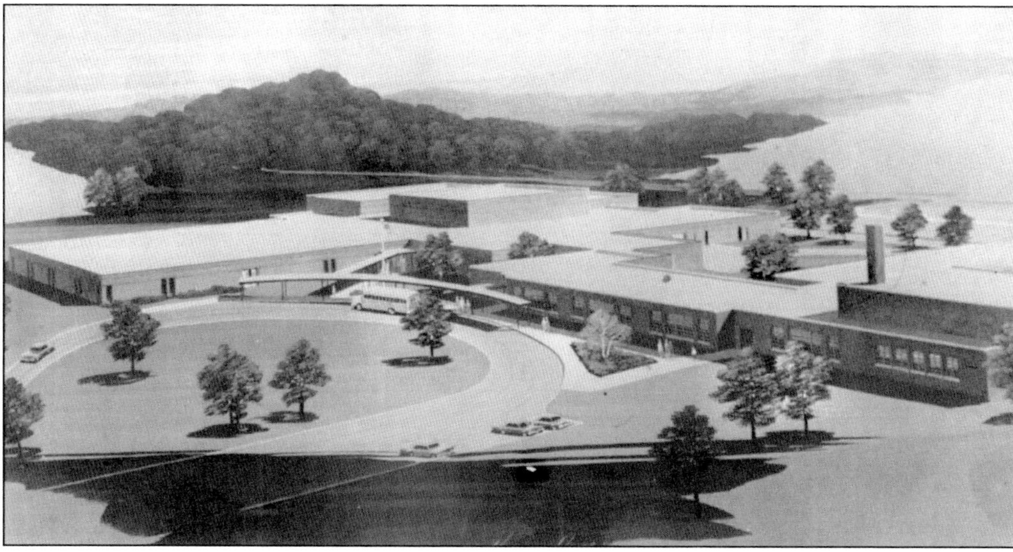

This is an architectural drawing of the combined Belmont Elementary School and the Pleasants County Middle School. The right side is the elementary, built in 1949 and renovated in 1951. In 1974, the middle school was built attached to the elementary school. This modern school uniquely includes a swimming pool. Author Ruth Ann Dayhoff taught for 36 years in these schools. (Courtesy of Pleasants County Schools.)

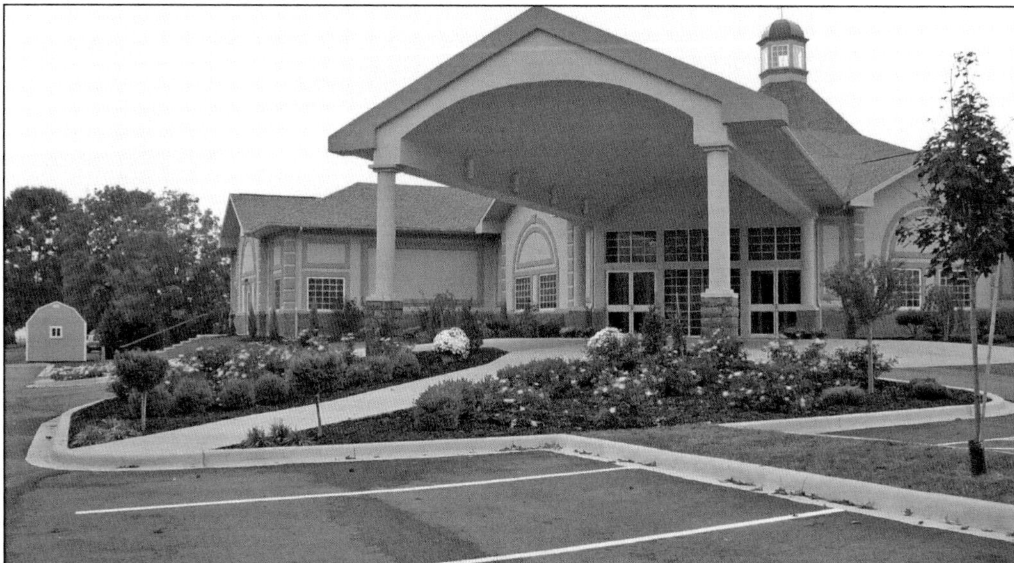

This beautiful, new North Pleasants Apostolic Church and Christian School was completed under the leadership of Pastor Terry Lough in 2005 and is located near Route 2 on Iron Horse Drive. Formerly the Apostolic Faith Church, it was established in 1939 by Rev. Chester S. Dayhoff (Ruth Ann Dayhoff's father) after a successful revival on Creel Street. It currently has the only Christian school in the county. (Courtesy of Ruth Ann Dayhoff.)

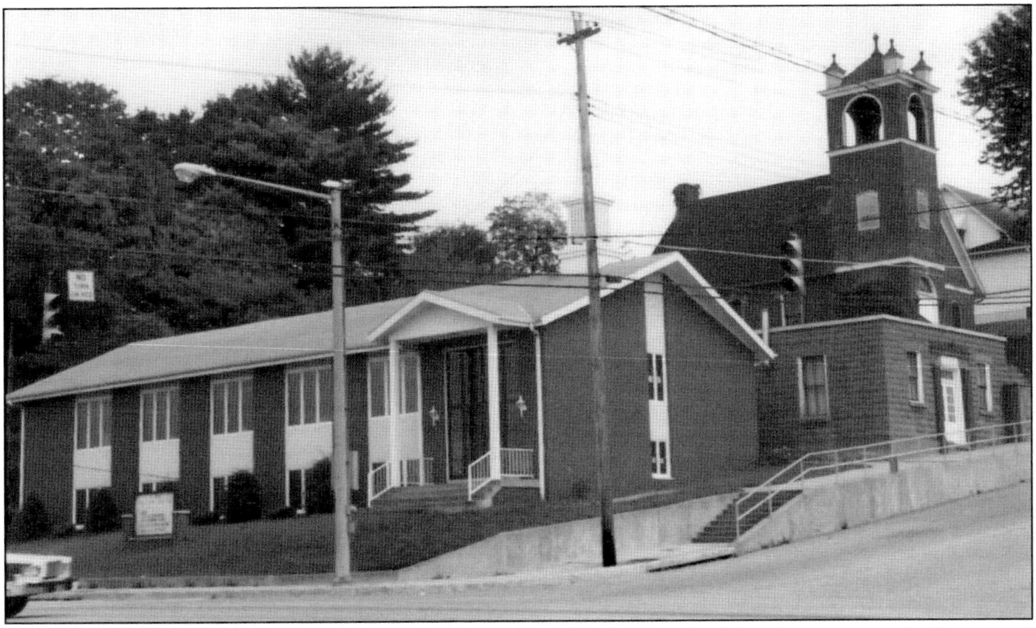

The St. Marys Presbyterian Church was organized on April 28, 1904. Members met in the Episcopal church until they built a church on Washington Street on land donated by the Ogdin family. The cornerstone was laid on February 12, 1908. In 1977, while Rev. Daniel Simmons was the pastor, a new church was built. St. Marys Presbyterian Church has been in service for 105 years. Rev. Michael Anderson is the current pastor. (Courtesy of Rev. Daniel Simmons.)

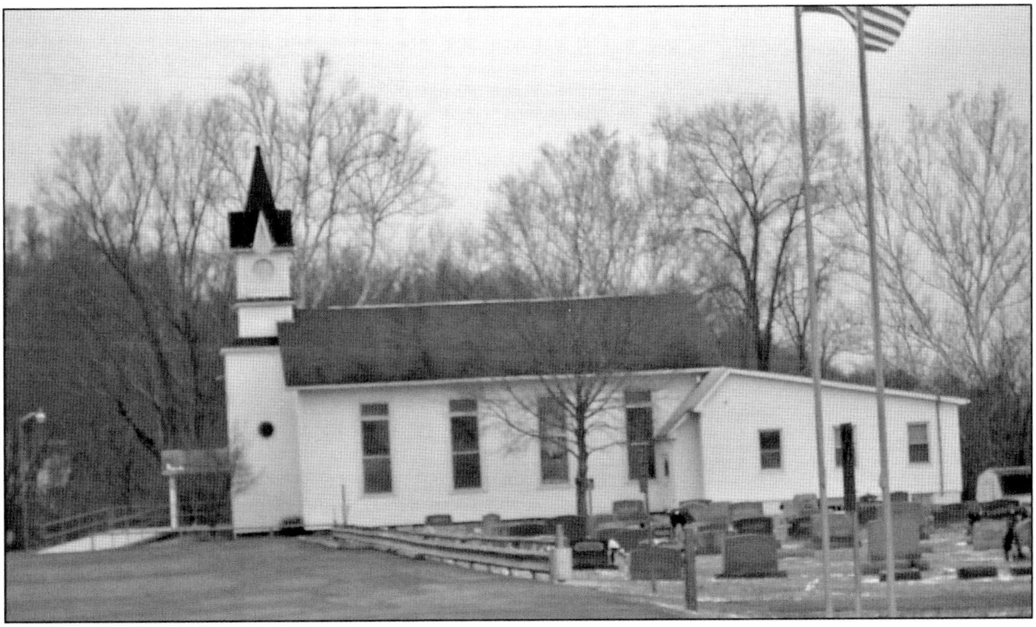

In January 1869, the Willow Island Baptist Church was organized. Members secured a building plot on Route 2 south of St. Marys, and on January 5, 1870, the new church was dedicated. It has been in service for 139 years. Many improvements have been made on this original church building. The church and cemetery create a lovely Pleasants County landmark. Rev. Richard Cale is currently the pastor. (Courtesy of Ruth Ann Dayhoff.)

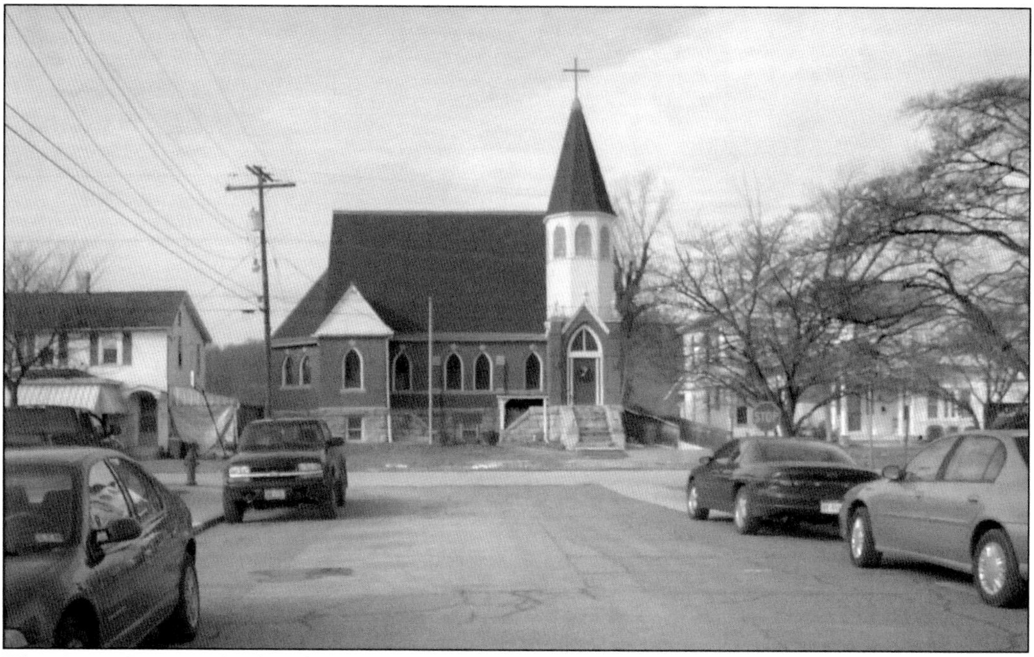

The Grace Episcopal Church began construction in 1895, making it the second oldest church building in St. Marys. The inside or nave of the church has been noted throughout the area as a most architecturally beautiful church. The nave, if turned upside down, portrays a ship of olden days. Rev. Lisa Heller Priest currently presides over services. (Courtesy of Ruth Ann Dayhoff.)

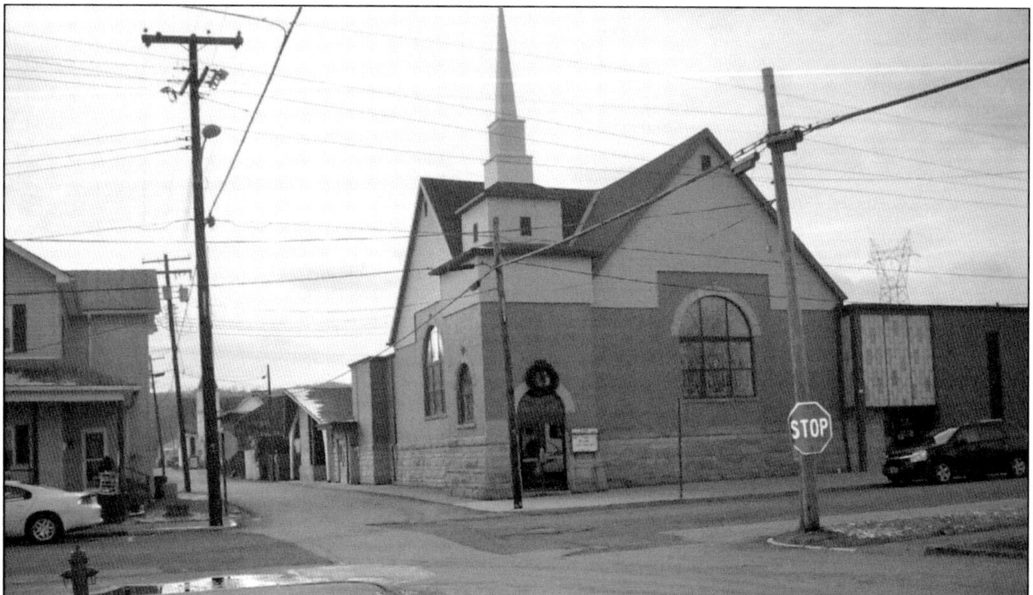

The official name, United Methodist Church, means the flowing together of three streams of Methodist plus the United Brethren Church. They were first organized in St. Marys in 1850, and a lot was purchased from Alexander Creel on Washington Street, where the current church stands. The present building was erected in 1906. Currently, Rev. Pam Shuman is the pastor. (Courtesy of Ruth Ann Dayhoff.)

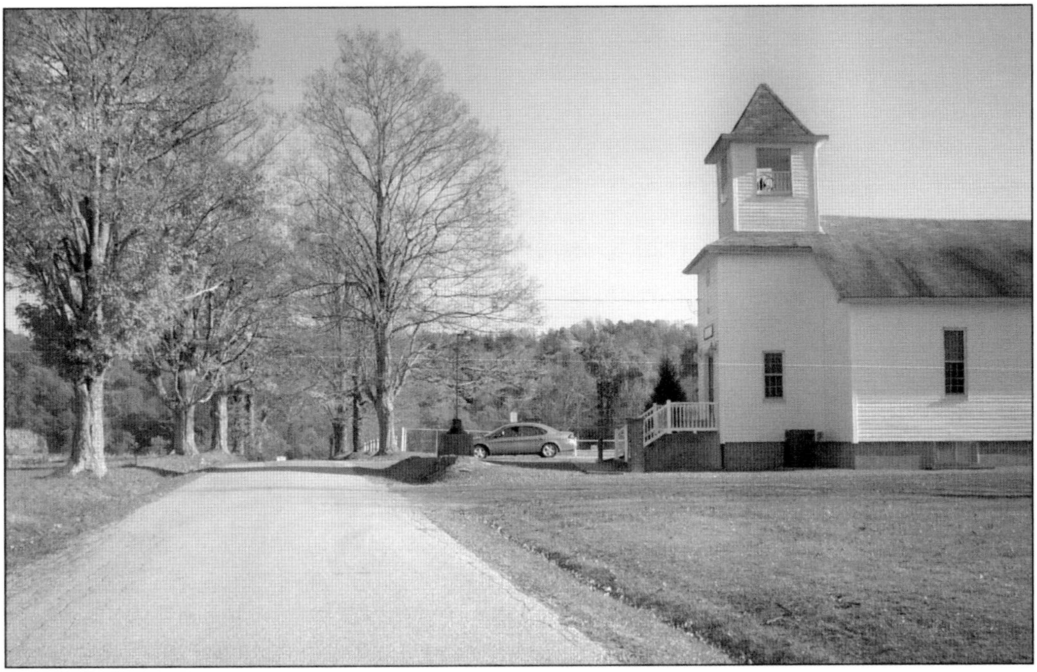

The Maple Lane Freewill Baptist Church is located near Hebron at the countryside village of Maple Lane. It was established October 6, 1968, under the leadership of Rev. George J. Burns with Rex Cox as interim pastor currently. A beautiful Masonic cemetery is located adjacent to the church. (Courtesy of Ruth Ann Dayhoff.)

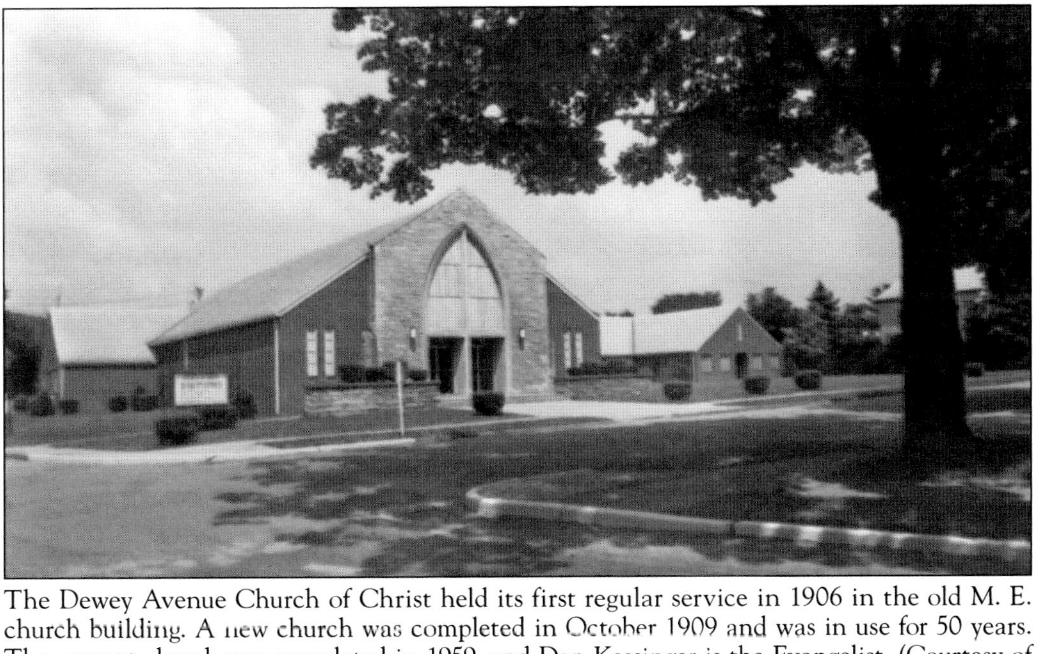

The Dewey Avenue Church of Christ held its first regular service in 1906 in the old M. E. church building. A new church was completed in October 1909 and was in use for 50 years. The current church was completed in 1959, and Dan Kessinger is the Evangelist. (Courtesy of Rev. Daniel Simmons.)

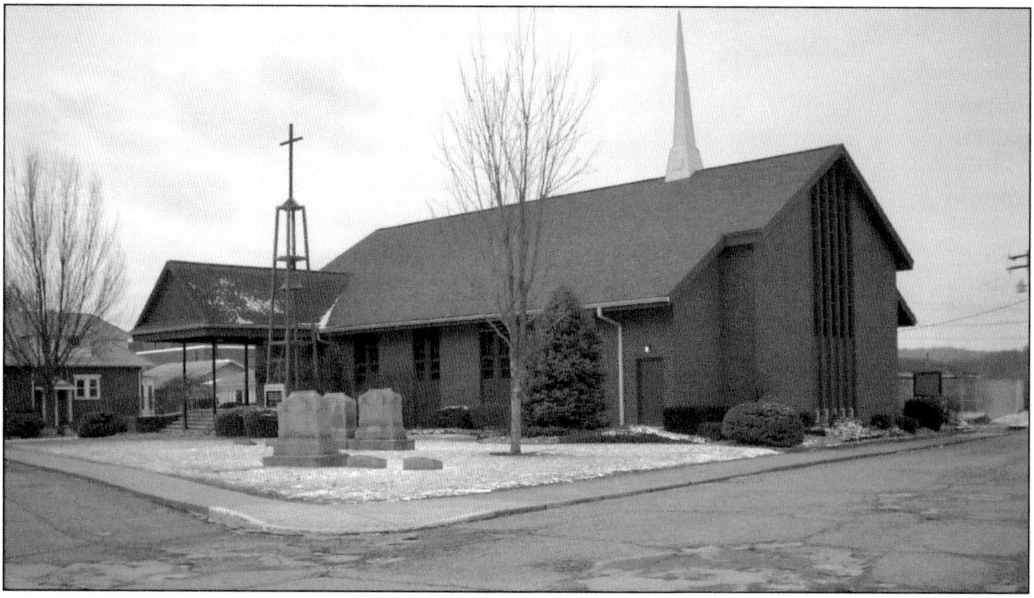

On October 22, 1898, the First Baptist Church of St. Marys was organized. They held services in the M. E. church until Samuel Barkwill donated land to build a church on the current site. The new church was dedicated May 26, 1901. This is a mission-centered church dedicated to lending a hand where needed. Paster John Strimer presides. (Courtesy of Ruth Ann Dayhoff.)

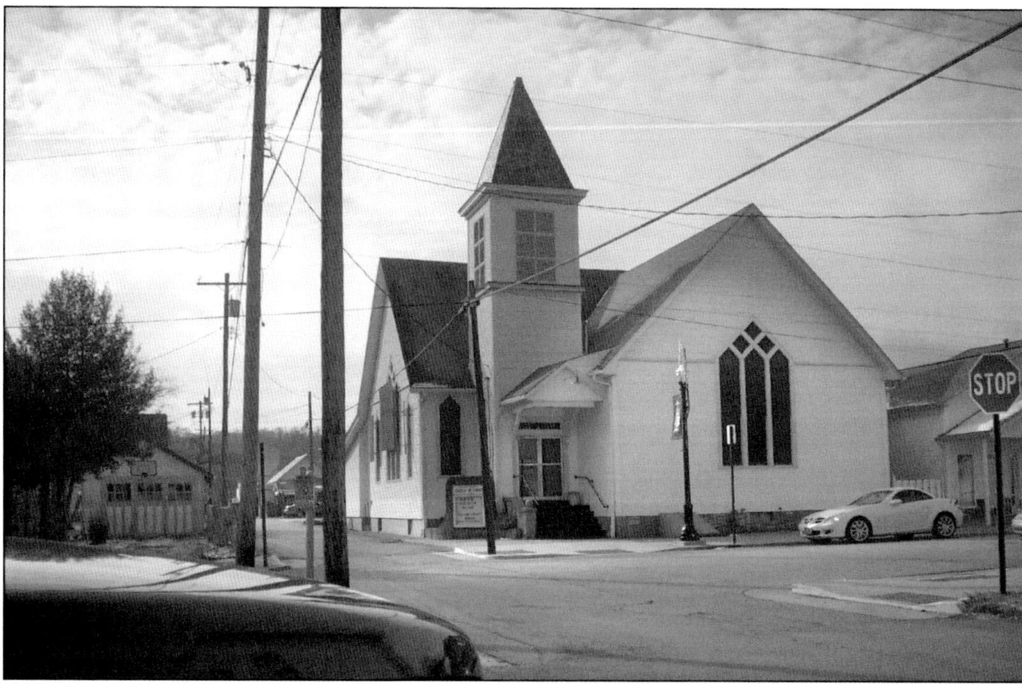

On January 20, 1935, the George Street Church of Christ was organized. The services were held in the Odd Fellows Hall until February 1, 1935. Then they moved to the present location of 108 George Street. They had purchased this building from the M. E. South Conference. Arnold Huyghebaert serves as Evangelist. (Courtesy of Ruth Ann Dayhoff.)

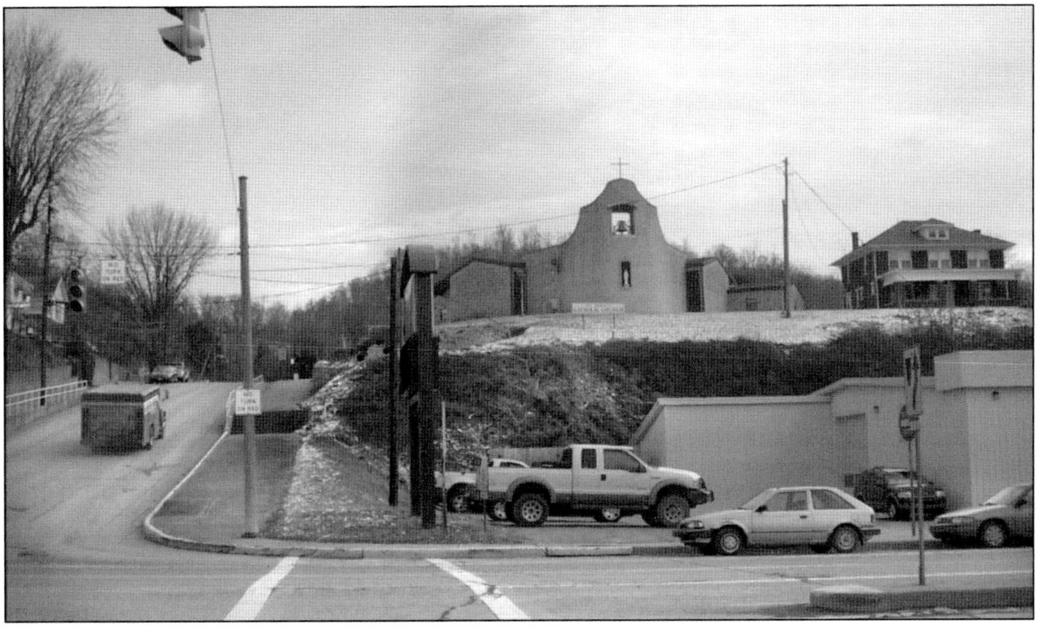

St. John's Catholic Church sits upon the Washington Street hill overlooking St. Marys. The first mass was held in the William Gale home in Belmont 1835. For many years, only infrequent mass was held in homes until 1913, when the United Brethren Church on Dewey Avenue was purchased. In 1978, they purchased and built the church above where the Grimm Hospital once stood. Fr. Shaju Abraham holds services. (Courtesy of Ruth Ann Dayhoff.)

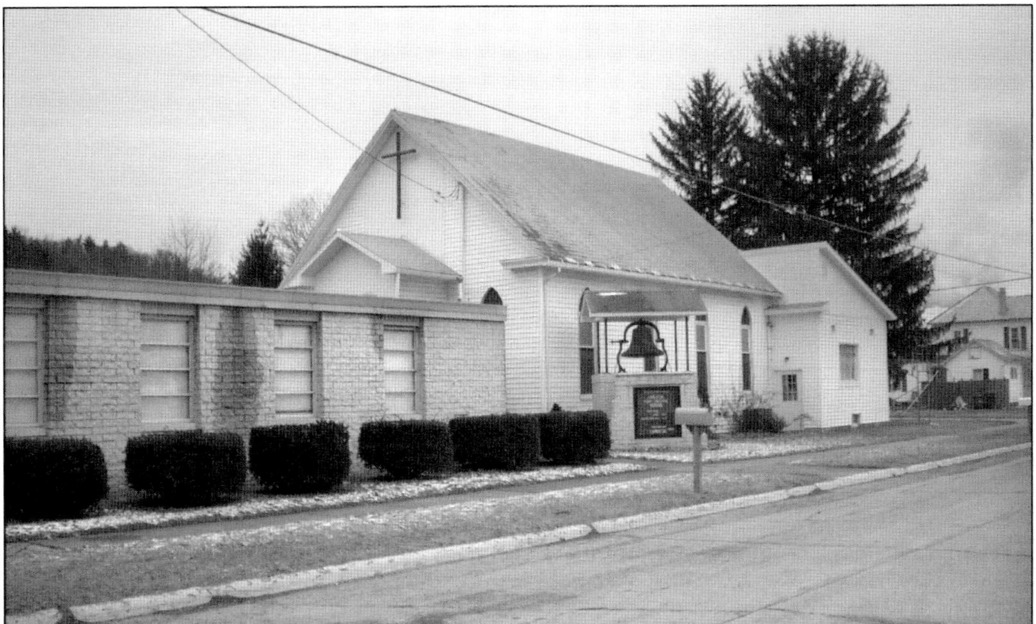

The Belmont United Methodist Church was organized in 1898. The building was erected around the beginning of the 20th century. Members started remodeling the church in 1951 and continued to add renovations throughout the years. In its earlier days, other churches also used the building until they could build their own. (Courtesy of Ruth Ann Dayhoff.)

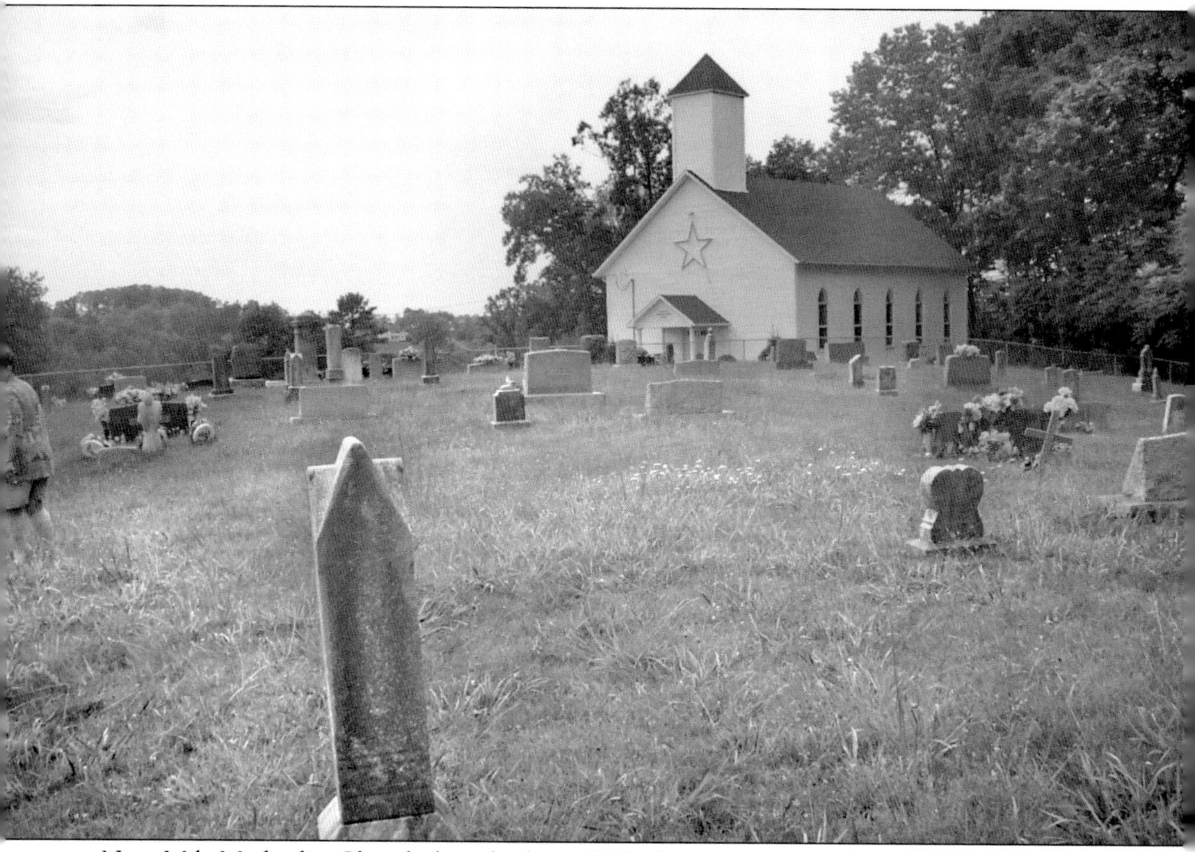

Nine Mile Methodist Church dates back to 1866, when it was started in a log cabin. In 1901, a frame building was constructed and is still standing today. It has been recently renovated, and a finished basement now provides room for classes and social events. Shauna Hyde is the current pastor. The beautiful, well-kept cemetery is the resting place for many early settlers as well as numerous local family members. (Courtesy of Sandra Cronin.)

All of the churches in Pleasants County cannot be pictured here because of lack of space. The churches below include all those not pictured that are listed in the county paper, the *St. Marys Oracle*: Beech Run Free Will Baptist, Bens Run Church of Christ, Bonds Creek Free Will Baptist, Calcutta United Methodist, Calvary Baptist, Cow Creek United Methodist, Community Church of Jesus Christ, Eureka Missionary Baptist, Belmont Baptist, French Creek Baptist, Good Hope Baptist, Mount Pleasant Church, Mount Nebo Church of Christ, Pine Grove Church of Christ, Pike Church of Christ, Pike Church of God, Pleasant Valley Church of Rock Run, Raven Rock United Methodist, Shadow Hill Baptist, St. Marys Church of the Nazarene, Zoar Baptist Church, the Celebration Center, the Victory Baptist, and the Waverly Church of Christ.

Ten

JUST PASSING THROUGH

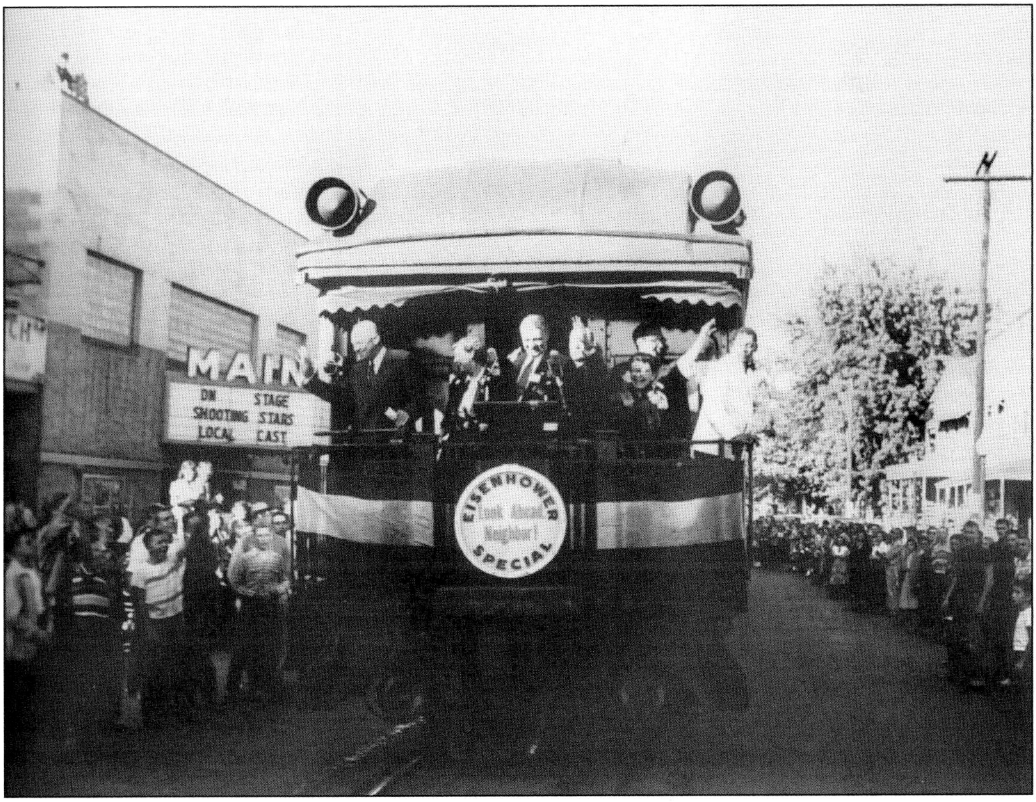

Dwight D. Eisenhower waves from the platform as his train picks its way up Main Street in St. Marys, West Virginia. It stopped at the Main Theater, which can be seen in the background. Schoolchildren were brought from school to see president-elect Dwight D. Eisenhower and Henry Cabot Lodge. To the left stands the author Ellen Dittman Pope. She shook hands with Eisenhower, and he said, "You are one of the new potential voters!" (Weirton Steel/Eisenhower Library, courtesy of Bob Withers.)

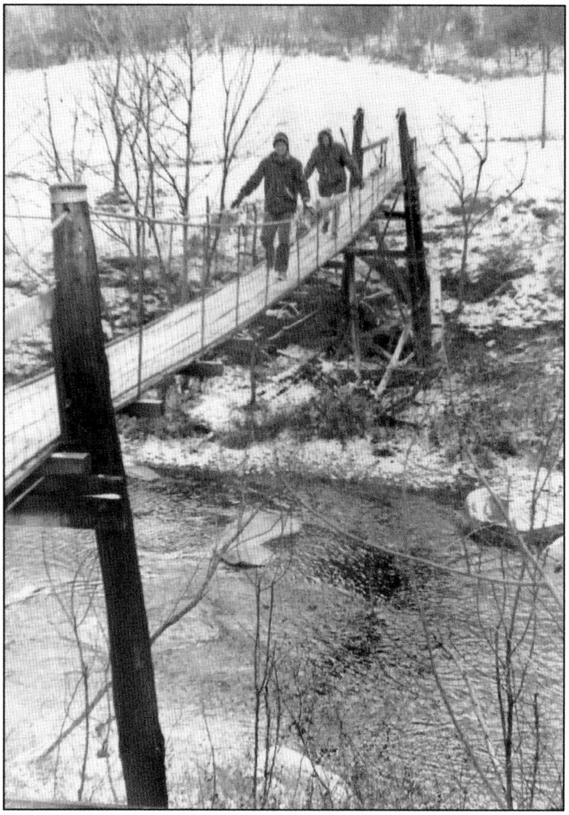

Footbridges like this one over McKim Creek were numerous in the early days of Pleasants County because of the many runs and creeks that flow into the Middle Island Creek and the Ohio River. A person often feels as if he were going to fall into the creek because the bridge often sways as one walks across. An old footbridge could be quite exciting and somewhat dangerous to cross. (Courtesy of Rev. Daniel Simmons.)

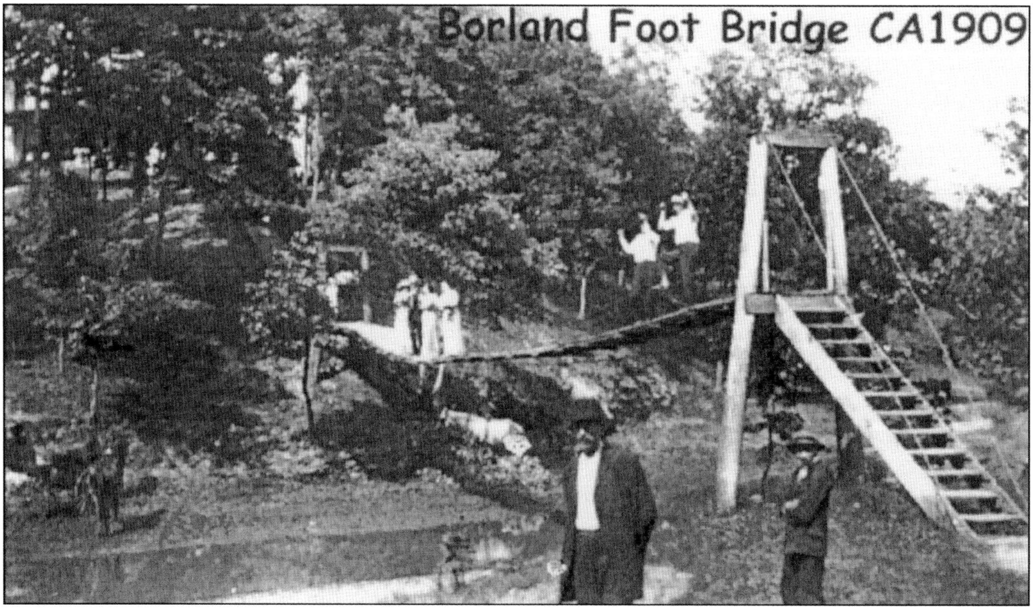

The Borland Springs footbridge was located over Bull Creek leading to the Borland Springs Hotel. In this photograph taken in 1909, one can observe ladies and gentlemen walking across to the hotel. The hotel was a delightful place of fun and relaxation for the local residents. The bridge as well as the hotel are long gone. (Courtesy of Mike Naylor.)

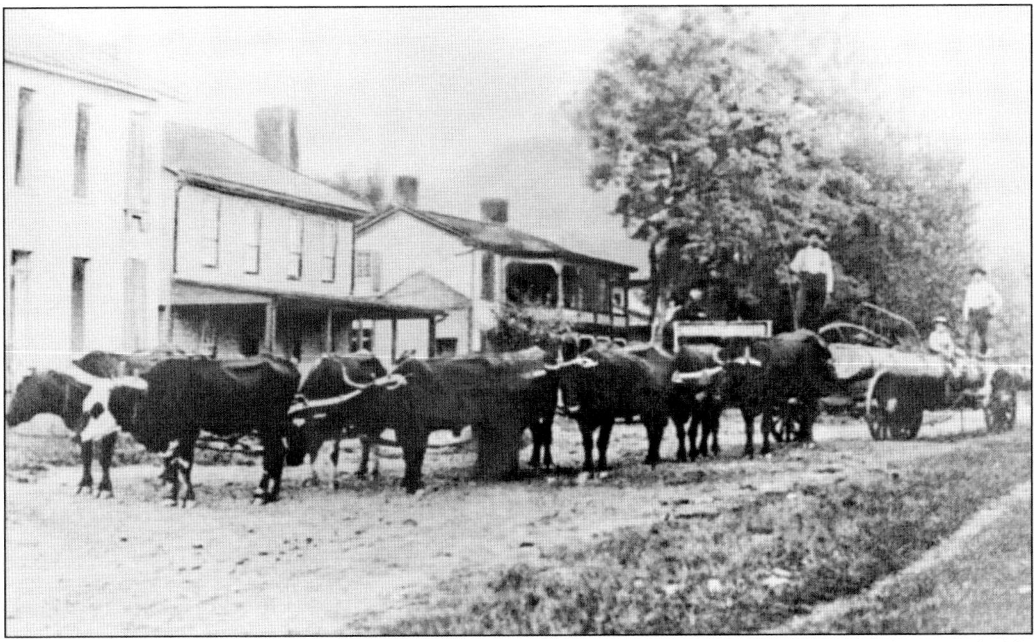

Levi Boley is driving his oxcart down Creel Street in St. Marys. He is hauling huge logs, probably taking them to a nearby sawmill. The many cooper shops could certainly use the wood as well as those preparing to build homes in the area. This picture was taken in 1884 before cars or trucks were available. (PCHSC, courtesy of WVDCHSA.)

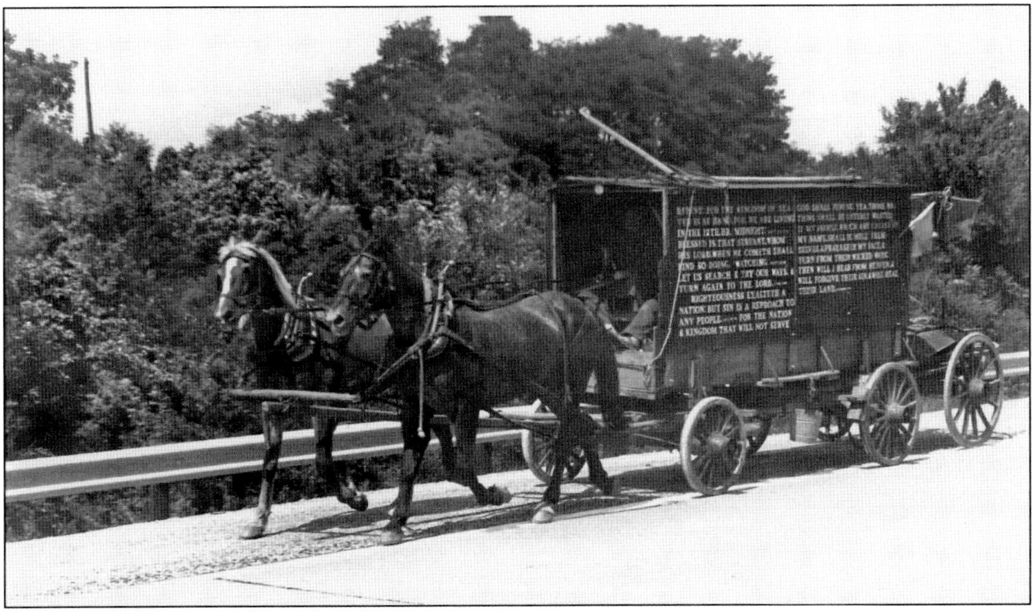

One more time, we see a horse-drawn wagon as it passes through the county. This time, a stranger with a message is traveling from state to state. This method of travel may be slow, but one can feel close to the countryside this way and meet many interesting people. (Courtesy of Rev. Daniel Simmons.)

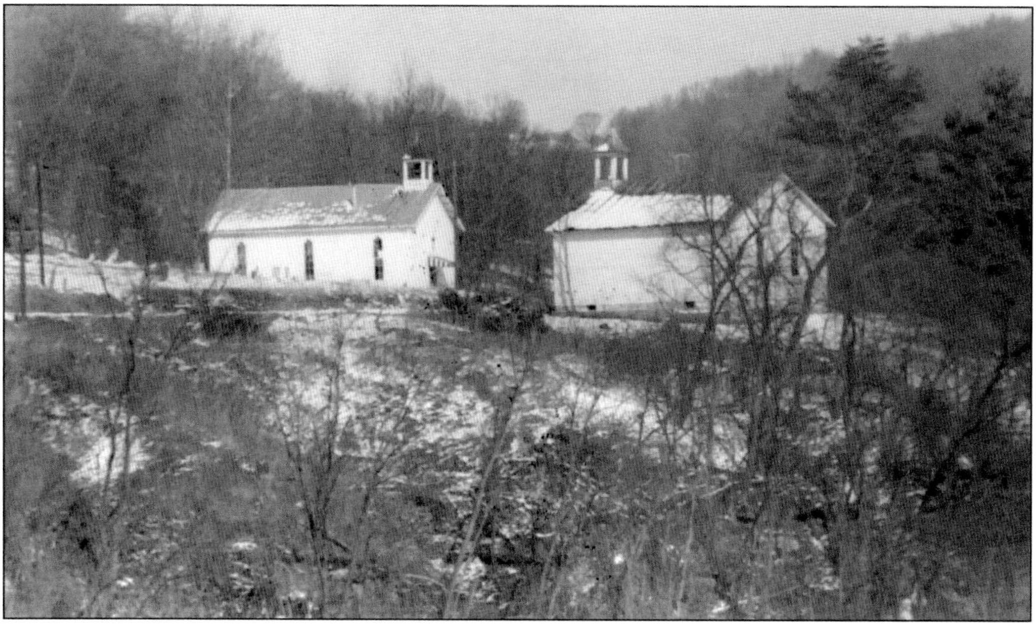

The first remembered church to hold services at Clay Point was the United Brethren in Christ. They met for about 100 years in the Clay Point School House. When they built the first actual church building, it was built with lumber from an old Methodist church at Grape Island. The church is now called the Clay Point United Methodist Church. The school has been out of use for many years. (Courtesy of Rev. Daniel Simmons.)

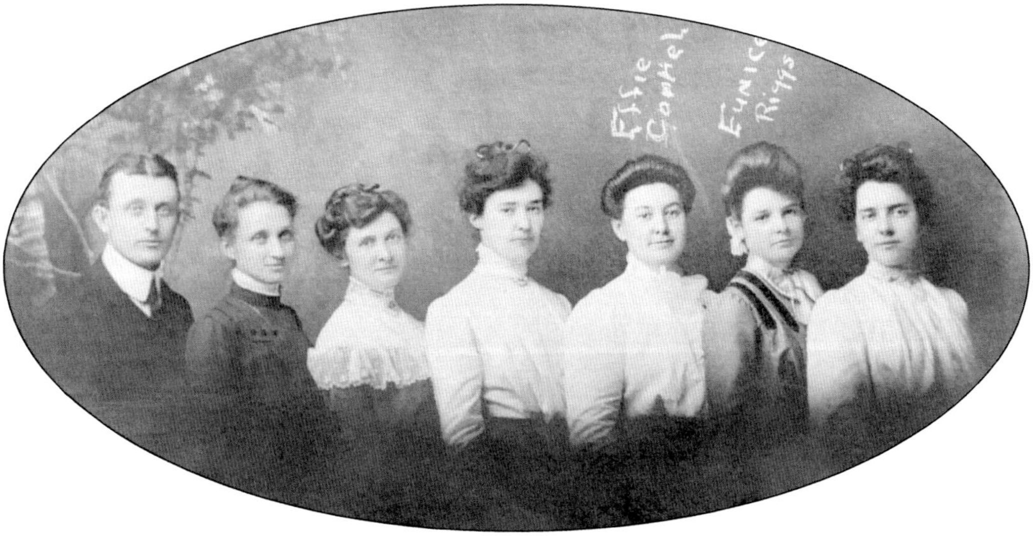

This photograph from 1903–1904 shows six women teachers and one man. Often male teachers were employed to aid in the students' discipline. As time went on, ideas such as these changed. The fifth teacher from the left, Ethel Gorrell (Effie), taught kindergarten on First Street. Many citizens of today hold very fond memories of this fine lady. (PCHSC, courtesy of WVDCHSA.)

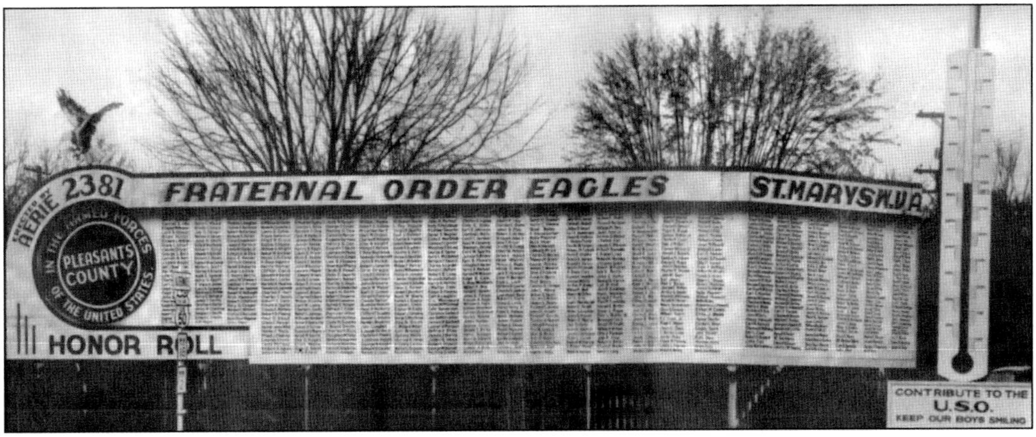

This is the honor roll of the World War II veterans from Pleasants County and St. Marys. The sign was erected by AERIE 2381 Fraternal Order Eagles. The Eagles took up a collection to send to the USO to keep our boys smiling. The thermometer on the right tracked the contributions. The sign was located next to Kramer Seller's business, on the property where the Davis Motor Company and parking lot were located for many years. The men and women of Pleasants County can be proud of service that was contributed to keep our country safe and free. Records show these approximate numbers of men and women serving in the following wars: Civil War, 529; World War I, 378; World War II, 568; Korean War, (killed) 4; Viet Nam War, (killed) 8, (POW) 1. (Above courtesy of the City of St. Marys; below courtesy of Frank and Ruby Sellers.)

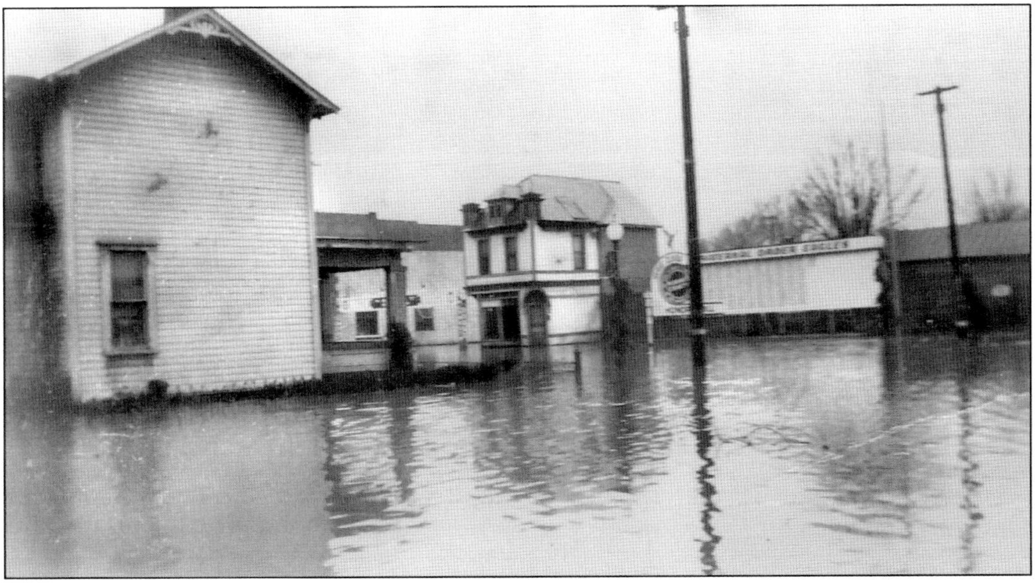

ACROSS AMERICA, PEOPLE ARE DISCOVERING SOMETHING WONDERFUL. *THEIR HERITAGE.*